There are many books on organizational change, but this one renews and transcends the genre! This book proposes an engaging view of how change leaders can travel inside "the spiral of sensemaking". I enjoyed reading this book because it intelligently demystifies why most organizational changes fail and translates a decade of practice-based research into a set of reflexive tools for practitioners.

Linda Rouleau, Professor of Organization Theory, Professorship in Strategy Organization and Social Practices, HEC Montreal, Canada.

By combining theory and practice, the authors have produced an excellent, informative and insightful book which addresses key issues in leading change, especially the vital role played by sensemaking processes.

Professor Bernard Burnes, Chair of Organisational Change, Stirling Management School, University of Stirling, UK.

I thoroughly enjoyed reading *Effective Organizational Change: leading through sensemaking.* Einar and Jacob have done a brilliant job in bringing the challenge of organizational change alive through their focus on individuals, personal realities, and sensemaking. The ability to understand (not necessarily agree with) and act on the very personal realities of others is crucial when initiating and leading organizational change. Indeed, a focus on people rather than on strict rules and structure is what will enable successful change. This view is not only embraced but strengthened through this work, and *Effective Organizational Change* is an essential read for both scholars and practitioners.

Professor Rune Todnem By, Editor-in-Chief, Journal of Change Management, and co-author of Managing Change in Organizations, Staffordshire University Business School, UK

This book is a successful combination of academic excellence and in-depth practical experience. The landscaping metaphor gives a breath of fresh air to a field that for too long has been dominated by superficial how-to handbooks and "best practice" statements. This is indeed a really important and needed contribution in a time of uncertainty and rapid change.

Jerry Karlsson, CEO, Swedish Institute for Quality

This is not just another textbook on organizational change. Instead of presenting a bunch of old and new theories about change, the authors have written a testimony that really captures the challenges of leading change in an imperfect world. It is obvious that they have been out there in the trenches. To put it simply: this is a must-read-book that really makes sense.

Anders Mellberg, former CEO, Agria Insurance

EFFECTIVE ORGANIZATIONAL CHANGE

Organizations are constantly evolving, and intelligent leadership is needed during times of transformation. Change leaders must help people become aware of, understand and find meaning in the new things that arise—they must oversee a sensemaking process.

Addressing this need, *Effective Organizational Change* explores the importance of leadership for organizational change based on sensemaking. Combining a theoretical overview, models and conceptual discussions rich with in-depth examples and case studies, this book uncovers what it is that leaders actually do when they lead change through sensemaking. It presents the most current sensemaking research, extends earlier work by developing the concept of 'landscaping', and provides guidelines on how leaders can drive sensemaking processes in practice.

This book is for undergraduate, postgraduate and MBA students of organizational change, as well as managers embarking on change projects within their organizations.

Einar Iveroth is Associate Professor at the Department of Business Studies, Uppsala University, Sweden. He is an expert in organizational change and IT-enabled change, and has published widely in leading journals such as the *California Management Review*, *Journal of Change Management*, *Journal of Environmental Management*, *European Management Journal*, and *Health Care Management Review*.

Jacob Hallencreutz, PhD, is a Change Expert and Group CEO of EPSI Rating Group, one of Europe's leading market research consultancies. He has 25 years' experience of leading change in both manufacturing and service organizations, including some of the largest in Northern Europe. Jacob is also a leading researcher and has published in a number of international scientific journals.

EFFECTIVE ORGANIZATIONAL CHANGE

Leading through sensemaking

Einar Iveroth and Jacob Hallencreutz

Routledge
Taylor & Francis Group

LONDON AND NEW YORK

First published 2016
by Routledge
2 Park Square, Milton Park, Abingdon, Oxon OX14 4RN

and by Routledge
711 Third Avenue, New York, NY 10017

Routledge is an imprint of the Taylor & Francis Group, an informa business

© 2016 Einar Iveroth and Jacob Hallencreutz

British Library Cataloguing in Publication Data
A catalogue record for this book is available from the British Library

Library of Congress Cataloging in Publication Data
    Iveroth, Einar.
    Effective organizational change : leading through sensemaking / Einar Iveroth and Jacob Hallencreutz.
        pages cm
    Includes bibliographical references and index.
    1. Organizational change. I. Hallencreutz, Jacob. II. Title.
        HD58.8.I94 2016
        658.4'06–dc23
                    2015006878

ISBN: 978-0-415-74772-1 (hbk)
ISBN: 978-0-415-74773-8 (pbk)
ISBN: 978-1-315-79688-8 (ebk)

Typeset in Bembo
by Taylor & Francis Books

CONTENTS

LIST OF ILLUSTRATIONS

Figures

Tables

Boxes

ACKNOWLEDGEMENTS

This work would not have been possible without colleagues and their respective organizations. We appreciate their patience during the bumpy writing and research process. A special thanks to Robert, the main character in Chapter 7—you really let us under the skin of your three-year change challenge. We are also grateful to Associate Professor Jan Lindvall for lengthy discussions about the spiral pattern of change a long time ago, and Professor Nils-Göran Olve for elaborating on decision making and myth cycles. We also want to thank Professor Fredrik Nilsson for being such an excellent leader and academic advisor in general. Many thanks also to our other colleagues at Implement Consulting Group, CASIP, Uppsala University and Linköping University for support, encouragement and fruitful discussions on organizational change and sensemaking along this project. An extra expression of gratitude to Professor Rickard Garvare at Luleå University of Technology and Assistant Professor Mathias Cöster at Uppsala University for valuable comments on earlier drafts of the book. Finally, and most importantly, the greatest and most loving thanks to our families, especially Jeanette, Sofie, Eije and Dorothea. Thank you for putting up with us. Without you, none of this would have happened.

PREFACE

We first met in a hotel lobby in Stockholm. Einar was holding a lunch seminar about results from his research on how organizational change is pivotal for successful technology-enabled change. Jacob and Implement Consulting Group were hosting the seminar. We had a cup of coffee afterwards, exchanged business cards and agreed to meet each other again. Little did we know that the coffee conversation would evolve into a full-scale book venture, but here we are.

The first project presented by Einar at the seminar concerned the global implementation of an enterprise resource planning (ERP) system within the multinational telecommunications company Ericsson. This was an IT-enabled change that affected the majority of the organizational sub-units of Ericsson, consisting of over 200 legal units situated in over 140 countries. The change was performed within its timeframe of three years, and from a managerial perspective was considered successful. The aim of the research project was to follow the practice of the change agents with the leading empirical question: What is it that these people actually do when they lead IT-enabled change successfully?

The second project presented lasted for four years and had also a practice focus with the guiding question of how to change individuals' behavior towards more sustainable practices. To answer this question, Einar examined the implementation of an IT system for sustainable transport logistics and procurement in Uppsala, a small municipality of Sweden. The purpose of the IT project was to attain a more sustainable transportation flow between goods deliverers and recipients within larger parts of the municipality. The overarching goal was to aid the municipality in being more sustainable by developing new local practices.

These two projects were similar because they both included large-scale implementation of IT and organizational change. They were also completely different in regards to being situated in two totally different organizational structures as well as two different environmental contexts. Yet the research projects came to the very same conclusion: one of the key factors for the success of the IT implementations was connected to the way the change agents manage to lead the change through different kinds of sensemaking processes.

For example, paramount for the success of the IT-enabled change in both cases was that they had formal and informal change agents that acted as sensemakers. These managers translated, for instance, the formal organizational change message and addressed questions such as, what does this new IT system, and the change that it brings, mean to me, my daily practice and my local organization? And how will I perform my work in the future? Throughout both projects these types of questions were intentionally talked about formally via workshops, training and conferences, as well as more informally through peer-to-peer conversations and discussions in corridors and at coffee machines. By doing so, the change agents acted as sensemakers by facilitating the sensemaking of employees who in most cases eased their uncomfortable feelings of ambiguity and equivalence.

Both these projects consisted of many small-scale change projects that together made up the whole respective transformations. During the years that the implementations took place there were small change projects within the respective transformations that were successful. At the same time there were others that were failures. What was noticeable was that the ones that were prosperous had in the main spent resources on enabling sensemaking processes. It was the other way around with the projects that failed as they had ignored many important sensemaking processes. These failed projects did not make the connection between IT and sensemaking— believing that IT is a tool that is robust, structured and tangible, and disregarding the important social elements of such technology.

Einar concluded that sensemaking processes are vital for leading successful IT-enabled change. However, none of them went far enough to explain how such processes can be driven in practice and therefore these research projects made call for further research on leading sensemaking processes. It was around this challenge that our cooperation took off. In this way, this book can be viewed as an extension of the two research projects and a way of contributing to the closing of this knowledge gap.

We are both organizational change geeks, but with different origins: Einar is the scholar, Jacob is the practitioner. Over the years, it has been obvious to us both that academic theories are one thing while the actual realization of these is another. No doubt there is a plethora of textbooks about organizational change. These textbooks introduce various models, concepts and ideas about organizational change in a clean and objectified manner. Leading change in real life, however, has always been less clear cut. Far too many change initiatives go wrong despite good intentions and plans.

During our meetings that followed the coffee break in the hotel lobby we shared many similar experiences from our craft of doing research and consultancy assignments. Our most vivid discussions revolved around the disturbing discrepancy between the rhetoric and the reality in the field of organizational change. To close this gap between theories, models and plans and the social systems on the ground we came to the conclusion that change leaders must improve their ability to lead sensemaking processes. Bluntly: managers must help people become aware of, understand and find meaning in new stuff. When leading through sensemaking, change is not just about following predesigned change management models. It is about acknowledging local, emerging interpretations and constructions of meaning through a series of dialogues.

Specifically, change leaders need to understand how people in a social system create for themselves systems of meaning of their world. These meanings are the foundation on which social life proceeds. That is what this book aims to address. *Effective Organizational Change* uncovers what it is that leaders actually do when they lead change through sensemaking. By doing so, the book provides the front-line of sensemaking research for researchers and graduate students, at the same time informing leaders of what they can do to excel in their change processes. The book combines theoretical overview, models and conceptual discussions with rich, in-depth and "thick" examples and cases from the field. Most importantly, *Effective Organizational Change* extends earlier work by developing the concept of land-scaping, and guidelines that explain how leaders drive sensemaking processes in practice.

1

INTRODUCTION

Imagine a hospital where more than half of all surgeries fail. Skills, routines and procedures might be in place, preparatory treatments fully completed, but nevertheless patients die, healthy organs are removed instead of damaged ones, and sometimes whole ventures end up in endless preparations, meetings and analysis while the patients perish.

Now visualize an airline where seven out of ten flights go wrong. The planes crash, pilots fly astray or vessels just never leave the runway.

Most of us would not tolerate that level of performance; we would demand studies of surgical procedures or airline safety, call for better regulations and legal actions against this carelessness. We would most certainly question the leadership of these organizations. However, when it comes to organizational change we seem to accept such poor outcome. In fact, in recent decades there has been a general consensus between practitioners and scholars that few are successful when leading organizational change (Burnes 2009). Although debated (Burnes 2011; Hughes 2011), it is estimated that around 70 percent of all organizational change initiatives fail to reach intended objectives. How can that be, in a time when societies and organizations experience change of a magnitude, speed, impact and unpredictability greater than ever before? These high failure rates are costing organizations around the world millions of dollars and wasted hours, year in, year out. Why do we accept that? Is there not an enormous need for effective organizational change?

First of all, we must admit the field of organizational change suffers from a gap between the rhetoric and the reality, both in academia and among practitioners. The literature is too conceptual and the empirical studies describing change processes are tricky to apply. Often-mentioned success factors like "strong leadership," "good communication" and "empowerment" are hard to argue against in theory, yet difficult to achieve in practice. "How-to" handbooks simplify a complex reality and offer off-the-shelf solutions based on anecdotal evidence. Managers learn of the benefits of these solutions through business publications that promote certain models or "gurus." The consulting industry is also party to the proceedings. Homemade solutions and quick fixes are offered as a remedy for complex change problems. However, from a more objective point of view there seems to be no universal, prescriptive and systematic change-management model to cover the diversified nature of change in organizations, despite the plethora of articles and books written in this field. So why burden you with yet another book on this matter? Do we not face the same pitfall as everyone else?

Why another book about organizational change?

Our own research and practical experience tell us that there are still aspects to unfold. For instance, in an effort just to get it done there is a tendency among organizations to dismiss the "people side" of organizational change in favor of using a set of quick prescriptive steps or no structure at all. In a stressful environment calling for quick fixes, managers simply do not have the time, focus and ability to apply complex models. In fact, we learn that most organizations do not have a conscious approach to organizational change at all. Rather, an "ad hoc mentality" prevails, especially concerning behavioral aspects of change (Hallencreutz 2012). No wonder change initiatives often go awry.

We have learnt that managers underestimate the effort it takes to create aware-ness, understanding and meaning. That is the great challenge for change leaders of today, and that is what leading through sensemaking is all about. The lack of contextual knowledge and ability to understand the human response to change leads to leaders who are unable to handle resistance and overcome obstacles (Andrews et al. 2008). This is where it all goes wrong. In real life, effective organizational change is very seldom just a matter of deploying the new organization chart or the new strategy with a few projects. It is about changing people's behavior, often a lot of people, and this is not trivial. So, behind all the complex theories and concepts about change failure lingers a very simple shortcoming: *management often fails to win over the hearts and minds of the people in the organization.*

This shortcoming happens because the underlying mechanisms of behavioral and sociocultural aspects of organizational change are constantly underestimated. A typical management approach to these matters is: "*Well, information is important. I presented the change project at our monthly meetings and no one had any questions. People nodded and seemed to understand. So everything should be okay.*" This attitude has nothing to do with not caring—our belief is that most managers strive to do a good job—but it has something to do with ignorance and interest, perhaps com-bined with a worldview stating that organizations are rational and logical places. "*I make decisions and communicate them, and I expect everyone to understand and therefore follow and if they do not I will just tell them again*"—almost as if communication is a simple transaction between a sender (i.e. manager) and receiver (i.e. employee or other stakeholder), and if the transaction fails it is because they did not listen enough and just repeating the message can easily fix the problem. However, in modern organizations, very seldom is a decision transformed into swift action just by sending an email, posting an intranet statement or speaking at meetings (Iveroth 2011; Iveroth and Bengtsson 2014). It takes a little more to address the "people side" of change.

There is an increasing amount of research which purports that the problems with the people side of change hinge on sensemaking and sensegiving activities (Maitlis and Christianson 2014; Sandberg and Tsoukas 2014; Weick 1995) of the managers leading change (Lüscher and Lewis 2008; Rouleau and Balogun 2011). In simple terms, managers fail to create widely the necessary awareness, understanding and willpower needed to make people change. From a theoretical standpoint, there are actually numerous research articles on sensemaking and organizational change. However, these are often very detailed and specific—as research articles tend to be. They generally lack a broader context and a discussion of how sensemaking fits into the theory of change. Overall, research articles on sensemaking and change are far too philosophical to disclose how sensemaking is performed in practice (Schatzki et al. 2001; Whittington 2006).

Sensemaking research is hard to make sense of. This is also another reason why managers overlook this aspect of organizational change. There are few, if any, books that explain how change can be led through a sensemaking approach. However, if we ever want to be able to confront and change the prevailing "failure paradigm," we advocate that leaders seriously explore their practices and attitudes toward the people side of change—especially on how to gain broad-based awareness, understanding and empowerment. By leading people through sensemaking, a change leader will have better conditions to gain sustainable behavioral change and thus handle what we see as the main reason for failed change initiatives. That is why this book is needed.

Let us give you a brief introduction to what this book tries to unfold. To decode sensemaking, we must first realize and accept that the world is complex and dynamic, and is constructed, interpreted and experienced by people in their interactions with each other and with wider social systems. Thus, sensemaking is not yet another instrumental management concept. Instead, we embrace that leading the people side of change is mainly about challenging and breaking up behavioral patterns triggered by social and biological habits—rational as well as irrational.

Research suggests that up to 45 percent of our time is spent on habitual patterns (see e.g. Neal et al. 2006). These patterns are maintained by a jumble of social conventions and interactions but also by core functions of the brain. For instance, we know from the neuroscientists that the brain's limbic system strives to make us run on autopilot because it consumes less energy. The autopilot in the brain consolidates habitual patterns—that is why you do many everyday things "without thinking." Moreover, the autopilot is also tuned to risk minimization and, as we all know, change means inherent risks. Thus, the nature of the brain can both trigger resistance and prevent change. To break with these habitual patterns, the changes we introduce must "make sense."

How can that be done? First, people must become aware of the need for change otherwise the mind will remain on autopilot and no sustainable behavioral change is likely to take place—at least, not to the extent we want to see as change leaders. However, if the need is clearly signaled and deeply and candidly discussed, the brain will alert the frontal lobes (where logic takes place) and people will start to reflect and ask themselves questions such as: Why? What? When? How? What will happen to me? If the sensemaking process is poorly managed, the limbic system will fight back and make us ready for fight, flight or freeze. As a response to these primitive reactions, the change leader needs to address the logos behind the change—people must understand the background and motives. Once again, it simply has to make sense. Finally, the next sensemaking challenge is to present solutions and processes to help people produce the willpower it takes to change. So in this respect, breaking with habitual patterns requires movement from the present towards creating awareness, understanding and then willpower. This is by no means an easy task but the models, approaches and guidelines that are presented in this book show how we can facilitate such a process.

However, when addressing the people side of change it is risky to talk about "people" as a unitary system. A population is seldom a homogeneous group of individuals. In our everyday life as civilians and professionals, we all cope with change in different ways and at different speeds. Some of us are eager to go forward and seek challenges; others are reluctant and suspicious of new things. Thus, the adoption of new ideas, work procedures, values, codes of conduct, etc. within a population will not likely be linear during a change process.

When we lecture about the diffusion of change in organizations, we use a childlike metaphor: we compare behavioral change with the process of popping popcorn (the old-school way—not in the microwave). If you put corn in a pot with oil and turn up the heat, the grains will not pop simultaneously. First, you will get a few "early poppers" flying out of the pot. Then, when the heat is stable the majority of the grains will go. After a burst of popping activity about 80 percent of the corn has popped, but 20 percent is still lurking in the oil. What to do? If we turn off the heat we will lose 20 percent of the grains, but if we persist we might burn the 80 percent already popped.

This popcorn ordeal is quite similar to what a change leader embracing "the people side" is facing. We know from theory that 15–20 percent of a normal population are early adopters and willing to take on change challenges (Rogers 2003). Their individual sensemaking processes are swift. We also learn that 60–70 percent will await the "right temperature in the pot" and then change. However, 15–20 percent will be late adopters, and some individuals might not want to pop at all. Surprisingly often we find that change leaders spend a great deal of their management time with the late poppers, coaxing and convincing them to change. This is a risky strategy. By focusing too much on the late adopters, the change leader sends subtle signals to the rest of the crowd: "*if you want my attention, resist change.*" Moreover, in this situation the speed of the change process adapts to the slowest moving which will trigger early adopters to check out and move on: "*at this place nothing happens."* Thus, our unorthodox recommendation is to focus on the 80 percent who actually pop. We should allow early adopters to experiment, conduct pilot testing and be forerunners. Good examples should be highlighted and quick wins celebrated. Then lead by logic of attraction, instead of logic of resistance or replacement. The late bloomers will eventually join in or seek new challenges in other organizations.

The popcorn metaphor highlights that behavioral change is not linear. We are dealing with living systems and you cannot in advance calculate exactly how and when individuals will act and react. Their respective sensemaking processes will take different amounts of time. Habitual patterns within an organization are strong hindering forces. Thus, you will most likely experience an exponential change process, where some individuals start, others follow and—suddenly—you get a burst of activity. According to this worldview, change should be seen as an organic diffusion and translation of ideas rather than an end to be achieved. Gladwell (2000) describes such a change process as a "social epidemic" which eventually reaches a tipping point. Herrero (2008) proclaims the need for "viral change" as an antipode to slow, painful and unsuccessful change projects.

So, what is the point in trying to lead this organic stuff? Our belief, which will be elaborated in this book, is that the blurry reality of the people side of change can, at least to some extent, be planned and managed. The good news is that enhanced focus on these underlying behavioral aspects will *accelerate change.* To put it in another way, leading through sensemaking will speed up the change process of going from where we are now to gaining awareness, then understanding and finally the willpower to execute change—making the change more effective. We believe that effective organizational change is neither a rigid, planned and linear project, nor a fully circular process of emergent change. Instead we suggest that it should be portrayed as a sensemaking spiral of events and activities moving upward. In this book we will explain this sensemaking trajectory of change in an individual and leadership perspective. As we will show you, leading through sensemaking will accelerate the change and make it more effective.

Making sense of the style and structure of the book

In the process of writing the book we had a dilemma about its style. As co-authors we span the spectrum of academic-consultant-practitioner. Should we adopt a scholarly and detached style or should we write in a personal and more engaged way? The final result is a "dual approach." It is our ambition to get under the skin of change to a larger extent than earlier research and practice accounts have provided. Strictly scholarly works are prone to approach change from afar and illustrating change from without, using aggregated data, high-level analysis or by rational recollection that lies far from the trenches of the practice of change (Iveroth 2010). We want to account for the change journey not by the snapshots we have already taken but rather by trying to show some of the ongoing, living experiences of feeling, seeing and experiencing that we use to make sense of change in real life. In this way, we want you to join us in an exploration of what goes on inside the minds of change leaders. Our ambition is to move our understanding of effective organizational change from the macro, external perspective, to an understanding from a more micro perspective, from within.

The book is divided into two parts. Part I is focused on theory and encompasses Chapters 2–5. Part II includes Chapters 6–8 and focuses on practice. If you are a researcher, you will probably find the earlier part of the book interesting. If you are a manager, we recommend the latter part of the book. However, when you have the time, we strongly recommend you read the whole book.

In Chapter 2 we cover some of the most important aspects of the theories of change. Here we will conceptualize organizational change, including discussions of what change actually is, what it is composed of, how it comes into being, and how we can study it. There is also an overview of the different perspectives of change, where the most important is if change is viewed as a planned event orchestrated by independent change managers or an emergent phenomenon composed of many loosely coupled activities that evolve over time. You will also read about more empirical and practical aspects of change as we discuss the maxim that 70 percent of organizational change projects fail.

In Chapter 3 we try to make sense of sensemaking theory. We do so by defining sensemaking and its closely associated concepts. This is followed by a deeper review of the different properties of sensemaking. Chapter 4 is more hands-on since it illustrates some of the cues that people extract to make sense of their reality. This includes different research-based models and approaches that leaders may use to their advantage in order to perform their sensegiving activities—and in so doing, to some extent steer people's sensemaking processes.

Moving on, Chapter 5 gets closer in exploring the connection between leadership and sensemaking. The chapter illustrates what research can tell us on the matter as well as developing eight guidelines for leading sensemaking processes which comprise different managerial activities. Besides these activities we also provide an answer to the question of how the sensemaking process—in a leadership perspective—emerges, develops, grows or terminates over time. In short, our answer is that it is a spiral moving (it is hoped) upwards, fuelled by the eight guidelines of sensemaking.

We dig deeper into this notion in Part II. In Chapter 6 we travel inside this spiral of sensemaking, and we present our concept of landscaping. This concept is used to visualize how the proactive change leaders guide people through four different imaginary landscapes of meaning: comfort, inertia, transformation and consolidation. Chapter 7 applies landscaping to a real-life context. Here we will take you on a ride through the bumpy change process of a department within a Swedish insurance company, which we followed closely for three years. The objective is to tell a rich story from the complex reality of organizational change and link it to the concept of landscaping outlined in the previous chapters. We will also show in detail how some of the aspects presented in earlier chapters manifest on the ground.

Finally Chapter 8 provides a summary of the book, lessons learned and conclusions. Here we resume the landscaping metaphor to visualize how a change leader guides people through four different imaginary landscapes of meaning. We conclude that the eight guidelines of sensemaking are key leadership tools. We advocate that a change process should be seen as a spiral, but we also argue that models are useful if we ever want to be able to capture, describe, understand and develop a complex contemporary organization. It is hoped that we leave the reader with a salient feeling that this book has shed some new light on how proactive sensemaking—landscaping—effectively can guide organizations through challenging change processes. All in all, in the end we also hope that the reader has a deeper understanding of the guiding key question of this book: What it is that managers actually do when they lead change through sensemaking?

Bibliography

Andrews, J., Cameron, H. & Harris, M. (2008) All change? Managers' experience of organizational change in theory and practice. *Journal of Organizational Change Management*, 21(3): 300–314.

Burnes, B. (2009) *Managing Change: A Strategic Approach to Organisational Dynamics*. New York: Prentice Hall/Financial Times.

Burnes, B. (2011) Introduction: why does change fail, and what can we do about it? *Journal of Change Management*, 11(4): 445–450.

Gladwell, M. (2000) *The Tipping Point: How Little Things Can Make a Big Difference*. Boston, MA: Little, Brown.

Hallencreutz, J. (2012) *Under the Skin of Change Meanings, Models and Management*. Doctoral thesis. Luleå: Luleå University of Technology.

Herrero, L. (2008) *Viral Change*. Beaconsfield: Meetingminds.

Hughes, M. (2011) Do 70 per cent of all organizational change initiatives really fail? *Journal of Change Management*, 11(4): 451–464.

Iveroth, E. (2010) *Leading IT-enabled Change inside Ericsson: A Transformation into a Global Network of Shared Service Centres*. Doctoral thesis no. 146. Uppsala: Uppsala University, Department of Business Studies.

Iveroth, E. (2011) The sociomaterial practice of IT-enabled change. *Journal of Change Management*, 11(3): 375–395.

Iveroth, E. & Bengtsson, F. (2014) Changing behavior towards sustainable practices using Information Technology. *Journal of Environmental Management*, 139(June): 59–68.

Lüscher, L.S. & Lewis, M.W. (2008) Organizational change and managerial sensemaking: working through paradox. *Academy of Management Journal*, 51(2): 221–240.

Maitlis, S. & Christianson, M. (2014) Sensemaking in organizations: taking stock and moving forward. *The Academy of Management Annals*, 8(1): 57–125.

Neal, D.T., Wood, W. & Quinn, J.M. (2006) Habits—A repeat performance. *Current Directions in Psychological Science*, 15(4): 198–202.

Rogers, E.M. (2003) *Diffusion of Innovations*. New York: Free Press.

Rouleau, L. & Balogun, J. (2011) Middle managers, strategic sensemaking, and discursive competence. *Journal of Management Studies*, 48(5): 953–983.

Sandberg, J. & Tsoukas, H. (2014) Making sense of the sensemaking perspective: its constituents, limitations, and opportunities for further development. *Journal of Organizational Behavior*, 36(1): 6–32.

Schatzki, T.R., Knorr-Cetina, K. & Savigny, E. (2001) *The Practice Turn in Contemporary Theory*. London: Routledge.

Weick, K.E. (1995) *Sensemaking in Organizations*. Thousand Oaks, CA: Sage.

Whittington, R. (2006) Completing the practice turn in strategy research. *Organization Studies*, 27(5): 613–634.

PART I
Theory

2

THE THEORIES OF CHANGE

This chapter discloses some of the underlying aspects of the theories of change. It does so by trying to conceptualize change in the first section. Here we use a fictional story to uncover some of the main themes of this concept. The next section dives deeper into the issue of different perspectives of change, illustrating some of the diverse ways in which change can be viewed and analyzed—revealing different lenses of the kaleidoscope of change. Most importantly we drill down into the perspectives of planned and emergent change as it is one resourceful way to compare the sensemaking perspective to other viewpoints of change. The following section shifts into illustrating some of the different arguments for or against planned and emergent change. Then we continue our journey deeper into the underlying notions of change by exploring the variance and process model of change. These two very different models of change carry with them certain assumptions about change which we will expose. We will then take a more empirical approach toward change compared with the earlier parts of the chapter, by examining the axiom that 70 percent of organizational change initiatives fail. This is done by looking more closely at the evidence of such a claim and the problems and complexities of measuring. Finally we will finish by providing a short reflective and philosophical stance on the effectiveness of organizational change and the claims of its success or failure.

The concept of change

The purpose of this chapter is to try to conceptualize change as a concept. This is by no means a simple task as there are innumerable organizational change definitions, models and explanations. For example, in Google, search using keywords connected to change: "change management" yields 8,170,000 hits; "organizational change" gives 4,580,000 hits; and sensemaking affords 2,170,000 hits.

Instead of presenting yet another model, we choose here to present a well-circulated anecdotal story of unknown origin that captures some of the most important aspects of change. This fictional tale is often used in workshops as well as in teaching and research. For example, Robert W. Scapens (2006) used this story when he tried to summarize decades of his research dedicated to the subject of management control and change (Burns and Scapens 2000).

Despite the unknown origin of the story, and despite being well circulated, we believe that it sends a powerful message about change from which we can learn, because learning in many cases comes not from aggregated metaphors, figures and models, or from atomic details of the empirical world, but rather from the stories that are crafted in between these two extremes. In this way, successful learning in many cases lies in the stories that are woven from both high and low aggregation of a study (Buchanan and Dawson 2007; Dumez and Jeunemaitre 2006; Iveroth 2010b):

> The story begins with a couple of scientists who place five monkeys in a cage together, with a ladder, and a bunch of bananas placed on top of the ladder. Very soon one of the monkeys is hungry and tries to climb the ladder in order to grab the bananas. However, as soon as it attempts to do so, the scientists spray all the remaining monkeys with cold water. Of course, they become terrified, and consequently immediately attack any monkey that tries to go up the ladder. This horrific behavior ultimately results in no monkey attempting to climb the ladder.
>
> Time passes, and after a while the scientists stop spraying the monkeys with cold water and replace one of them with a new monkey. The new monkey grows hungry and tries to climb the ladder, but as soon as it does so, all the remaining monkeys rush forward and attack it. The new monkey never gets up the ladder and learns that if it tries to climb, it will be assaulted.
>
> The process continues and the scientists replace yet another monkey. The same thing happens. The second new monkey tries to get the bananas by climbing the ladder and the rest of the monkeys spring forward and attack it. However, this time round the first new monkey participates in the attack. So it continues, and the scientists replace one monkey after another. Every time this happens the newcomer tries to climb the ladder and is attacked by the other monkeys.
>
> After some time has passed the cage contains five new monkeys. The astonishing thing is that none of these monkeys tries to climb the ladder, despite the fact that none of them has ever been sprayed with water.
>
> Question: Why is this so?
>
> Answer: Because this is the way we have always done things around here.

This story has a clear connection to organizational change because it shows how organizational routines and policies are developed over time and how after a while they become part of the assumptions taken for granted in a culture. Nobody actually knows why we do the things we do because it is the way we have always done so—in this way we often forget the original circumstances that gave rise to a certain behavior.

These assumptions are powerful and are in fact the very heart of organizational change. Deep down it is these assumptions that leaders are trying to alter when they lead and drive organizational change. However, in many cases these forces are overlooked. Managers become obsessed with control and cling on to the formal, structural, top-down aspects of change such as planning, change message, goals, the functionality of technology, increasing shareholder value, numbers, analyses, etc.

A simple example is the implementation of an information system, like an enterprise resource planning (ERP) system. The implementation of such a system is so much more than just the technical artifact and the software. When an ERP system is implemented some people will feel threatened because they will lose power and control, some people will have to re-learn how to do things because it has to be aligned with the ERP system, some people will have to do totally new things and get a new role, and so forth. In this way, the implementation of the ERP system not only requires changes to technology and organizational structure, but also requires that people change what they are doing.

In other words, the greatest challenge for you as a leader is to make people change "how we do things around here." Yet, research recurrently shows that leaders are preoccupied with the hard and technical stuff of change (Davenport 1998; Dedrick et al. 2003; Jørgensen et al. 2009). People too easily believe that as long as they get the right change program and best practice and communicate it to everybody in the organization, then people will understand its brilliance and adopt the change. Such blind faith towards planning and structure is common. What they fail to realize is that the hard factors need to be combined with the soft factors of change that encompassess sensemaking processes (Beer and Eisenstat 1996; Iveroth 2010a).

Hard factors of change should not, however, be ignored. In fact, these factors of change create a foundation on which to build. They are essential because they provide the power that influences the efficiency of the change. Such power is nevertheless limited if it is not combined with the social, softer side of change which primarily consists of sensemaking processes. In this way, the hard factors of change are the "order qualifiers" and the soft factors are the "order winners."

Besides this aspect, there are four other characteristics of change that can be drawn from the story. First, in order to change an organization a leader should try to understand the unique culture, values and social structure of the organization— how and why people do the things they do in a particular organization. Every organization and change situation is unique and change as such is therefore to a certain extent a highly situated and context-dependent phenomena. More simply put, there is no one-size-fits-all solution to change. However, one factor that increases the probability for success is first to make sense of the organization that you are trying to change, and *then* change it.

This sensemaking can take the form of just talking to people in the organization to get a feel and sense of "how they do things around here." It can also take a more structured approach with the use of instruments and models (a classical example is the cultural web; see Johnson 1992) that (it is hoped) are not used bluntly as truths but as a way to make sense and discuss the organization and the change. Neither the less structured nor the structured approach is a panacea and using both approaches at the same time is probably most effective (together with some critical thought).

Without such structured and unstructured approaches we would probably fail at our first attempt to change the monkey's behavior because we did not take the time to make sense and understand why in this case the monkeys were reluctant to climb the ladder. So in conclusion, change is deeply connected to the culture, social structure and values of an organization. Therefore, the probability for success is higher if a leader tries to make sense of these unique circumstances before implementing change.

A second characteristic of change that we can draw from the story of the five monkeys is that change is highly political. Say, for example, that you wanted to change the situation of the monkeys and try to alter their behavior to make them climb the ladder and grab the bananas. Then you could increase your chances of success by speaking to the leader of the monkeys—the alpha male. If he could be convinced, then others would most likely follow. By extension, leaders who take change seriously and acknowledge its political aspect understand that it requires various strategic, diplomatic and subtle activities. For instance, successful leaders are proactive and perform different kinds of stakeholder analyses, and in doing so try to avoid excessive conflict. This leader also values "rallying the troops" through roadshows and building a network of "change sponsors" before the formal change is launched. When the change is in motion, conflicts and change resistance are dealt with immediately and delicately.

The third characteristic is that history plays a key role in change. If you as a leader can understand the circumstances that originally gave rise to a certain behavior, than the situation will be easier to change. For example, if the new monkeys in the cage understood the circumstances of being sprayed with water, then it would be much easier to change the situation. Remember that none of the new monkeys has any information about being sprayed with cold water. In their world, every monkey that tried to climb the ladder was attacked simply because that was the way things were. In short, the behavior becomes detached from its historical roots. So one of the first tasks for a change leader is in fact not to look into the future but instead to look into the rearview mirror and make sense of the past. It is only when we understand the past that we can effectively move forward.

Finally, change is in part composed of tacit properties such as ideas and emotions. In our story the monkeys' behavior was controlled by strong, terrified feelings of getting sprayed with cold water and being attacked by the other monkeys. Likewise, there were ideas that controlled the situation such as avoiding climbing up the ladder. These properties of change are tacit, intangible and imperceptible in nature. This is one of the reasons why change can seem slippery and hard to manage, and this is why a large part of the literature is occupied with activities such as coming up with a strategy for change resistance and crafting an inspiring change vision. Here lies also part of the reason why successful change agents score high in having people-management skills and emotional intelligence. This is presumably also the reason why change is more effective where there is an increasing willingness to move away from rational argument, figures and numbers, towards stories, feelings and sensemaking.

In conclusion the story of the five monkeys has provided us with a number of important characteristics for change that we will directly and indirectly re-visit throughout this book. These are in summary:

- Change is deeply connected to the taken-for-granted-assumptions that are developed over time.
- Driving change is a combination of managing the hard factors and the soft factors of change. The hard factors only provide a foundation and it is the soft factors (including sensemaking) that ultimately determine the success of the change.
- There is no panacea for managing change as it is situated and dependent of context and culture.
- Change is highly political.
- History plays a key-role in managing change.
- Large parts of a change process contains tacit and intangible properties.

Different perspectives of change

There have been numerous reviews of organizational research that try to categorize change in different ways, and here we will use the work of Senior and Swailes (2010) and By (2005), as they have one of the most intuitive ways of doing so.[1] They suggest that change theories can be classified in three ways: scale and scope, rate of occurrence and how it comes about.[2] We will look closer at these three ways of categorization. First, we will give examples of the first two types and then elevate both into a matrix that snares more of the details and complexities of the elusive concept of change. By doing so, the framework provides us with a roadmap that can facilitate discussion and comparison of different change projects. The second part of this section covers "how change comes about," and this provides us with some specific arguments and discussions that aid our understanding of sense-making and how to frame and compare the concept with other perspectives. Altogether, these three different ways to categorize change—scale and scope, rate of occurrence and how it comes about—provide us with a language that we can use to aid our understanding and discussions of change. In this way, they function as a kaleidoscope revealing different facets of change.

Classifying change according to scale and scope

The first type of categorization, scale and scope, refers to the extent of the change (By 2005; Senior and Swailes 2010). One of the most referenced examples of such a classification is Dunphy and Stace (1993), who categorize change as in Figure 2.1.

Both Modular transformations and Corporate transformations can be seen as radical change, whereas the others are more minor changes. Overall, this kind of classification is rather straightforward and this is also probably why there is less debate and dispute regarding it among researchers. The strength of Dunphy and Stace's work is that it is in its original form fairly detailed; however, it assumes that change is planned and orchestrated.

There are also less detailed classifications that often focus on a two-fold category about the scope. For example, Marshak (2002) distinguishes change depending on if it influences only parts and segments of the organization or if it influences patterns and the whole organizational system. In a similar manner, Balogun and Hailey (2008) differentiate between transformational change that includes a reappraisal of the central assumptions of the organization, versus realignment change that refers to organizational alterations performed within an existing framework.

Classifying change according to the rate of occurrence

Rate of occurrence, the second type of classification, denotes how often change happens. Some researchers claim that change is discontinuous and occurs in radical moves and revolutions. Here change is often a dramatic alteration of the organization as a whole which includes strategic reorientation. Organizations experience relatively long periods of stability which suddenly end in an outburst of radical change. In turn, this is followed by another period of balance and equilibrium that ends with another period of revolutionary change (Gersick 1991). This type of discontinuous change is often triggered by a new disruptive and innovative technology (e.g. smartphones and digital photography), redesign of processes (e.g. Business Process Re-engineering), or profound changes to policies and regulations (e.g. the deregulation of the telecommunications market in the 1980s in parts of Europe). As Burke (2008) points out, these types of change models can also be identified in theories of individual change, such as the transformation into parenthood. They can also be detected in many theories of group change: "Groups do not develop in

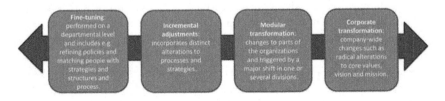

FIGURE 2.1 Classifying change according to scale and scope
Source: Based on Dunphy and Stace 1993.

a linear set of stages, rather, they proceed with not much happening and then recognize (almost suddenly) a need to move forward rapidly in a new way" (Burke 2008: 66).

There is another camp, on the other hand, which argues that change is less radical than some want us to believe. Instead, it is suggested that change is continuous rather than discontinuous and takes the form of many small steps and adjustments which together make up the change in a larger system. After every incremental step there are feedback loops and reviews to determine if the change step was in the right direction. If not, then attempts will be made to improve the incremental change.

In this way, continuous change arises not from revolutions but from evolution and is often driven bottom-up. Typical examples include Japanese practices such as Kaizen and continuous improvement. Theories that are labeled continuous often make connection between the nature of change and the nature of living systems and biology. They often claim, for instance, that organizations are like all living things in that they evolve over time in an ongoing fashion and with a constant struggle for survival.

There is evidence for both radical and evolutionary change, and both types are equally beneficial for an organization. What matters, though, is the particular change situation and people's ability to make sense of the challenge ahead: "The point is: Over time (and even concurrently) organizations need evolution and revolution [...] The trick is to clearly identify the nature of the challenge and then use the right tool for the right task" (Pascale et al. 2000: 38).

Now, if we combine the two ways of categorizing (i.e. scale and scope, and rate of occurrence) into a matrix we get four different types of change, as illustrated by Figure 2.2.

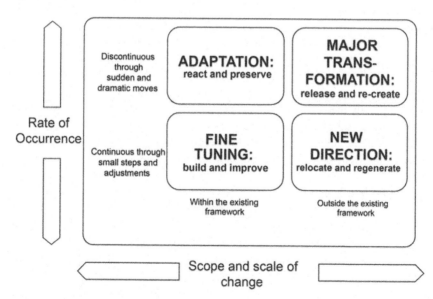

FIGURE 2.2 Four different types of change
Source: Based on Marshak 2002; Nadler and Nadler 1998.

Starting from the upper left corner of the matrix, we have what is referred to as Adaption. Here change is discontinuous that occurs through sudden and dramatic moves. However, it is not transformational for the whole organization as the scope of the change is within the existing framework. This type of change is often the result of, for example, a gap analysis and alterations are only done to individual subunits and components of the organization. One of the purposes of Adaption is to react to external triggers such as new legislation, new competition, environmental changes which lead to adjustment and alignment parts of strategy, structure and processes. However, core aspects of the organizations operation are not really affected as the needed changes are within existing frames. A spectacular example could be when the Icelandic volcano Eyafjattnajökul erupted in April 2010. The eruption as such was nothing to bother about except for people living nearby, but the volcano produced an enormous cloud of ash that drifted more or less all over Northern Europe and halted air traffic. From 15 to 20 April about 20 countries (most of European IFR airspace) stopped all commercial jet traffic. Consequently, a very high proportion of flights within, to and from Europe were canceled, creating the highest level of air travel disruption since World War II. About 100,000 flights and 10 million travelers were affected and overnight many organizations in the area needed to adapt to new circumstances. The eruption affected economic, political and cultural activities in Europe and across the world. Several sectors depending on air freighted imports and exports were badly affected by the flight disruption.

Moving to the lower left corner of the matrix we find Fine tuning. This is the type of change that is done on a continuous basis through small steps and alterations and is performed with an existing framework. The aim here is to build and improve existing practices through ongoing operational adaptations and improvements. Change practices such as Kaizen and Total Quality Management bear the mark of this type of change. A resilient organization strives to be in this corner. Toyota is a well-known and often-used example here. In the mid-1960s Toyota and the Swedish car manufacturer SAAB both produced around 30,000 units per year. Toyota followed its long-term fine-tuning philosophy while SAAB chose another path. By the end of 2012 Toyota produced 10,000,000 units per year while SAAB filed for bankruptcy after decades of strategic, structural and cultural problems.

Moving to the right, we have New directions which is still change that occurs on a continuous basis but is more radical in nature because the scope of the change lies outside the existing framework. This type of change strives to relocate the organization by changes to its culture, structure and processes, as well as to regenerate the competitive advantage through ongoing alteration to its products, services, capabilities and resources. This type of change is usually the result of deliberate decisions taken by key stakeholders. An example could be when the global IT player IBM during the fall of 2004 decided to sell its PC division to China-based Lenovo Group and take a minority stake in the former rival. IBM is one of the few IT companies with a continuous history dating back to the 19th century. The company has been well known through most of its recent history as one of the world's largest computer companies and systems integrators. Thus, at the time, the disposal of the company's PC unit definitely meant a new strategic, structural and cultural direction—from the traditional focus on hardware to a more software-oriented strategy.

Finally, in the upper right corner, Major transformation is situated. This type aims to release the organization from its current position and recreate what the company does by radical changes to its strategy, structure and processes. In this way, this is a dramatic change to the "spinal cord" of the organization. A Major transformation is often the outcome of a crisis due to profound disruptive external events. The impact of new technology has definitely over time affected many mature industries such as photography, telecoms and media, where the business logic faces new ways of thinking. However—and this is important—the experience of a major transformation is also context dependent. For instance, the Eyafjattna-jökul eruption in 2010 implied a major transformation for smaller organizations within the traveling industry. In the United Kingdom alone, 13 travel firms collapsed during the summer of 2010. The ash cloud disruption was cited as one of the contributing factors.

In summary, the four types of change displayed in Figure 2.2 offer one way to structure and make sense of the myriad types of change that exist. Such classifications can be of value because the term "organizational change" often means different things to different people. In fact, practitioners and researchers often talk past each other when they converse about change, or use different words, phrases and concepts when referring to the same thing. When using this matrix in practice, this is often the scene. A senior executive might call a change initiative a fine tuning: "*Ah, this change is not really a big thing. We merge two departments that do pretty much the same thing. It's a tune up.*" However, the middle managers in charge face a different reality: "*For us, this is big. All our employees will be affected. I would call it a major transformation.*" As a result, we not only get stuck intellectually exploring different avenues for change but also it obstructs our decisions and actions which in turn can impede the change process as such (Jabri 2012; Marshak 2002; Pettigrew et al. 2001). Indeed, we concur with Marshak (2002: 285) when he reminds us that: "Talk is never 'just talk.' Language is not a neutral medium. Language both enables and limits what and how we think and therefore what we do."

Classifying according to how change comes about

The final category is how change comes about. This refers to how change is accomplished and comes into being. This is also the main concern of this book as it is a way of comparing and framing the sensemaking approach. Here there are two major camps: those who argue that change is an intentional and planned activity, and those who argue that true change is instead an emergent activity that is mainly driven bottom-up.

Planned change is the most prominent paradigm and views change as a progressive movement from one (worse) stable state to another (better) state through time, often with a clear end state—like an arrow from the present to the future.

This movement is the result of a disequilibrium that has arisen from a divergence from the internal deep structure of the organization or from the external environment (such as adjusting to new market conditions). Change as such follows a linear trajectory towards a specific end state which is defined by a vision. An understanding of change is mainly acquired from examining it from outside and viewing it from afar with a macro, distant and global perspective. In practice, a planned change is often described as having a number of clear steps, such as Explore, Plan, Action and Integrate.

From the standpoint of planned perspective, change is an intentional activity with one or several autonomous change agents which are not directly part of the system that is undergoing the change—driving the change from outside. These actors are the prime movers of change which through analyzing and planning activities orchestrate the change. Ford and Ford (1995: 543) explain that planned change:

> occurs when a change agent deliberately and consciously sets out to establish conditions and circumstances that are different from what they are now and then accomplishes that through some set or series of actions and interventions either singularly or in collaboration with other people. The change is produced with intent, and the change agent is at cause in the matter of making the change.

The planned approach stems from the seminal work of Kurt Lewin, who after a successful academic career in Germany fled to the USA before World War II. His continued work across the Atlantic amounted to numerous influential theories, models and ideas including, for example, action research, group dynamics, force field analysis and the three-step model of change. Among these it is probably the three-step model that has had the most impact on organizational research. The underlying idea is to split up the change process into a three-face model consisting of the parts displayed in Figure 2.3.

The three-step model has inspired numerous researchers by introducing the idea of dividing the change process into phases (Beckhard and Harris 1987; Beer 1980; Bullock and Batten 1985; Burke 2008; Lippitt et al. 1958). For example, Lippitt and his colleagues (1958) continued Lewin's work and suggest that the change process can be stretched out even further and divided into seven steps:

1. Diagnose the problem—unfreeze
2. Assess the motivation and capacity for change—unfreeze

FIGURE 2.3 Lewin's three-step model of change

3. Assess the motivation, resources and commitment of change agent—unfreeze
4. Choose progressive change object and develop to-do lists and strategy—move
5. Select and clarify the role and responsibility of the change agent—move
6. Uphold change through communication, coordination and feedback—refreeze
7. Progressively let go of the helping relationship where the change agents withdraw their responsibility and the change is integrated into the culture of the organization—refreeze

Lewin can be considered one of the forefathers of change research and his overall influence on social science, and in organizational change in particular, cannot be understated:

> There is little question that the intellectual father of contemporary theories of applied behavioral science, action research and planned change is Kurt Lewin. His seminal work on leadership style and the experiments on planned change which took place in World War II in an effort to change consumer behavior launched a whole generation of research in group dynamics and the implementation of change programs.
>
> *(Schein 1988: 238; also noted by Burnes 2004)*

Indeed, Lewin's impact is profound and many of today's influential change-management models can be seen as a result of the Lewinian heritage, for example organizational development, the open system approach and large group interventions.

The other major camp argues that change can also come about as an *emergent* and constantly evolving activity. This is the counterpoint to planned change and is also where the sensemaking perspective is situated. The proponents for the emergent change perspective argue that if you follow the people who are actually driving the change in the field then another picture arises that is very different compared with that argued by the planned approach advocates. Here change seems to be an everyday activity consisting of many loosely coupled acts that are interdependent and over time can build up, accumulate and gain momentum to create substantial change. With this view, change is something constantly present in our daily lives and is the accumulation of many small alterations of, for example, processes and practices. As such, change occurs all the time and is often the consequence of improvisation, experimentation and a way of acting as a response to the absence of *a priori* explicit plans and intentions. Knowledge of change is predominately gained from exploring it "from within" and by examining change up close with a micro, close and local perspective. A deep understanding of change, it is argued, can only be gained from experiencing or exploring it at the front line.

As we noted earlier, planned change follows a linear trajectory that resembles an arrow from the present to a clearly defined future end state, which along the way is divided into different clear steps (Lindvall and Iveroth 2011). In contrast, the emergent perspective follows a cyclical, processual trajectory (Marshak 1993; Tsoukas and Chia 2002; Weick and Quinn 1999). With this perspective the change is a process that goes through different phases in a cycle and when the cycle has been completed it revisits these phases. However, when the change returns to the phases of the change cycle the phases are (it is hoped) different from earlier, being altered as a result of going through the cycle. There is no end state; instead, the change process is journey oriented and strives to make improvements along the way and to restore balance.

Popular examples of the phase and trajectory of emergent change are continuous change processes and feedback loops: plan–do–check–act (PDCA, the Deming cycle) or plan–implement–assess–modify. Other common examples are often based on the idea of a "life cycle" that is applied to different things that change. For example, a product can be seen to go through the phases of development, introduction, growth, maturity and decline. Similarly, we all go through life in a process of the phases of birth, adolescence, maturity, aging and decline, and ultimately death.

Marshak (1993) illustrates the difference in the trajectory of planned and emergent change by the change process that high-performing groups often go through, displayed in Figure 2.4. In planned change that follows a progressive path the group goes through the states of Form, Storm, Norm, and finishes in the end state of Perform.[3] Marshak (1993: 402) notes

> "When change is viewed as linear and progressive, it is logically inappropriate and/or impossible to go back to something that came before" (in the less effective past). The focus of attention and action(s) is on striving toward the (better) future. As a result, redoing something in the linear-progressive model is likely to be viewed as "going backward," "not making progress" or "going around in circles." To repeat something is almost synonymous with failure and is frequently avoided even when needed. Thus in a team-building intervention, the focus might be to move the team through various stages of group

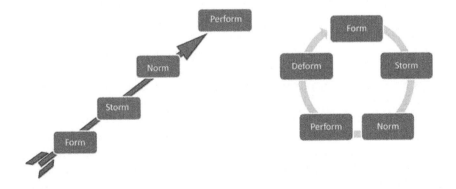

FIGURE 2.4 Group development according to planned and emergent change
Source: Based on Marshak 1993: 405.

development until it becomes a "high-performing team." Returning at that point to an earlier stage, such as group formation or norm setting, would be viewed negatively because the (implicit) objective is to achieve and maintain (permanently) the high-performance stage.

In contrast, Marshak illustrates the cyclical trajectory of group development in an emergent perspective by explaining that it goes through five (instead of four) phases which are constantly revisited but in different form: form, storm, norm, perform, deform. Marshak (1993: 402–403) explains:

> returning to some stage/phase/state, albeit in a different form perhaps, is normal and needed to maintain continuing harmony and equilibrium. In a cyclical model, after all, "going around in circles" is both normal and necessary. Returning to something is not only expected but, in fact, needed to "keep things moving." Furthermore, in a cyclical-processional model no stage is presumed to be better than another. Each stage is just different and necessary to maintain the natural cycle. Consequently, in the cyclical-processional model, one would assume there is a stage after high performance (perhaps decline or deforming) that the team would naturally move into after achieving peak performance. Deforming or decline would then inherently lead to team re-forming, re-norming, and so on, back to high performance and decline in endless cycles.

Emergent change is mainly driven with a bottom-up approach where sensemaking is of central concern. The different models, lower-level theories and approaches that are presented mainly in Chapters 3–5 are a cornerstone for this perspective. As we will elaborate in Chapter 5, the leader functions as a sensemaker who has the ability to sense the change before it comes into full being and then tries to redirect and translate the change for employees or other stakeholders.

An illustrative way to explain some of the details of emergent change is the work of Orlikowski (1996: 66):

> Each variation of a given form is not an abrupt or discrete event, neither is it, by itself, discontinuous. Rather, through a series of ongoing and situated accommodations, adaptations, and alterations (that draw on previous variations and mediate future ones), sufficient modifications may be enacted over time that fundamental changes are achieved. There is no deliberate orchestration of change here, no technological inevitability, no dramatic discontinuity, just recurrent and reciprocal variations in practice over time. Each shift in practice creates the conditions for further breakdowns, unanticipated outcomes, and innovations, which in their turn are responded to with more variations. And such variations are ongoing; there is no beginning or end point in this change process.

A summary of different aspects of planned and emergent change is displayed in Table 2.1.[4]

Arguments for and against the emergent and planned perspectives

There is, and has been for quite some time, a discussion of arguments for and against planned or emergent perspectives.[5] Researchers often discuss which theoretical

TABLE 2.1 Comparison of planned and emergent change

	Planned change	*Emergent change*
Rhythm, pattern and frequency of change	Change is intentional and is infrequent and discontinuous	Change is constant and is evolving and cumulative
View of change and inertia	Change is an occasional disruption or divergence from equilibrium that is driven and managed externally	Change is a pattern of ceaseless modifications and alterations in processes and practices
	Change is the outcome of the failure of adapting the deep structure of the organization to the altered outer context and environment	Change is the outcome of organizational instability and alert reactions to daily contingencies
Level of aggregation and standpoint of the observer	Understanding change from outside by viewing it from afar with a macro, distant and global perspective	Understanding change from within by exploring it up close on the front line with a micro, close and local perspective
Role of change agent	The change agent is an autonomous actor that functions as a prime mover that orchestrates change	The change agent is a sensemaker who senses the underlying dynamics of upcoming change and tries to redirect change accordingly through translation and conversation
Type of intervention	Predominantly top-down	Predominantly bottom-up
Change trajectory	Linear and progressive trajectory from one stable state to another that is oriented toward a clear end goal and destination	Continuous, processual and cyclical trajectory that seeks equilibrium and goes through different phases that are revisited in (it is hoped) altered form
Examples of related theories, models and applications	Lewinian three-step model, organizational development, large group interventions, gestalt psychology, evolutionary economics, punctuated equilibrium, variance model	Sensemaking, population ecology, contextualism, organizational learning, antenarrative, dialogue, sociomateriality, process model

Source: Adapted from Weick and Quinn 1999: 366; Marshak 1993: 403.

lens to use when analyzing their data, and practitioners often want to know which perspective is the most effective in propelling change forward.

Arguments from the advocates for emergent change

On the one hand, advocates for the emergent perspective criticize planned change for being unrealistic because their ideas do not align with how things really are at the front line of change. Weick (2001: 231), for example, argues that:

> the liabilities of planned change include a high probability of relapse; uneven diffusion among units; large short-term losses that are difficult to recover; less suitability for opportunity-driven than for threat-driven alterations; unantici-pated consequences due to limited foresight; temptations toward hypocrisy (when people talk the talk of revolution but walk the talk of resistance); adoption of best practices that work best elsewhere because of a different context; ignorance among top management regarding key contingencies and capabilities at the front line.

Besides this, there are four other recurrent criticisms of the planned perspective. First, the planned approach can be criticized for not coping with the current global and fast-changing business environment because "the change plan" becomes obsolete even before it is implemented. Planned change is insufficient since "the change plan" becomes outdated and management cannot adapt quickly enough.

Second, the perspective assumes that the change strategy is crafted by well-informed and knowledgeable managers. However, many of the leaders high up in the hierarchy of the organization often do not have a clear picture of what is needed to accomplish the change. There is an overreliance on the leaders who are too far away from the vanguard of change (By 2005; Poole and Van de Ven 2004; Wilson 1992). As Weick (2000: 229) puts it, there is often an overestimation of and blind faith in "the centrality of managerial planning."

Third, the planned approach underestimates the power and interests of different stakeholders. The perspective is based on the assumption that change is a project where agreement can be reached and that the people involved have a willingness and interest in participating (Burnes 2009; Caldwell 2006; Dawson 1994). However, such a view ignores the politics of change because in reality there are often great conflicts and power plays between different stakeholders (Constantinides and Barrett 2006; Hill 2003; Hope 2010).

Fourth, the planned approach has also been criticized for being too rational. For example, the planned approach departs from the perspective where the world can be objectively observed and measured. These measurements and observations can then be used to conduct sequential analyses and action. History, context, experience and emotion are neglected. An illustrative example of the rational nature of planned change is the work of Beckhard and Harris (1987). They argue that successful change is mainly the product of a cognitive and analytical process. Such change is achieved when the recipients have intellectually understood the problems of maintaining a status quo and have received clear communication about the future end state. In this way, change per se is merely a transactional event between a sender and a receiver. They summarize their argument in their change formula:

$$C = [ABD] > X$$

where C refers to change, A denotes the recipients' level of dissatisfaction with the status quo, B stands for the recipients' desire to achieve the proposed change and end state, D stands for practicality of change, and finally X is the cost of the change.

According to this formula, unsuccessful change and change resistance are often merely a question of failed cognitive and analytical transaction between the agent and recipient. In other words, the employees have not truly understood the message of change. This failed transaction can then be corrected by repeating or reinventing the form and message of change. When they at last understand the rational arguments in the message of change then change will follow rapidly.

Arguments from the advocates of planned change

On the other hand, the proponents for the planned perspective argue that it is almost impossible to manage change with an emergent approach since change with this perspective consists of micro-processes, circular trajectory and a mish-mash of unpredictable activities and events. They argue that the emergent perspective provides little hands-on guidance for what actually should be done (Hughes 2010). In short, the action steps are very unclear and ambiguous.

Another weakness is that the emergent perspective as a movement is very fragmented. There is a lack of a clear and united focus on how to manage, deal with and drive change as well as a dearth of any agreement on model or approach. At best, the proponents of emergent change can settle on a number of overarching principles of different kinds (Dawson 1994, 2003; Pettigrew 1997). However, these are often broad and ambiguous. By (2005: 375) notes that the movement "consists of a rather disparate group of models and approaches that tend to be more united in their skepticism to the planned approach to change than to an agreed alternative."

Another criticism is that the emergent approach departs from the notion that organizations are situated in a dynamic and ever-changing environment. However, as Burnes (2009) reminds us, this is not always the case and there can be situations where the market and environment are stable, and where planned change can indeed be a fruitful approach. The emergent approach is therefore not universally applicable.

A final critique is that emergent change scholars often criticize the planned approach for reducing change into a number of simple steps. However, if you examine some of the writings of the advocates of the emergent approach in detail, they too suggest that change has stages in the form of, for example, a start, middle and end (Hayes 2002; Hendry 1996). For instance, Hendry (1996: 624) notes: "Scratch any account of creating and managing change and the idea that change is a three stage process which necessarily begins with a process of unfreezing will not be far below the surface."

Complicating things further

The above arguments are just some of the many opinions and considerations connected to planned and emergent change. Overall, however, such discussions of "for" or "against" the two different perspectives are a hazardous play that can cloud the mind: "The danger in discussing emergent change as a counterpoint to planned change is that a polarized either/or divide is encouraged" (Hughes 2010: 96–97). As Hughes (2010: 97) also notes, if you look closely enough at the writing of, for example, Weick (2000) and Burnes (2009), it actually "favours a more balanced approach" where both theories exist depending on perspective. We align ourselves with these and other researchers with similar notions by arguing that reality lies in covering some of the aspects of both ends of the spectrum (e.g. Marshak 1993: 410; Poole and Van de Ven 2004: 6; Tsoukas and Chia 2002: 572; Weick 2000: 239).

The question is not one of either/or: change as such can be both planned and emergent at the same time. There are many complex underlying reasons for such a claim (e.g. Burnes 2009; Bushe and Marshak 2009; Farjoun 2010; Hernes 2014; Marshak 1993; Purser and Petranker 2005; Tsoukas and Chia 2002) and here are five.

First, if you extend your examination of the literature from the aforementioned reflections over change towards actual change theories, you will most likely discover that many of these include both planned and emergent change (Van de Ven and Poole 1995). Greenwood's institutional theory and McGrath and Tschan's complex adaptive systems theory are two examples (Poole and Van de Ven 2004).

Second, the complexities of contemporary business yield a situation where leaders often have to have a duality of approach to manage their business—being able to manage planned *and* emergent change at the same time. In a broad perspective, social science has been dominated by an either/or perspective (e.g. planned or emergent), but an increasing body of research now underlines that driving forces such as technology and globalization require organizations to be flexible enough to handle "and" situations instead of "either/or" ones (Agarwal and Helfat 2009; Farjoun 2010; Netz and Iveroth 2011). A classic example of this phenomenon is in strategy, where some argue that organizations today have to be flexible enough to have both a low-cost and a differentiation strategy, and sometimes two organizations have to compete and cooperate at the same time (Calori 1998; Collins and Porras 1994; Hamel and Prahalad 1994). Similarly, studies in international business show that multinational corporations need to be and act both on global and local levels (Bartlett and Ghoshal 1989). Likewise, studies about information technology show how technology enables organizations to be centralized and decentralized at the same time (Boland et al. 1994; Lindvall and Iveroth 2011).

A brief and crude example of being able to manage planned and emergent change at the same time is the implementation of information systems. When such a change project follows a planned approach it starts by analytically assessing the situation in the organization (e.g. the current situation, as-is analysis), drawing up a strategic plan with different milestones and a predetermined end state (e.g. determining IT requirements, crafting goals and a vision), conducting necessary organizational change and then designing and rolling out the IT project in accordance with the plan. In this way, the IT is treated as a simple and stable tool that can be constructed and implemented following some simple pre-designed and planned steps (Avgerou and McGrath 2007; Iveroth 2011). However, the success of the implementation partly hinges on managers' openness to the emergent change that occurs during the process, and that is spread across the organization and its willingness to rewrite the plan accordingly. In this respect they have to "stick to a plan," but at the same time be open to emerging evidence that gathers momentum across the organization and amounts to a redirection of the change process. In other words, the leaders have to try to stick to the plan but at the same time constantly be open to rewriting the plan according to emerging evidence from the people who are actually implementing the change.[6]

To be able to do so, leaders have to be receptive to the sensemaking that is performed at the front line where change managers are dealing with behavioral and organizational change, and where the technicians discover different ways to tailor the system to the organization. Further important activities are the ability to look closely and be updated on what is happening; conversing candidly with people to discover what is actually going on; facilitating learning to learn from trials and mistakes during the change journey; making sense of the emerging evidence and translating it into concrete action of what to do next and then redirecting and providing a new direction. Altogether, these and other aspects are in fact precisely what we refer to as the eight guidelines for sensemaking, which we will return to in Chapters 5 and 6.

Third, there is no universal remedy for managing change. Neither planned change nor emergent change is universally applicable and they both have their benefits and their shortcomings. Indeed, there are several ways to approach change. Every organization is in itself unique and faces novel challenges that cannot be compared with others. There are, for example, situational variables that need to be accounted for (Burnes 2009; Stace and Dunphy 1994). On one hand emergent change can be attractive for organizations that face global competition and rapidly changing environments. One the other hand there are organizations that are situated in a stable environment with predictable situations where planned change most likely is a better choice. Then there are the internal organizational aspects that need to be accounted for as some organizational cultures can be more aligned and attuned with emergent change than others. In this respect, there is a certain truth to the statement that "one best way to manage change" should be replaced with "one best way for each" (Burnes 1996). An organization should manage change depending on its unique circumstances. Neither planned nor emergent change will offer a blueprint—both are needed, depending on the situation.

However, that being said, such a contingency approach also has its drawbacks. For example, a contingency approach to change does not adequately address the fact that change consists of numerous different stakeholders with different opinions that are often in conflict. In reality things are much more complex and you cannot just "pick" an approach and implement change accordingly. What complicates things even further is that many organizations today have change processes that bear the mark of being both planned and emergent at the same time. The sheer scale and complexity of contemporary organizations has amounted to a situation where there are several different types of sub-organizations, social structures, sub-cultures and so forth within the same larger organization (Iveroth 2012). Therefore, treating an organization as a single, monolithic entity and leading change with one type of approach is obsolete. In this respect, "one best way for each" should be replaced with "several best ways for each."

Fourth, whether change is planned or emergent depends on the level of aggregation and how close you are to the actual change. In other words, it depends on the standpoint of the observer. Weick and Quinn (1999: 362) explain:

> From a distance (the macro level of analysis), when observers examine the flow of events that constitute organizing, they see what looks like repetitive action, routine, and inertia dotted with occasional episodes of revolutionary change. But a view from closer in (the micro level of analysis) suggests ongoing adaptation and adjustment. Although these adjustments may be small, they also tend to be frequent and continuous across units, which mean they are capable of altering structure and strategy.

Tsoukas and Chia (2002: 572, emphasis in original) illustrate this point by taking an example from Bateson (1979) about an acrobat balancing on a high wire (see also Hernes 2014):

> We say the acrobat on the high wire maintains her stability. However, she does so by continuously correcting her imbalance [...] For example, at a certain level of analysis (or logical type)—that of the body—the statement "the acrobat maintains her balance" is true, as is also true the statement "the acrobat constantly adjusts her posture," but at another level of analysis—that of the *parts* of the body. The apparent stability of the acrobat does not preclude change; on the contrary it presupposes it.

More crudely put, if you look at the acrobat from a distance, like watching from the audience, the acrobat appears to be very stable in her posture and what she does. However, if you look closer you will notice that her stability is composed of many small changes and balancing acts of her entire body.

So at the very front line and in the details of change, things are to some extent always continuous, consisting of numerous small, interconnected changes. As such, these continuous alterations seem to be the result of improvisation, learning, real-time experimentation, daily conversations and discussions, quick feedback loops, meaning making, sensegiving, reinterpretation, translation, social interactions and so forth.

From another perspective, if you are viewing the same change from afar—like being senior managers far away from where change actually happens and being preoccupied by planning—than change appears to be much more stable. For them, change is composed of infrequent changes, revolutions, aggregated analytical data, linear paths, coordination and rational management control systems, central management planning and so forth. The main point is that indeed change can be viewed as planned; however, in the forefront where change actually happens, change is continuous.

In summary, if you take change seriously and if you examine change in practice then you will notice that in most cases there is no planned change that is not also emergent, and no emergent change that is not planned. All changes have ingredients of both perspectives but the degree of planned or emergent varies. Change, life and our world are far too complex for clear-cut distinctions and it is unrealistic to presume otherwise. This is also why in this book we present case studies and new theories (i.e. landscaping, see Chapters 6 and 7) that to some extent include both a planning and emergent perspective. If you look close enough you can detect traces of both perspectives depending on which theoretical lens you are applying and which aspect of the case studies you are examining—but you will also find a strong dominance of the emergent view.

Our belief in change as an emergent phenomenon is firm but at the same time we do acknowledge the complexities of reality and therefore are inclined to incorporate some of the aspects of planned change in our analyses and writing. By doing so, we choose a less radical way than others, and a more practice-oriented approach than earlier research has offered. Together, this amounts to a middle way between planned and emergent change with a preference for the latter.

There are many practitioners who avoid embracing the benefits of emergent change and focus too much on the routines, managerial planning, numbers and figures, top-down interventions, distinct change phases, visions and goals, best practice of the planned change. Not all of these changes fail, but the majority of such changes could have a higher certainty of success if they opened up to the theories and guidelines that we present in this book and combined them with their current planned change interventions. Indeed, we concur with Weick (2000: 237) when he notes that, "if leaders take notice of emergent change and its effects, however, they can be more selective in their use of planned change." One reason why many managers earlier have ignored this is because there is a considerable amount of knowledge about planned change and significantly less understanding of emergent change. We simply do not have enough knowledge about what it is that managers actually do when they drive sensemaking processes. This is precisely the knowledge gap that this book addresses.

Variance and process perspectives

We ended the earlier section by arguing that in reality change can be both planned and emergent, dependent on such things as the situation and the standpoint of the observer. Here we extend this discussion by trying to explain that planned and emergent perspectives are also in some cases a matter of which theoretical and methodological lens you choose. The lens in the glasses of planned change will allow you to see certain things and in certain ways, while the lens in the glasses of emergent change will make you see things in a totally different light. Accompanying the choice of glasses are certain assumptions about change: what change actually is, what it is composed of, how it comes into being, and how we can study it. This is the main subject of this section.

Overall, there are two approaches that are used in studies of change: the variance model and the process model (Langley 1999; Mohr 1982). The former views change as a "thing" and as an entity and is most prominent in the planned approach. The variance model functions on an input-process-output model (e.g. Rogers 1962) as the focus is on understanding the variables that go into the "black box" and then explaining what comes out at the other end. The variance model is beneficial for studies focusing on the causes, outcomes and mechanisms behind organizational change. The underlying assumption is that an outcome will constantly come about when the sufficient and required conditions are present (Poole et al. 2000).

Since the approach examines the relation between an independent and a dependent variable—a "black-box" perspective—it puts less emphasis on how change occurs across time. In other words, the model sheds less light on what happens inside the black box. A typical research question for studies that use a variance model is "*What* are the antecedents or consequences of the issue" (Van de Ven 2007: 145, emphasis in the original).

Instead of examining change through the lens of the variance model you can choose the process model. This model is chiefly concerned with understanding how change evolves and develops over time. This model is most commonly used in studies of emergent change scholars and here the focus is on the different events, activities and choices that are made across the change process. Van de Ven explains that a typical research question for studies that uses a process model is: "How does the issue emerge, develop, grow, or terminate over time?" He continues to explain that the process model seeks "'event-driven' explanation of the temporal order and sequence in which a discrete set of events occur based on a story or historical narrative" (Van de Ven 2007: 145). An illustrative example of such narratives is the case studies that are presented in this book (see Chapter 7). The researcher Pettigrew (1997)—who can be considered one of the earliest supporters of the process model—has summarized a set of guiding assumptions for processual analyses to which most studies using this model ascribe. See Box 2.1 for some of these.

A further underlying notion of the variance and process models is the matter of how you view change in connection to your belief of the nature of the world and its composition (i.e. ontology). Van de Ven and Poole (2005: 1377–1378) use an example from Rescher (1996) to illustrate this point by connecting it to the ideas of the philosophers Democritus and Heraclitus from antiquity. As they explain, Democritus favored viewing the world as stable, consisting of "things" and "entities" as he "pictured all of nature as composed of stable material substance or things that changed only in their positioning in space and time. Here the identity or substance of things does not change, only their development and adaptation in relation to other dimensions and properties."

Heraclitus, on the other hand, viewed the world from a process perspective as he "argued that substantializing nature into enduring things (substances) is a fallacy because they are produced by varied and fluctuating activities. 'Process is fundamental: The river is not an object but an ever-changing flow; the sun is not a thing, but a flaming fire. Everything in nature is a matter of process, of activity, of change' (Rescher 1996: 10)" (Van de Ven and Poole 2005: 1377–1378).

BOX 2.1 GUIDING ASSUMPTIONS FOR PROCESSUAL ANALYSES

- A non-linear and multifaceted view of process: change is seen as non-linear and a dynamic view is sought. The aim is not to get lost in variables when trying to determine how one independent variable affects the dependent variable. Instead of looking for a unifying theory of change, the researcher strives for a holistic explanation and is open to multiple viewpoints.
- Path dependency and temporal interconnectedness: from a process perspective, history is important. The past, which is brought forth through the consciousness of people, affects the present as well as the future. History is alive in the present but not to the extent that it becomes a solely deterministic factor.
- Process is entrenched in the context: both the organization's inner context (e.g. structural, political and cultural forces) and outer context (e.g. competitive forces) affect the process of change. In other words, the change process is situated and embedded in the context. Hence, in order to study process, the context has to be examined. This implies that a complete analysis of change should include multiple levels of analysis and seeing multiple processes at the same level of analysis.
- Change is asymmetrical: the change process is embedded in different contexts and the rate of change differs from one place to another. For example, change in the sales department might be higher than in other departments due to pressures from contextual factors of the market.

(Pettigrew 1997)

In these different views illustrated by the arguments of Democritus and Heraclitus lie also one of the explanations and connections to planned and emergent change. How you view the nature of the world and change—either as stable "things" and "entities" or as a "flowing river" and a "flaming fire"—ultimately influences how you choose to lead and manage change. When you see change as a "thing" using a variance model you are preoccupied with diagnosing change. You are also interested in examining the causal relationships that take place in an organization since you view an organization as a system with underlying law-like mechanisms. Leading change here is mainly about managing the different states that together make up the change process (which we discussed earlier in connection to planned change).

Books and articles based on a variance model are prone to give us advice and guidelines on how managers should deal with certain issues in different stages or steps. For example, at the planning step of change there is often a preoccupation with diagnosing (Beckhard and Harris 1987; Burke and Litwin 1992; Cummings and Worley 2008). In the action step there is a focus on constructing the change message (Armenakis and Harris 2002; Bernerth 2004; By 2007) or vision (Kotter 1996). At the integration step there is an emphasis on feedback and reward (Nadler 1993; Sirkin et al. 2005). Because of this preoccupation with different states, the variance model using the planned perspective has often been criticized for only giving a simple overview and synopsis—what is often referred to as a "synoptic account of change." Tsoukas and Chia (2002: 570) explain:

> Synoptic accounts view change as an accomplished event whose key features and variations, and causal antecedents and consequences, need to be explored and described. Such knowledge is generated by approaching "change" from the outside and, typically, it takes the form of a stage model in which the entity that undergoes change is shown to have distinct states at different points in time. Synoptic accounts have been useful insofar as they have provided us with snapshots of key dimensions of organizations at different points in time, along with explanations for the trajectories organizations followed.

They continue, saying: "Given its synoptic nature, it does not do justice to the open-ended micro-processes that underlay the trajectories described; it does not quite capture the distinguishing features of change—its fluidity, pervasiveness, open-endedness, and indivisibility." They finish of their argument by asking in what way you choose to understand the character of a city: Is it by the photographs that you take or by walking around and talking to its citizens, getting a feeling for the town?

What Tsoukas and Chia are basically saying is that a planned perspective that departs from viewing change as a "thing" is problematic because it only gives snapshots of change and relies on high-level, aggregated data about overall conditions. This macro perspective recurrently explores the transition from different aggregated states and therefore misses the micro-processes that exist in between the states, such as sensemaking and sensegiving processes. As a result, we know more about what we should do "at" different stages or steps of the change process, but less about what we should do "between" the different states. For example, what are the significant activities and decisions that take place in the field and are situated between the exploration and planning steps, or between the action and integration steps (or between any other steps for that matter)?

This is precisely where the emergent approach with a process view of change comes in handy. This perspective puts less emphasis on the different steps and is more concerned with what goes on between steps, while the focus is on events, activities and choices that emerge across time. By doing so, we move away from viewing change as a "thing," toward viewing it as a process. At the same time we are moving away from understanding change through a macro perspective and from outside, toward understanding change from within through micro processes. We are getting under the skin of change.

The riddle of success and failure of organizational change

The current axiom is that approximately 70 percent of all change initiatives fail. Either intended changes are not fully launched, or fail, or are achieved but are over budget, late and met with great frustration (Burnes 2011). However, there is a lack of empirical evidence for such a claim and there are often no clear standards or performance indicators to define "failure" and "success." Who would be the judge? Different stakeholders might arrive at different conclusions. Perceived success and failure are context dependent and socially constructed: it depends on whom you ask.

Another challenge is how to measure success and failure during organic emergent change processes that unfold over time. This kind of change process can hardly fail, since it is constantly growing and adapting to new circumstances. Likewise, you can hardly proclaim success since you often have no clear outspoken objectives or plans. Even if you have clear plans and objectives, these are often in reality continuously altered during the change process as new ideas, facts and circumstances arise. What complicates things further is the fact that outcomes are always to some extent subjective and stakeholder dependent. In reality, claiming that a change has been a success or a reality is deeply problematic. This section will explain some of the reasons why this is so.

Evidence and reasons for failure

Let's start at the very beginning. There is a considerable amount of writing that claims that the failure rate is significantly high (Beer and Nohria 2000; Hammer and Champy 1993; Kotter 2008; Markus 2004; Smith 2002, 2003; The Standish Group 2009). Not all of these studies provide the same figure, but most claim that the failure rate is around 70 percent. In addition, the figure has been relatively high and stable during recent decades (see e.g. Bessant and Haywood 1985; Crosby 1979; The Standish Group 1994).

The studies of success and failure are often connected to the examination of a popular and contemporary concept that is used as a reason for change. For instance, according to Helms-Mills et al. (2008), the statistics suggest that 75 percent of all studied American Total Quality Management (TQM) initiatives during the last decade failed. Studies of TQM in European countries found a failure rate of 70 percent or more (Burnes 2009). A study of major European, Asian and North American companies by Bain & Co. found that the failure rate for culture change initiatives was 90 percent (Rogers and Meehan 2007). Studies of major change projects involving new technology found failure rates of between 40 and 80 percent (Berggren and Lindkvist 2001; Burnes 2009). Zook and Allen (2001) learn that between 80 and 90 percent of organizations fail to execute their strategies. It is also claimed that 70 percent of all Balanced Scorecard implementations fail (De Waal and Counet 2009). The concept of Business Process Re-engineering scores no better, with failure rates between 60 and 80 percent reported (Bryant 1998). Some scholarly research has been carried out on Six Sigma's influence on management theory and application (Goffnett 2004; Schroeder et al. 2005) and the deployment of Lean seems to follow the general trend—studies indicate failure rates of around 80 percent (Bhasin and Burcher 2006).

Such high change failures are generally explained by referring to lack of communication and weak management. Other reasons cited include the lack of attention given to the human dynamics of change and a lack of knowledge of the underlying processes of change (Armenakis et al. 1993; Iveroth 2010b; Iveroth and Bengtsson 2014). In the organizational leader's efforts just to "get it done," there has been a tendency to dismiss all the theoretical aspects of organizational change and the underlying assumptions, knowledge and understanding of the change process in favor of using a set of quick prescriptive steps (Burnes 1996; Sanwal 2008).

Most recent studies reveal the crucial role of cultural and behavioral change during transformational projects (Iveroth 2011; Iveroth and Bengtsson 2014; Jørgensen et al. 2009). The underlying mechanisms of behavioral and sociocultural aspects of organizational change must not be underestimated. Organizations are complex social systems. Change management, by means of models, must also construct meaning, and meaning lies in sensemaking and not in external elements (Lythcott and Duschl 1990). Oakland and Tanner (2007) emphasize that people are the essential contributor to successful change, and managing change within the culture is important. According to a survey conducted by The Economist Intelligence Unit (2008), a root cause of failure is that management fails to win over the hearts and minds of the people in the organization. The lack of contextual knowledge and ability to understand the human response to change leads to change leaders who are unable to handle resistance and overcome obstacles (Andrews et al. 2008).

Altogether, one of the biggest problems with the axiom of a 70 percent failure rate is that there seems to be no reliable evidence (Burnes 2011; Hughes 2010, 2011; Randall 2004). There is simply no hard evidence to back up such a claim. For example, Hughes (2011: 460), who has performed an extensive review of the high failure rate statements, says that "the 70 per cent organizational-change failure rhetoric was largely informed by magazine articles and practitioner books lacking discussion of methodologies, epistemologies, and reference to organizational-change research and scholarship." He concludes by saying that, "the implication is that any inherent change failure rate is inappropriate. The belief that organizational change is a code which once cracked/broken will result in lower change failure rates misrepresents the ambiguous and dynamic practice of managing change and what is now known about processes of changing" (Hughes 2011: 461).

Hughes also argues that the claims of a rate of success or failure ignore the contextual aspect of change—that every change project is always to some extent novel since the project is tied to unique circumstances of the environment. The exact same circumstances can never reappear elsewhere. Another reason why rates are inappropriate is the ambiguity of change. For example, measuring and establishing rates ignores the emergent properties of change and improvisation. Other ambiguities of change that rates ignore are the plurality of change and the multiple accounts of change outcomes. What is success for one individual is an utter failure for another.

There are, of course, more subtle cases when the literature makes claims of "best practice"—hinting about a recipe for success but not providing any concrete rate of success or failure. Many of these writings (Sanwal 2008) try to ground their argument on change stories about "real" companies where they affirm the types of practice that have been executed. This has provided us with a plethora of guru statements and how-to handbooks that is hard to navigate.

Here Hallencreutz and Turner (2011) have contributed by reviewing how the terms "organizational change," "change management" and "best practice" have been used in the literature, to explore whether there are existing widespread common models and definitions for organizational change best practice. Their findings are no surprise and confirm that different terms appear to be used for a variety of perspectives and research applications.

This extends the review made by Hughes that there are no consistent definitions of best practice in the literature, that there is no evidence-based "best" or "worst" way to manage change, and that the expression "best practice" is not substantiated by empirical evidence. More interestingly, by using the lens of organizational change on the work of Todaro (2002), Hallencreutz and Turner (2011) attempt to classify best practice into different categories, as displayed in Table 2.2. By doing so, they decode the term "best practice" and offer a way to organize the plethora of change concepts and models on offer.

The problems and complexities of measuring

The question of success and failure of change is closely connected to measuring. To measure change is extremely complex, if not impossible. Markus and her colleagues (2000) provided some in-depth knowledge of three of these complexities. First, the outcome of measuring depends on "whom you ask". Within all types of change projects there are always different stakeholders who have different views of the value of the change and what is "at stake." Take, for example, the implementation

TABLE 2.2 Different types of "best practice"

Type of "best practice"	Description
Icon practice	Practices implemented by admired companies and/or prominent executives—"*if IKEA does it, it must be the best*"
Award-winning practice	Practices adopted by winners of business excellence awards such as the Malcolm Baldrige National Quality Award—"*if the winner does it, it must be the best*"
Common practice	Practices that have industry-wide diffusion, adoption and acceptance—"*if everyone else is doing it, it must be the best*"
Anecdotal practice	Practices based on anecdotal evidence and widespread success stories—"*if it worked for them, it must be the best*"

of a new information system, with stakeholders including a project manager, a user or customer, and a decision maker. Success for the project manager is when a project has been accomplished on time and within budget. The user or customer, on the other hand, is happy when he or she has experienced a smooth change process and can make use of what the change set out to do—such as being able to use all the functionalities of a newly implemented information system. However, for a decision maker things are very different. He or she is most likely to deem the change project a success when the expensive technology is shown to provide information that enables swifter and better decisions.

Second, it depends on "when you measure". Using the same above example, the project manager is thrilled and thinks the new information system is a success when it passes all the milestones and actually works in the go-live stage. The user is more concerned with what happens after the go-live stage and wants fully functional information when he or she is actually using the system (i.e. post-implementation). Finally, the decision maker will consider the implementation a success when sufficient time has passed to enable him or her to take high-quality decisions. This, however, could take a considerable amount of time, as it often takes several years for an information system to be integrated into an organization. What complicates things even further when it comes to when to measure is the notion that a change could be considered a success but in later years be shown to be a clear and utter failure. Similarly, a complete failure can over time—when people adjust to the change—turn out to be a real success.

Finally, Markus and her colleagues (2000: 247, emphasis added) underline "*the yardstick* or criterion against which to compare an actual level of achievement" as a third complexity of measurement. For instance, the yardstick for the users and adopters of an information system is their perception that the system meets their objectives and expectations. This approach has a number of problems, such as, for example, comparing different objectives and expectations across organizations. Users' objectives and expectations can also be unrealizable, for instance.

In conclusion, with regard to measuring and the numbers it provides, it is imperative to bear in mind that qualitative information can be at least as important as quantitative. There is a danger that managers rely too much on technology, structure and praise, and blindly follow all things that you can measure (Iveroth 2010a). Such a hazardous approach can be illustrated by the so-called McNamara fallacy:[7]

> The first step is to measure whatever can be easily measured. This is OK as far as it goes. The second step is to disregard that which can't be easily measured or to give it an arbitrary quantitative value. This is artificial and misleading. The third step is to presume that what can't be measured easily really isn't important. This is blindness. The fourth step is to say that what can't be easily measured really doesn't exist. This is suicide.
>
> *(Handy 1995: 221)*

Another reason why measuring success and failure is problematic is that it is often not a formal project per se that determines a success, but instead, in many cases, the changes that are enabled by the project. What makes this even more complicated is that these changes—which come as an effect of a project—often take years to reveal themselves. One illustration of this is the so-called Solow Paradox or Productivity Paradox: "you can see the computer age everywhere but in the productivity statistics" (Solow 1987: 36). What Solow was trying to convey is that it is almost impossible to identify and measure the outcome of IT investments in terms of higher productivity. It is difficult to find any direct gains in productivity.

One reason for this is because for IT, productivity and measurement do not capture the actual benefits enabled by the new technology. More specifically, studies show that IT does not have a value in itself (Dedrick et al. 2003; Fryk 2009; Kohli and Devaraj 2003; Lucas 1999). Instead the value that can be gained from investments in technology is based on the organizational, operational and behavioral changes that the technology enables. However, these changes do not come automatically. They take time and usually only occur when the organization has managed to develop and establish, for example, new work processes, roles, routines, environments and competencies that reap the full benefits of the investment (i.e. time lag). Dedrick et al. (2003: 27) note, for example:

> At the firm level, the review further concludes that the wide range of performance of IT investments among different organizations can be explained by complementary investments in organizational capital such as decentralized decision-making systems, job training, and business process redesign. IT is not simply a tool for automating existing processes, but is more importantly an enabler of organizational changes that can lead to additional productivity gains.

Here lies also part of the answer to why we can see different productivity gains in similar organizations that have implemented the same technology. This is because various organizations are making use of the advantage that can be reaped from IT to varying degrees. The degree of benefit and value that different organizations gain from their IT investment also varies. For example, the learning curve of using new software can vary between organizations depending on the employees' background and level of earlier experience of using similar software. Even though the Solow Paradox or Productivity Paradox is mainly concerned with technology, the same underlying reasoning can be applied to most change projects.[8]

A philosophical stance

A final and important task before the end of this chapter is to raise some deeper philosophical questions. The managers and researchers who praise evidence-based best practice and measurement and rates for success and failure operate under certain different assumptions about the world around us. For example, they take for granted that there is a single unitary reality apart from our perception. They also believe that this world can not only be measured, but also managed according to a certain recipe. They want to believe that if we can measure this world that is situated "out there," then we can also construct a panacea consisting of rules for success.

Another departure point is to acknowledge that there is a world out there but that our individual understanding of it will always be limited (Van de Ven 2007). Of course, we can make some relatively stable assumptions about physical and material things, but understanding the reflexive and emergent social processes that involve people (and which is often the essence of the change process) is considerably more difficult—if not impossible. With such an approach there are no absolute, universal or error-free truths or laws. Every individual is unique, and their work and opinions will always be biased by earlier experience. In this sense, there is no point in trying to establish validity in any external or objective sense because each of us have experiences from our own point of view and each of us experiences a slightly different reality from anyone else. My landscape of meaning varies from yours. Therefore, there might not be such a thing as a single, generalized, organizational change best practice to be found.

If only organizational change—or life in general, for that matter—were as simple as just identifying the successes and then replicating them. Instead of implicitly accepting the traditional notion that organizations are rational, logical places we should consider the wider evidence from other domains which reflect a different reality. If managers instead see that the world is complex, dynamic and constructed, interpreted and experienced by people in their interactions with wider social systems, they should be a little cautious in drawing hasty conclusions in early stages of change processes.

We have met some brilliant leaders over the years but more often skilled specialists who have qualified for managerial positions due to expertise rather than leadership talent. In an urge to manage and control, we have seen rigorous operating procedures and performance-management systems. We have met management teams that try to grasp the whole by measuring and controlling fragments. We believe this should come to an end. Instead, we should zoom out and understand the complex reality of organizational change before we tamper with new claims of best practice, stories of success, models and tools. All new change-management models and best practices should be labeled with a warning: "Leadership not included. Read instructions before use."

In conclusion, we encourage scholars as well as practitioners to follow the advice of Gummesson (2000: 97): "As long as you keep searching for new knowledge and do not believe you have found the ultimate truth but, rather, the best available for the moment, the traditional demand for generalization becomes less urgent."

Summary

This chapter has framed and discussed change both conceptually and empirically. We have conceptualized change by showing different perspectives and their adjacent arguments, and we have explored different philosophical and methodological approaches. The chapter has also afforded some answers to the practice-oriented riddle of the success and failure of organizational change. Having portrayed some aspects of the vast canvas of change in the hope of aiding the framing of change, we will now zoom into one particular detail: sensemaking.

Notes

1 For other reviews and overviews of change theories, see for example Caldwell 2006; Poole and Van de Ven 2004; Armenakis and Bedeian 1999; and Van de Ven and Poole 1995.
2 In practice, change projects connected to implementing, for example, Total Quality Management and Six Sigma often have characteristics of several of these classifications (By 2005).
3 Marshak uses the classical group-development model developed by Tuckman. In short, in the Form stage, for example, plans, roles and routines are established and the group is mobilized; in Storm, conflicts surface and boundaries are tested; in the Norm stage issues are resolved and the group is more confident with each other; and in the Perform stage the group acts without friction, with the support of structures that have been built up in earlier stages.
4 It is not our intention to combine Figure 2.2 with planned and emergent change. These are two different ways to conceptualize change. However, there are some patterns. For example, in a broad perspective emergent change is often a frequent type of change in "Fine-tuning: build and improve," and planned change is most likely common in "Major transformation: release and recreate." However, elements of both emergent and planned change are more or less present in all four different types of change in Figure 2.2.
5 See for example Burnes 2009; Caldwell 2006; By 2005; Weick 2000; Burnes 1996; Wilson 1992; Kanter et al. 1992; Quinn 1980.
6 For detailed accounts of this phenomenon, see Harris & Davenport 2006: 2; and Lindvall & Iveroth 2011: 299.
7 This fallacy is named after Robert McNamara, a businessman who became US secretary of defense between 1961 and 1968. According to Bass (1996), the likely background to the statement was that the USA measured its battle successes in the Vietnam War by body count.
8 Managing technology-enabled change is increasingly important for organizations to prosper since almost everything we do is connected to technology. For example,

technology is deeply ingrained in our organization in such a way that if it were to cease to exist overnight, then the whole organization would abruptly come to a halt. In addition, the technology that we use on a daily basis is continuously changing. Just think how many times the software we use is updated. In this way, mastering technology-enabled change is crucial for organizations' long-term survival, and the information provided by this book is highly relevant to both academics and practitioners who are interested in the connection between technology and change.

Bibliography

Agarwal, R. & Helfat, C. (2009) Strategic renewal of organizations. *Organization Science*, 20(2): 281–293.

Andrews, J., Cameron, H. & Harris, M. (2008) All change? Managers' experience of organizational change in theory and practice. *Journal of Organizational Change Management*, 21(3): 300–314.

Armenakis, A.A. & Bedeian, A.G. (1999) Organizational change: a review of theory and research in the 1990s. *Journal of Management*, 25(3): 293–315.

Armenakis, A. & Harris, S. (2002) Crafting a change message to create transformational readiness. *Journal of Organizational Change Management*, 15(2): 169–183.

Armenakis, A.A., Harris, S.G. & Mossholder, K.W. (1993) Creating readiness for organizational change. *Human Relations*, 46(6): 681–703.

Avgerou, C. & McGrath, K. (2007) Power, rationality, and the art of living through socio-technical change. *MIS Quarterly*, 31(2): 295–315.

Balogun, J. & Hailey, V. (2008) *Exploring Strategic Change*. Harlow: Prentice Hall.

Bartlett, C.A. & Ghoshal, S. (1989) *Managing Across Borders: The Transnational Solution*. Boston, MA: Harvard Business School Press.

Bass, B.M. (1996) Theory of transformational leadership redux. *The Leadership Quarterly*, 6(4): 463–478.

Bateson, G. (1979) *Mind and Nature: A Necessary Unity*. New York: Dutton.

Beckhard, R. & Harris, R. (1987) *Organizational Transitions: Managing Complex Change*. Reading, MA: Addison-Wesley.

Beer, M. (1980) *Organization Change and Development: A Systems View*. Santa Monica, CA: Goodyear.

Beer, M. & Eisenstat, R.A. (1996) Developing an organization capable of implementing strategy and learning. *Human Relations*, 49(5): 597–621.

Beer, M. & Nohria, N. (2000) *Breaking the Code of Change*. Boston, MA: Harvard Business School.

Berggren, C. & Lindkvist, L. (2001) *Projekt: organisation för målorientering och lärande*. Lund: Studentlitteratur.

Bernerth, J. (2004) Expanding our understanding of the change message. *Human Resource Development Review*, 3(1): 36–52.

Bessant, J. & Haywood, B. (1985) *The Introduction of Flexible Manufacturing Systems as an Example of Computer Integrated Manufacturing: Final Report*. Brighton: Brighton Polytechnic, Innovation Research Group.

Bhasin, S. & Burcher, P. (2006) Lean viewed as a philosophy. *Journal of Manufacturing Technology Management*, 17(1): 56–72.

Boland, R.J., Jr, Tenkasi, R.V. & Te'eni, D. (1994) Designing information technology to support distributed cognition. *Organization Science*, 5(3): 456–475.

Bryant, A. (1998) Beyond BPR-confronting the organizational legacy. *Management Decision*, 36(1): 25–30.

Buchanan, D. & Dawson, P. (2007) Discourse and audience: organizational change as multi-story process. *Journal of Management Studies*, 44(5): 669–686.

Bullock, R.J. & Batten, D. (1985) It's just a phase we're going through: a review and synthesis of OD phase analysis. *Group & Organization Studies*, 10(4): 383–412.

Burke, W.W. (2008) *Organization Change: Theory and Practice*. Thousand Oaks, CA: Sage Publications.

Burke, W. & Litwin, G. (1992) A causal model of organizational performance and change. *Journal of Management*, 18(3): 523–545.

Burnes, B. (1996) No such thing as … a 'one best way' to manage organizational change. *Management Decision*, 34(10): 11–18.

Burnes, B. (2004) Kurt Lewin and the planned approach to change: a re-appraisal. *Journal of Management Studies*, 41(6): 977–1002.

Burnes, B. (2009) *Managing Change: A Strategic Approach to Organisational Dynamics*. New York: Prentice Hall/Financial Times.

Burnes, B. (2011) Introduction: why does change fail, and what can we do about it? *Journal of Change Management*, 11(4): 445–450.

Burns, J. & Scapens, R.W. (2000) Conceptualizing management accounting change: an institutional framework. *Management Accounting Research*, 11(1): 3–25.

Bushe, G.R. & Marshak, R.J. (2009) Revisioning organization development diagnostic and dialogic premises and patterns of practice. *The Journal of Applied Behavioral Science*, 45(3): 348–368.

By, R.T. (2005) Organisational change management: a critical review. *Journal of Change Management*, 5(4): 369–380.

By, R.T. (2007) Ready or not … *Journal of Change Management*, 7(1): 3–11.

Caldwell, R. (2006) *Agency and Change: Rethinking Change Agency in Organizations*. London: Routledge.

Calori, R. (1998) Essai: philosophizing on strategic management models. *Organization Studies*, 19(2): 281–306.

Collins, J.C. & Porras, J.I. (1994) *Built to Last: Successful Habits of Visionary Companies*. New York: HarperBusiness.

Constantinides, P. & Barrett, M. (2006) Large-scale ICT innovation, power, and organizational change: the case of a regional health information network. *Journal of Applied Behavioral Science*, 42(1): 76–90.

Crosby, P.B. (1979) *Quality is Free: The Art of Making Quality Certain*. New York: McGraw-Hill.

Cummings, T. & Worley, C. (2008) *Organization Development and Change*. Mason, OH: South-Western.

Davenport, T.H. (1998) Putting the enterprise into the enterprise system. *Harvard Business Review*, 76(4): 121–131.

Dawson, P. (1994) *Organizational Change: A Processual Approach*. London: Paul Chapman.

Dawson, P. (2003) *Understanding Organizational Change: The Contemporary Experience of People at Work*. London: Sage.

Dedrick, J., Gurbaxani, V. & Kraemer, K.L. (2003) Information technology and economic performance: a critical review of the empirical evidence. *ACM Computing Surveys*, 35(1): 1–28.

De Waal, A.A. & Counet, H. (2009) Lessons learned from performance management systems implementations. *International Journal of Productivity and Performance Management*, 58(4): 367–390.

Dumez, H. & Jeunemaitre, A. (2006) Reviving narratives in economics and management: towards an integrated perspective of modelling, statistical inference and narratives. *European Management Review*, 3(1): 32–43.

Dunphy, D. & Stace, D. (1993) The strategic management of corporate change. *Human Relations*, 46(8): 905–920.

The Economist Intelligence Unit (2008) *A Change for the Better—Steps for Successful Business Transformation*. London: The Economist.

Farjoun, M. (2010) Beyond dualism: stability and change as a duality. *The Academy of Management Review*, 35(2): 202–225.

Ford, J.D. & Ford, L.W. (1995) The role of conversations in producing intentional organisational change. *Academy of Management Review*, 20(3): 541–570.

Fryk, P. (2009) *Modern Perspectives on the Digital Economy: With Insights from the Health Care Sector*, Doctoral thesis no. 146. Uppsala: Företagsekonomiska institutionen, Uppsala universitet.

Gersick, C.J.G. (1991) Revolutionary change theories: a multilevel exploration of the punctuated equilibrium paradigm. *Academy of Management Review*, 16(1): 10–36.

Goffnett, S.P. (2004) Understanding Six Sigma: implications for industry and education. *Journal of Industrial Technology*, 20(4): 2–10.

Gummesson, E. (2000) *Qualitative Methods in Management Research*. Thousand Oaks, CA: Sage.

Hallencreutz, J. & Turner, D.-M. (2011) Exploring organizational change best practice: are there any clear-cut models and definitions? *International Journal of Quality and Service Sciences*, 3(1): 60–68.

Hamel, G. & Prahalad, C.K. (1994) *Competing for the Future*. Boston, MA: Harvard Business School Press.

Hammer, M. & Champy, J. (1993) *Reengineering the Corporation: A Manifesto for Business Revolution*. New York: Harper Business.

Handy, C. (1995) *The Age of Paradox*. Boston, MA: Harvard Business Press.

Harris, J.G. & Davenport, T.H. (2006) *New Growth from Enterprise Systems: Achieving High Performance through Distinctive Capabilities*. Wellesley, MA: Accenture Institute for High Performing Business.

Hayes, J. (2002) *The Theory and Practice of Change*. Basingstoke: Palgrave.

Helms-Mills, J., Dye, K. & Mills, A.J. (2008) *Understanding Organizational Change*. Abingdon: Routledge.

Hendry, C. (1996) Understanding and creating whole organizational change through learning theory. *Human Relations*, 49(5): 621–641.

Hernes, T. (2014) *A Process Theory of Organization*. Oxford: Oxford University Press.

Hill, L. (2003) *Becoming a Manager: How New Managers Master the Challenges of Leadership*. Boston, MA: Harvard Business School Press.

Hope, O. (2010) The politics of middle management sensemaking and sensegiving. *Journal of Change Management*, 10(2): 195–215.

Hughes, M. (2010) *Managing Change: A Critical Perspective*. London: CIPD Publishing.

Hughes, M. (2011) Do 70 per cent of all organizational change initiatives really fail? *Journal of Change Management*, 11(4): 451–464.

Iveroth, E. (2010a) Inside Ericsson: a framework for the practice of leading global IT-enabled change. *California Management Review*, 53(1): 136–153.

Iveroth, E. (2010b) *Leading IT-enabled change inside Ericsson a transformation into a global network of shared service centres*. Doctoral thesis no. 146. Uppsala: Uppsala University, Department of Business Studies.

Iveroth, E. (2011) The sociomaterial practice of IT-enabled change. *Journal of Change Management*, 11(3): 375–395.

Iveroth, E. (2012) Leading IT-enabled change across cultures. *European Management Journal*, 4(3): 340–351.

Iveroth, E. & Bengtsson, F. (2014) Changing behavior towards sustainable practices using information technology. *Journal of Environmental Management*, 139(June): 59–68.

Jabri, M. (2012) *Managing Organizational Change: Process, Social Construction and Dialogue*. Basingstoke: Palgrave Macmillan.

Johnson, G. (1992) Managing strategic change—strategy, culture and action. *Long Range Planning*, 25(1): 28–36.

Jørgensen, H., Owen, L. & Neus, A. (2009) Stop improvising change management! *Strategy & Leadership*, 37(2): 38–44.

Kanter, R.M., Jick, T. & Stein, B. (1992) *The Challenge of Organizational Change: How Companies Experience it and Leaders Guide it*. New York: Free Press.

Kohli, R. & Devaraj, S. (2003) Measuring information technology payoff: a meta-analysis of structural variables in firm-level empirical research. *Information Systems Research*, 14(2): 127–145.

Kotter, J. (2008) *A Sense of Urgency*. Boston, MA: Harvard Business School Press.

Kotter, J.P. (1996) *Leading change*. Boston, MA: Harvard Business School Press.

Langley, A. (1999) Strategies for theorizing from process data. *Academy of Management Review*, 24(4): 691–710.

Lindvall, J. & Iveroth, E. (2011) Creating a global network of shared service centres for accounting. *Journal of Accounting & Organizational Change*, 7(3): 278–305.

Lippitt, R., Westley, B. & Watson, J. (1958) *The Dynamics of Planned Change: A Comparative Study of Principles and Techniques*. New York: Harcourt, Brace.

Lucas, H.C. (1999) *Information Technology and the Productivity Paradox: Assessing the Value of Investing in IT*. Oxford: Oxford University Press.

Lythcott, J. & Duschl, R. (1990) Qualitative research: from methods to conclusions. *Science Education*, 74(4): 445–460.

Markus, M. (2004) Technochange management: using IT to drive organizational change. *Journal of Information Technology*, 19(1): 4–20.

Markus, M.L., Axline, S., Petrie, D. & Tanis, S.C. (2000) Learning from adopters' experiences with ERP: problems encountered and success achieved. *Journal of Information Technology*, 15(4): 245–265.

Marshak, R. (1993) Lewin meets Confucius: a review of the OD model of change. *Journal of Applied Behaviour Science*, 29(December): 393–415.

Marshak, R.J. (2002) Changing the language of change: how new contexts and concepts are challenging the ways we think and talk about organizational change. *Strategic Change*, 11(5): 279–286.

Mohr, L.B. (1982) *Explaining Organizational Behavior*. San Francisco, CA: Jossey-Bass.

Nadler, D. (1993) "Concepts for the management of organizational change." In C. Mabey & B. Mayon-White (eds), *Managing Change*. London: Paul Chapman, pp. 85–98.

Nadler, D.A. & Nadler, M.B. (1998) *Champions of Change: How CEOs and their Companies are Mastering the Skills of Radical Change*. San Francisco, CA: Jossey-Bass.

Netz, J. & Iveroth, E. (2011) "Strategic renewal overlap: do practices matter?" In J. Netz, M. Ek Lopes, L. Melin, E. Brundin & M. Nordqvist (eds), *In Search of Practice. JIBS Research Report Series No. 2011–1*. Jönköping: Jönköping University Press, pp. 99–126.

Oakland, J. & Tanner, S. (2007) A new framework for managing change. *The TQM Magazine*, 19(6): 572–589.

Orlikowski, W.J. (1996) Improvising organizational transformation over time: a situated change perspective. *Information Systems Research*, 7(1): 63–92.

Pascale, R.T., Millemann, M. & Gioja, L. (2000) *Surfing the Edge of Chaos: The Laws of Nature and the New Laws of Business*. New York: Three Rivers Press.

Pettigrew, A. (1997) What is a processual analysis? *Scandinavian Journal of Management*, 13(4): 337–348.

Pettigrew, A., Woodman, R. & Cameron, K. (2001) Studying organizational change and development: challenges for future research. *Academy of Management Journal*, 44(4): 697–713.

Poole, M.S. & Van de Ven, A. (2004) "Central issues in the study of change and innovation." In M.S. Poole & A. Van de Ven (eds), *Handbook of Organizational Change and Innovation*. New York: Oxford University Press, pp. 3–31.

Poole, M.S., Van de Ven, A., Dooley, K. & Holmes, M. (2000) *Organizational Change and Innovation Processes: Theory and Methods for Research*. Oxford: Oxford University Press.

Purser, R.E. & Petranker, J. (2005) Unfreezing the future exploring the dynamic of time in organizational change. *The Journal of Applied Behavioral Science*, 41(2): 182–203.

Quinn, J.B. (1980) Managing strategic change. *Sloan Management Review*, 21(4): 3–20.

Randall, J. (2004) *Managing Change, Changing Managers*. Hove: Psychology Press.

Rescher, N. (1996) *Process Metaphysics: An Introduction to Process Philosophy*. Albany: State University of New York Press.

Rogers, E.M. (1962) *Diffusion of Innovations*. New York: Free Press of Glencoe.

Rogers, P. & Meehan, P. (2007) Building a winning culture. *Business Strategy Series*, 8(4): 254–261.

Sanwal, A. (2008) The myth of best practices. *Journal of Corporate Accounting & Finance*, 19(5): 51–60.

Scapens, R.W. (2006) Understanding management accounting practices: a personal journey. *The British Accounting Review*, 38(1): 1–30.

Schein, E. (1988) *Process Consultation: Vol. 1, its Role in Organisation Development*. Reading, MA: Addison-Wesley.

Schroeder, R.G., Linderman, K. & Zhang, D. (2005) Evolution of quality: first fifty issues of production and operations management. *Production and Operations Management*, 14(4): 468–481.

Senior, B. & Swailes, S. (2010) *Organizational Change*. Harlow: Pearson Education.

Sirkin, H.L., Keenan, P. & Jackson, A. (2005) The hard side of change management. *Harvard Business Review*, 83(10): 108–118.

Smith, M.E. (2002) Success rates for different types of organizational change. *Performance Improvement*, 41(1): 26–33.

Smith, M.E. (2003) Changing an organisation's culture: correlates of success and failure. *Leadership & Organization Development Journal*, 24(5): 249–261.

Solow, R. (1987) We'd better watch out. *New York Times Book Review*, 12(July): 36.

Stace, D. & Dunphy, D.C. (1994) *Beyond the Boundaries: Leading and Re-creating the Successful Enterprise*. Sydney: McGraw-Hill.

The Standish Group (1994) *The Chaos Report*. Yarmouthport, MA: The Standish Group International Inc.

The Standish Group (2009) *CHAOS Summary 2009*. Yarmouthport, MA: The Standish Group International Inc.

Todaro, J.B. (2002) Change for the right reason: what is a best practice? *Community & Junior College Libraries*, 11(1): 27–36.

Tsoukas, H. & Chia, R. (2002) On organizational becoming: rethinking organizational change. *Organization Science*, 13(5): 567–582.

Van de Ven, A. (2007) *Engaged scholarship: a guide for organizational and social research*. Oxford: Oxford University Press.

Van de Ven, A.H. & Poole, M.S. (1995) Explaining development and change in organizations. *Academy of Management Review*, 20(3): 510–540.

Van de Ven, A. & Poole, M.S. (2005) Alternative approaches for studying organizational change. *Organization Studies*, 26(9): 1377–1404.

Weick, K.E. (2000) "Emergent change as a universal in organizations." In M. Beer & N. Nohria (eds), *Breaking the Code of Change*. Boston, MA: Harvard Business School, pp. 223–241.

Weick, K.E. (2001) *Making Sense of the Organization*. Oxford: Blackwell Business.

Weick, K.E. & Quinn, R.E. (1999) Organizational change and development. *Annual Review of Psychology*, 50(1): 361–386.

Wilson, D. (1992) *A Strategy of Change: Concepts and Controversies in the Management of Change*. London: Routledge.

Zook, C. & Allen, J. (2001) *Profit from the Core*. Cambridge, MA: Harvard Business School Press.

3

MAKING SENSE OF SENSEMAKING THEORY

The objective of this chapter is to explain sensemaking theory and illustrate some of its underlying claims. This is achieved first by defining the concept as well as the closely associated concepts of organizational sensemaking and sensegiving. This is followed by a section that reviews the seven original properties of sensemaking as postulated by Weick. The section also includes more recent research on the subject as it covers the additional properties of prospective sensemaking that focus on how it shapes future events, decisions and actions.

The social process of sensemaking and sensegiving

Sensemaking

"When I leave our meetings, I think I get this … but hell, you have to explain this once again. It just doesn't make sense." This quote could be valid in many social interactions in our professional lives. We all experience situations where we have to cope with mixed messages, ambiguities, incomplete information and facts that we simply do not like to hear. This blurry reality has to make sense, and *sensemaking* means just that: to make sense out of something. It is this process by which we give meaning to our experience and socially construct the world around us and the actions we take. Thus, sensemaking is a real-time process and a live broadcast. When we engage in an activity and thereby begin really to understand what we are doing in the act itself, we induce structure and meaning into the unknown. We produce a landscape of meaning.

In theory, the purpose of sensemaking is to reduce equivocality and ambiguity by supplying a pattern of meaning so that we can understand what we have just done and experienced. In simpler words, sensemaking creates some sort of order of the flow of events that we are undergoing, and in so doing the world becomes structured in such a way that it becomes meaningful and workable.

In the many writings of Weick—who is the originator of the concept—there exists a great repertoire of sensemaking definitions emphasizing different aspects of the concept. Three of these are:

> Sensemaking is about such things as placement of items into frameworks, comprehending, redressing surprise, constructing meaning, interacting in pursuit of mutual understanding, and patterning.
>
> *(Weick 1995: 6)*

> The basic idea of sensemaking is that reality is an ongoing accomplishment that emerges from efforts to create order and make retrospective sense of what occurs.
>
> *(Weick 1993: 635)*

> Sensemaking involves the ongoing retrospective development of plausible images that rationalize what people are doing. Viewed as a significant process of organizing, sensemaking unfolds as a sequence in which people concerned with identity in the social context of other actors engage ongoing circumstances from which they extract cues and make plausible sense retrospectively, while enacting more or less order into those ongoing circumstances.
>
> *(Weick et al. 2005: 409)*

As a process, and in its smallest form, sensemaking includes one thing, a relationship, and another thing, frame ↔ relationship ↔ cue. Frame is constituted by earlier attained schemata or knowledge structures such as rules, values or knowledge gained through, for example, professional training. A cue is more immediate and refers to present stimuli and triggers that indicate that things do not yet make sense. The relationship signifies that in order to create meaning the individual has to connect the cue with the frame and see them in relation to each other. In the words of Weick: "the content of sensemaking is to be found in the frames and categories that summarize the past experience, in the cues and labels that snare specifics of present experience, and in the ways these two settings of experiences are connected" (Weick 1995: 111).

Let us roughly exemplify and simplify these aspects in relation to effective organizational change: Carl is an engineer and has been working with operations planning for many years at a medium-sized Swedish manufacturing company in a small town in the southern part of the country. For decades, the business has moved on, and that is also Carl's current frame: stability and contentment. However, now the company is suffering from intensive attacks from new low-cost competitors. The managing director is about to introduce a cost-cutting program. When Carl hears about this need for change at a staff meeting, this information becomes an immediate cue that does not make sense. He asks himself why. He tries to match this cue with his current frame, and build a relationship that makes sense. By doing so, Carl becomes aware of the change to come, and can see and understand the background and motives.

Organizational sensemaking

The sensemaking process is connected to the daily life of an individual but sensemaking can also been seen in a wider organizational context: organizational sensemaking (Starbuck and Milliken 1988). Here the focus is on the shared meanings of, for instance, corporate objectives among managers, employees and stakeholders which they gain through different types of social interaction. When things do not make sense for the employee, he or she experiences ambiguity, equivocality and uneasiness. The employee, alone, does not understand what they have experienced or the information they have been given.

To reduce these feelings of uncertainty, they seek a meaning through socializing and interaction with others in the organization—which is probably what Carl would do in the case above. Collectively people together interpret and translate information, events and experiences of the organization with the aim of constructing a commonly shared meaning that makes the organizational world more workable and sensible (Maitlis 2005; Stensaker et al. 2008). To some extent, organizational sensemaking is often seen as a more complex and less stable process compared with individual sensemaking in everyday life. This is presumably because it includes a greater variety of different actors, negotiations, events, language, symbols and implications (Weick 1995: 63–64).

In organizational change, sensemaking is paramount for the emergent process of change because such processes influence the way people interpret, understand and act upon change initiatives. As such, sensemaking is powerful because it can alter people's mindsets and actions connected to organizational change. When change is introduced, employees and stakeholders feel that things are "up in the air." They question what they have been doing, as well as the information and behavior of senior managers. They face an unknown future. In such a situation people have a hard time making sense of what is happening and what they are supposed to be doing (Senior and Swailes 2010). This is precisely the type of situation with which organizational sensemaking is concerned. Weick et al. (2005: 410) note that occasions of sensemaking happen when there is an "experience of being thrown into an ongoing, unknowable, unpredictable streaming of experience in search of answers to the question, 'what's the story?'"

Sensegiving

Closely associated with sensemaking is the concept of sensegiving, which is the process whereby an individual tries to influence others' sensemaking processes (Gioia and Chittipeddi 1991; Maitlis and Lawrence 2007). A sensegiver provides open communication and cues in such a way that it affects the construction of meaning of others—for example, a manager who tries to influence the way employees interpret a strategic change that is underway in their organization. The manager does so by, for example, communicating his perspective of the change with the aim of creating a buy-in and influence stakeholders' behavior, with the ambition to affect the outcome. In short, through sensegiving the manager tries to make the organizational change a workable certainty for employees and stakeholders (Rouleau 2005). However, the manager will be unable to control the construction of meaning and sensemaking processes fully (Stensaker et al. 2008). Employees and stakeholders will also be influenced by others in their sensemaking, such as cues picked up from newspapers or internal discussion with peers during coffee breaks, and so on.

Typical examples involving organizational change are the everyday sensegiving and sensemaking processes going on around coffee and lunch tables in every organization, often regarding if and how different aspects will affect the organization. For instance, colleagues trying to make sense of cues of information delivered at a meeting where a change leader performed sensegiving. By doing so, they construct their own meanings:

What did the CEO say at the monthly meeting?
She talked about the need for change and improved productivity. Apparently we don't reach our strategic objectives.
Okay, but do we have a problem? I mean here at our site?
No, I don't think so. Our figures look pretty good.
Well ... she also said something about the financial situation in the EU or something.
And this international crisis she talked about, will it affect us?
It probably won't affect us in Europe, but perhaps the US division.
All right, but her talk about the need for improved productivity, what does it mean in practice for us?
I don't know. I suppose management will launch a new project or two, probably nothing to worry about. But she looked quite stiff so there is definitely something going on.
Okay, but our figures look good, eh? We can relax, eh?
Aha ... pass me the sugar please. By the way, did you see the match yesterday?

Sensemaking and sensegiving are both equally important for people's social construction[1] and meaning. The sensemaker and sensegiver try to influence each other through communication and interactive behavior. This together creates a shared future frame that consists of common perspective, cognition and interpretation of a strategic change. In this way, they are "two sides of the same coin" (Rouleau 2005: 1415): sensemaking cannot exist without sensegiving, and vice versa.

These complementary processes are reciprocal and iterative in nature, and progress from a current frame into a future one (Ahmad et al. 2013; Gioia and

Chittipeddi 1991), as is crudely simplified in Figure 3.1. For example, a manager performs sensegiving through communication of vision and goals of a strategic change (A in Figure 3.1). The purpose is to make employees and stakeholders reframe reality. This is then picked up by employees and stakeholders who try to interpret and make sense of the change (B). In turn, they perform sensegiving processes towards the change leaders (e.g. try to influence the vision and the goals of the change, C). In the next phase the leader tries to make sense of the information provided by the employees and stakeholders (D). Based on this, the manager then makes alterations to his or her sensegiving processes, and so forth (back to A).

Properties of sensemaking

Sensemaking is often confused with concepts like interpretation, understanding and attribution (Schwandt 2005). However, sensemaking has seven attributes which set it apart from other processes, often referred to as the seven properties of sense-making. These are: social context, identity construction, retrospect, salient cues, ongoing projects, plausibility, and enactment. We will now explain each of these concepts.[2]

Social context

Organizations are very social as they are "a network of intersubjectively shared meanings that are sustained through the development and use of a common language and everyday social interaction" (Walsh and Ungson 1991: 60). Weick (1995) is resourcefully using this quote to underline that there are numerous underlying core aspects of what we call organization that are significantly social in nature. Making sense of something is to a large extent done in interaction with the social context that surrounds us. For example, the meaning of something is in part influenced by the conversations and interactions that you have with employees,

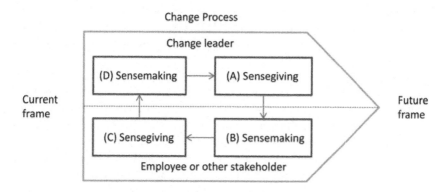

FIGURE 3.1 The reciprocal process of sensemaking and sensegiving

friends, peers, trade union representatives, line managers, senior managers, suppliers, customers and so forth.

This has several implications. First, since we make sense in an interaction with the social context, what and how we make sense is influenced by the different actors around us. Therefore, the "sense" has to be "sensible" in the eyes and ears of others. For example, what you say and what you do will be influenced by the audience that you expect will assess you. Further, since sensemaking is situated in a social context you are not only being influenced by the presence of others but in the process of making sense on your own, you are at the same time contributing to the sensemaking processes of others. It is a two-way process: you are helping them and they are helping you in your respective sensemaking processes.

Another important factor within this component is the role of symbols, rules, routines and language. Sensemaking not only arises from human beings in a social context but also from symbolic interaction. These are constantly present in social context and they are an integral part of our constant creation of meaning. They supply some of the bricks that you need to make your house of meaning and which are usually constantly present in your surroundings. However, the sudden lack or alteration of such symbols, rules, routines and language in our social surroundings can trigger sensemaking and change. When a new IT system is implemented, for example, it can alter the organizational processes and employees have an occasion for sensemaking because they can no longer fall back on the old routine. Similarly, when the precious logotype of the company is replaced by a new one, this triggers a process among employees to make sense of it all. In the next chapter, which discusses triggers of sensemaking, we will look at some of these symbolic aspects.

Identity construction

The sensemaking process is strongly influenced by our identity as it filters our meaning and understanding of the world, which ultimately shapes our actions: "Our identity is continually being redefined as a result of experiences and contact with others, for example, parents, friends, religion, where we went to school, where we work and what type of job we do all affect how we view certain situations" (Mills et al. 2010: 184).

This property of sensemaking also suggests that identity is dynamic and is partly shaped by people around us (Weick et al. 2005). Think, for example, about your identity during puberty, think about all the different aspects that influenced your identity at that time, think about how your identity shaped your sensemaking, and then compare it with your current identity. Who we are, what we think, what matters to us depends upon our identity, and this identity is to a large part socially negotiated with the people with whom we interact daily: "people learn about their identities by projecting them into an environment and observing the consequences" (Weick 1995: 23; also noted by Helms-Mills 2002). In this sense, our identity and concept of the "self" influence how we make sense and act, and this in turn shapes how others make sense of and treat us. When our identity is questioned, it has the potential to become unstable. When this happens there is a window of opportunity to reconstruct our identity into something new (Gioia and Chittipeddi 1991), and this is the very moment when we become open to new ideas and meanings.

A dramatic example of the property of identity construction is when people get fired. Losing our job often leads us to question who we are and if we can mentally renegotiate our identity (i.e. who I am) in such a way that we may apply for a new type of job. From a more organizational point of view, a reconstruction of identity often happens when the supervisor suddenly announces that the business is actually going bankrupt. Overall identity construction is one of the most powerful properties of sensemaking. It often occurs when there is some sort of crisis that provides us with the opportunity to reflect and ask challenging questions of ourselves and of other employees in the organization (Maitlis and Sonenshein 2010). As in the above examples, on such occasions leaders (it is hoped) make the call for increased attention and a sense of emergency. This type of instance is often an underestimated occasion for sensemaking that forms and influences the subsequent change process.

Retrospect

When you perceive something that is happening, it is actually after it has taken place because it takes time for the information to travel to your retina and up to your brain. Even if we are just talking about microseconds, the stimulus from the world that we see, perceive and process is from the past. Therefore, in reality we always unconsciously make sense of something not when it happens, but after it has happened. This is also why Weick argues that people first act and then make sense of their action—meaningfulness comes after we have acted and not before.

For example, people often come up with explanations after they have committed an action to justify what they have done and rationalize their behavior. This also means that sensemaking is a comparative process since we compare "what is happening now" with a similar episode or event from our past, and thereby give meaning to the present (Mills et al. 2010). Weick explains: "whatever is occurring at the moment will influence what is discovered when people glance backward" (Weick 1995: 26). The rationale of retrospect is neatly summarized in the phrase "meaningful lived experience," as you cannot call something an experience and induce it with meaning until after you have been through it.

A further aspect that Weick underlines in retrospective sensemaking is that there are many possible meanings and therefore the sensemaker will be overwhelmed with equivocality. For example, a manager will be confused because there exist simply too many multiple meanings of a project. In such a situation managers "need values, priorities, and clarity about preferences to help them be clear about which projects matter. Clarity on values clarifies what is important in elapsed experience, which finally gives some sense of what that elapsed experience means" (Weick 1995: 27–28).

Salient cues

When we create meaning we use many small indicators consisting of ideas and actions to help us build a story that makes sense. Weick calls these indicators for cues, and defines them as "simple, familiar structures that are seeds from which people develop a larger sense of what may be occurring" (Weick 1995: 50). When people start lumping cues together and connecting them, they start to create meaning. This grouping and bracketing of cues that makes meaning arise is influenced by three important aspects: a) our broader frame consisting of, for example, earlier experience, training and routines—what we have done earlier in our lives; b) the use of organizational vocabulary and language; and c) the context and milieu from which it is derived.

Clampitt (2010: 9) has provided a simple yet powerful example of how organizational vocabulary and context matter in interpreting cues. The phrase "I have a bug" can have different meanings depending on the organizational context. For a nurse in a hospital environment this would mean that the person has some sort of bacteria. For a computer programmer working at Google this would mean that there is a coding error in the program on which they are working. For an undercover detective at Scotland Yard this would mean that they are being surveilled by an eavesdropping device. For a biologist it would refer to an interesting insect specimen.

From a change leadership perspective, cues are specifically relevant since the cues that employees draw upon—from sources such as gossip, tabloids, speeches by the CEO and so forth—are small components in their process of making sense of the organizational change that is underway. The sensegiver should be aware of the different cues that employees draw upon in their sensemaking processes, since this influences employees' interpretation of the change program. This can have an impact on how the change emerges and its trajectory. In this way, "control over which cues will serve as a point of reference is an important source of power" (Weick 1995: 50).

Ongoing

Sensemaking never stops, nor does it start clean as it is a continuous process, a constant and ongoing flow. In short, we always try to make sense of things. This means that sensemaking changes over time as there is a constant new flow of cues and experiences. It also means that no sensemaking is performed in isolation and it is always constrained or facilitated by the past. For example, when you come up with an idea, it is influenced by your experience and your prior knowledge (Helms-Mills et al. 2008).

However, the constant flow of sensemaking can be interrupted by a shock: "The reality of flows becomes most apparent when that flow is interrupted. An interruption to a flow typically induces an emotional response, which then paves way for emotion to influence sensemaking" (Weick 1995: 45). Translated into an organizational context, such situations are when there is an interruption of what is expected and planned for, such as a break of standard operating procedure. Such situations are occasions for sensemaking that are induced by emotions, because "[i]t makes good evolutionary sense to construct an organism that reacts significantly when the world is no longer the way it was" (Weick 1995: 46).

The property of ongoing is also connected to the perspective of emergent change that we discussed in Chapter 2. As we described there, this perspective reflects an understanding of change as an ongoing learning process that emphasizes the evolutionary nature of change rather than following predefined steps of planned change (Alvesson and Sveningsson 2008). Empowering managers to "plan" for change ignores this evolving nature of change. Therefore leaders who are open to see change as an ongoing process rather than a one-off and planned event are also likely to be more successful in realizing desired change outcomes (Rowland and Higgs 2008).

Plausibility

A sensemaking process seeks to be as plausible as possible rather than accurate (Weick 1995: 55). People act on information that they believe is plausible rather than finding the exact right information with 100 percent accuracy. When we perform sensemaking, we constantly seek new data and information that increases the plausibility, makes things more comprehensible than they were earlier, and less subject to criticism. This is a continuous process as we will never arrive at a point where there is a maximum level of plausibility and we will never find "the truth." It is a constant, endless struggle.

Weick explains:

> sensemaking is about plausibility, coherence, and reasonableness. Sensemaking is about accounts that are socially acceptable and credible [...] It would be nice if these accounts were also accurate. But in an equivocal, postmodern world, infused with the politics of interpretation and conflicting interests and inhabited by people with multiple shifting identities, an obsession with accuracy seems fruitless, and not of much practical help, either.
>
> *(Weick 1995: 61)*

So when is something plausible? Helms-Mills puts it simply: "Plausibility is a feeling that something makes sense, feels right, is somehow sensible, and fits with what you know" (Helms-Mills 2002: 67). Of course, if something is plausible, it is also deeply connected to the dominant social construction and the social context where the sensemaking process is taking place. In other words, a piece of information is seen as more plausible not only if it fits with what you know, but also needs to be aligned with what other people think of as the momentum of the time.

What seems plausible for one group of people in one type of organization might be considered highly implausible by other people in another organization. In a broader perspective, this property, and sensemaking as a whole for that matter, is a critique against perspectives such as rational decision making, strategic planning and planned organizational change. Such a perspective argues, for example, that change can be planned because we can collect data that are accurate, which are then used to make rational decisions that subsequently help us to change a situation from one stable state to another.

Enactment

The last property of sensemaking can be considered as stimulus for action and therefore this part is crucial for the sensemaking process as a whole. In this sense, without action there is no sensemaking and all the other properties have been built up to support this last stage of execution. However, Weick goes further than action by referring to it as enactment (Weick 1995: 30–38). By doing so, he underlines that by our very action we create our environment and this environment can both enable and constrain our action (Maitlis and Sonenshein 2010; Schwandt 2005).

Here the crucial point of enactment is that our environment and organizations are social constructions. We socially construct the environment around us when we perform actions, and this social construction provides us with both limits and possibilities for new actions. Therefore, organizations are part of our actions, not something that exist "out there" but instead something "in here" which all employees partake in creating through their enactment. This also means that we do not individually construct our environment but instead co-create with others.

By extension, this also means that interpretations become shared, confirmed, objectified and internalized and the dominant part of what is "out there" when we enact it (Van der Heijden et al. 2012). In essence, enactment "refers to the construction of social reality through action that is then (retrospectively) made sense of by the actor or actors involved" (Helms-Mills 2002: 70).

Prospective sensemaking

The above seven properties are the original aspects that Weick illustrates in his book from 1995. However, a growing stream of research has highlighted an additional property: prospective sensemaking (Gephart et al. 2010; Kaplan and Orlikowski 2013; Stigliani and Ravasi 2012; Wiebe 2010; Wright 2005). Or in other words, future-oriented sensemaking. Traditionally, sensemaking is in most cases described as focusing on making sense of retrospective accounts. Sensemaking of what has already transpired with a focus of studying the relation between the present reality (as it is interpreted) and what we expected it to be (Stigliani and Ravasi 2012). There is increasing research that now underlines that sensemaking also has an important role to play in shaping future events, decisions and actions.[3]

One of the first research accounts that explicitly addresses the future-oriented nature of sensemaking is the work of Gioia and his colleagues (1994: 378; Maitlis and Christianson 2014). They define prospective sensemaking as: "the conscious and intentional consideration of the probable future impact of certain actions, and especially nonactions, on the meaning construction processes of themselves and others." Weick agrees that this aspect of sensemaking does exist (see e.g. Weick et al. 2005), but has put less emphasis on it in the majority of his research and writing.

Future-oriented sensemaking is concerned with trying to interpret what is going on at the moment, as well as what has happened, with the aim of weaving plausible futures. This draws attention to notions that the process of making sense builds on three levels of temporality: past, present and future (Wiebe 2010). For example, Kaplan and Orlikowski (2013) have demonstrated how actors engaged in strategy-making use multiple interpretations of an organizational historical trajectory (past), as well as different understandings of present problems (present), when they make forecasts (future). Such studies want to remind us that when we perform sensemaking it is indeed based on retrospection, but when we do so we are at the same time thinking forward, trying to figure out sensible images of the future: what could we be doing and what do we want to become (Jabri 2012)?

Sensemaking and cartography

A colorful and illustrative way of explaining and to some extent summarizing the nature of sensemaking is to compare it with cartography (Weick 2001: 9). The nature of making maps is very similar to the rationale of sensemaking:

- Cartographers use different kinds of projection to make their representation (i.e. map) of "reality."
- There is no "true" or "best" map of the world. Instead there exist an indefinite number of plausible maps that can be constructed.
- The map, or the output of the cartography, is dependent on such things as what it represents, what it looks for, how it looks, where it looks and the tools that enable it to do so.
- The work of the cartography is endless because the areas and terrain of the world are continuously changing. The challenge, therefore, is to try to supply some form of temporary stability of the ever-changing world.
- Maps can, at least to some extent, explain and generalize blurry realities and serve as a means to replicate a common understanding of a certain context.

In this way, we as individuals are constantly drawing our own maps, based on our landscapes of lived experience. Our own map will never fully match that of any other human being. However, as we go about our private and professional daily lives we interact with other people and by doing so our map becomes slightly more aligned with (but not identical to) those of other people.

Thus, searching for a generic recipe for effective organizational change that can be replicated in every possible organization around the globe is pointless. There is such a distant gap between measurable facts and social constructs, and there is no perfect match between the maps and the landscapes out there. The social context, where the actual change is taking place, seems to override no matter what management concept we introduce. However, to learn more about the landscapes of meaning in organizations that are about to undergo change seems like a good investment for change leaders. We will return to this aspect of sensemaking and cartography and its connection to maps and social context in Chapter 6, where we develop the concept of landscaping.

Summary

The ambition of this chapter has been to get closer to the underlying notions of sensemaking. In doing so we have communicated that one important part of this concept is the cues that people draw upon to make their world more structured, meaningful and workable. This essential component—cues—is the main subject of the next chapter. There we will look at some of the origins of these cues: the sounds from narratives and conversation, the subtle symbolic messages that we perceive, and the more material and technological artifacts that we use.

Notes

1 A social construction is an aspect, information or knowledge that can be considered true in a certain context and in a particular point in time. This is usually something of which we are not aware and is based on a collection of people's judgment of a phenomenon that becomes institutionalized over time. Social construction is dynamic and changes over time depending on, for example, generation and culture. For example, the fact that "the world is flat" was once upon a time considered in the Western world to be true. Likewise, what can be considered "justice" or "disgusting" is also a social construction.
2 Those who are interested in an in-depth explanation of the seven properties can find this in Weick 1995: 17–62.
3 However, there are some who would disagree on this point. See Maitlis and Christianson 2014: 96.

Bibliography

Ahmad, R., Ferlie, E. & Atun, R. (2013) How trustworthiness is assessed in health care: a sensemaking perspective. *Journal of Change Management*, 13(2): 159–178.
Alvesson, M. & Sveningsson, S. (2008) *Changing Organizational Culture: Cultural Change Work in Progress*. London: Routledge.
Clampitt, P.G. (2010) *Communicating for Managerial Effectiveness*. Los Angeles, CA: Sage.
Gephart, R., Topal, C. & Zhang, Z. (2010) Future-oriented sensemaking: temporalities and institutional legitimation. *Process, Sensemaking, and Organizing*: 275–312.
Gioia, D. & Chittipeddi, K. (1991) Sensemaking and sensegiving in strategic change initiation. *Strategic Management Journal*, 12(6): 433–448.
Gioia, D.A., Thomas, J.B., Clark, S.M. & Chittipeddi, K. (1994) Symbolism and strategic change in academia: the dynamics of sensemaking and influence. *Organization Science*, 5(3): 363–383.
Helms-Mills, J. (2002) *Making Sense of Organizational Change*. New York: Routledge.
Helms-Mills, J., Dye, K. & Mills, A.J. (2008) *Understanding Organizational Change*. Abingdon: Routledge.

Jabri, M. (2012) *Managing Organizational Change: Process, Social Construction and Dialogue.* Basingstoke: Palgrave Macmillan.

Kaplan, S. & Orlikowski, W.J. (2013) Temporal work in strategy making. *Organization Science*, 24(4): 965–995.

Maitlis, S. (2005) The social processes of organizational sensemaking. *Academy of Management Journal*, 48(1): 21–49.

Maitlis, S. & Christianson, M. (2014) Sensemaking in organizations: taking stock and moving forward. *The Academy of Management Annals*, 8(1): 57–125.

Maitlis, S. & Lawrence, T.B. (2007) Triggers and enablers of sensegiving in organizations. *Academy of Management Journal*, 50(1): 57–84.

Maitlis, S. & Sonenshein, S. (2010) Sensemaking in crisis and change: inspiration and insights from Weick. *Journal of Management Studies*, 47(3): 551–580.

Mills, J.H., Thurlow, A. & Mills, A.J. (2010) Making sense of sensemaking: the critical sensemaking approach. *Qualitative Research in Organizations and Management: An International Journal*, 5(2): 182–195.

Rouleau, L. (2005) Micro-practices of strategic sensemaking and sensegiving: how middle managers interpret and sell change every day. *Journal of Management Studies*, 42(7): 1413–1441.

Rowland, D. & Higgs, M. (2008) *Sustaining Change: Leadership that Works.* Chichester: John Wiley & Sons.

Schwandt, D.R. (2005) When managers become philosophers: integrating learning with sensemaking. *Academy of Management Learning & Education*, 4(2): 176–192.

Senior, B. & Swailes, S. (2010) *Organizational Change*, fourth edn. Essex: Pearson.

Starbuck, W.H. & Milliken, F.J. (1988) "Executives' perceptual filters: what they notice and how they make sense." In D. Hambrick (ed.), *The Executive Effect: Concepts and Methods for Studying Top Managers.* Greenwich, CT: JAI Press, pp. 35–65.

Stensaker, I., Falkenberg, J. & Grønhaug, K. (2008) Implementation activities and organizational sensemaking. *Journal of Applied Behavioral Science*, 44(2): 162–185.

Stigliani, I. & Ravasi, D. (2012) Organizing thoughts and connecting brains: material practices and the transition from individual to group-level prospective sensemaking. *Academy of Management Journal*, 55(5): 1232–1259.

Van der Heijden, A., Cramer, J.M. & Driessen, P.P. (2012) Change agent sensemaking for sustainability in a multinational subsidiary. *Journal of Organizational Change Management*, 25(4): 535–559.

Walsh, J.P. & Ungson, G.R. (1991) Organizational memory. *Academy of Management Review*, 16(1): 57–91.

Weick, K.E. (1993) The collapse of sensemaking in organizations: the Mann Gulch Disaster. *Administrative Science Quarterly*, 38(4): 628–652.

Weick, K.E. (1995) *Sensemaking in Organizations.* Thousand Oaks, CA: Sage.

Weick, K.E. (2001) *Making Sense of the Organization.* Oxford: Blackwell Business.

Weick, K.E., Sutcliffe, K.M. & Obstfeld, D. (2005) Organizing and the process of sensemaking. *Organization Science*, 16(4): 409–421.

Wiebe, E. (2010) *Temporal Sensemaking: Managers' Use of Time to Frame Organizational Change.* Oxford: Oxford University Press.

Wright, A. (2005) The role of scenarios as prospective sensemaking devices. *Management Decision*, 43(1): 86–101.

4

DECIPHERING SOME SOURCES OF SENSEMAKING CUES

The purpose of this chapter is to explore some of the sources of the cues that people extract to give meaning to their experience and to their current and future actions.[1] We will do this by looking at the cues that people extract from the narratives and subjects of discussion in their everyday life, from the conversations and dialogue they have with co-workers, from the symbols carried to them by different communication vehicles, from their bodily movement, and from the IT and material artifacts that enable their work. In other words, cues from the sources of hearing, seeing, feeling and using. We will finish the chapter by providing some real-world examples of how three workshop exercises, based on the sources of cues, can be used to enhance sensemaking.

The cues that are extracted from such sources provide a point of reference from which people make sense of the organization and from which their work emerges. As Weick (1995) contends, this is an important foundation of power for leaders because if to some extent you can control people's point of reference, you can redirect their attention, influence their attitude towards change, and ultimately influence the change process as a whole.[2]

When we say that we will decipher the sources of cues of sensemaking, we mean that we will try to convey the managerial implications of the research that is done in this area. In doing so, we hope that this "translation" will elucidate examples of how leaders consciously and unconsciously influence sensemaking and sensegiving activities in their social interaction. This chapter by no means covers all earlier research, but it serves as an insight into both classical studies and more recent sensemaking-related research. We also want to underline that this chapter does not aspire to provide a recipe for successful sensemaking. Instead, we hope that it affords some well-informed and research-based road maps and examples of the numerous studies that exist about the myriad aspects of sensemaking cues.

However, let us first revisit one of the main points of the earlier chapter: organizational sensemaking is inherently a social process. It is something that we do in relation to other people in a world outside ourselves. Maitlis (2005: 21), for example, underlines the social aspect by explaining that organizational sensemaking is when "organization members interpret their environment in and through interactions with others, constructing accounts that allow them to comprehend the world and act collectively." This means that sensemaking and sensegiving processes arise if different social interactions between people are facilitated. In fact, sensemaking is triggered by different types of activities which enable an "intersubjective process" to arise between people (Maitlis and Christianson 2014). That is, flows and activities that spark a psychological relation between two or more conscious minds which ultimately results in action. This chapter provides different examples of what can ignite these psychological relations and how leaders can influence them.

Narration

One of the most immediate ways in which we perform social sensemaking is by the narratives we have with colleagues in the workplace (Abolafia 2010; Boje 1991; Brown and Humphreys 2003; Brown et al. 2008). We engage in conversation, trying to convey a personal meaning, and in return we get narratives from others that include their personal meaning.

Narratives often contain such things as good guys, bad guys, obstacles, struggles and so forth (Jabri 2012). The narrations we create are part of what we do, who we are, and they take place where there are people conversing. In this constant act of unfolding narration we co-create a meaning and make sense of events, activities and plans. By doing so, we also evaluate and give legitimacy to some and at the same time illegitimacy to others.

Narratives are about the past but at the same time they play an important role in understanding what is happening at the moment. Jabri (2012: 76) explains: "Narrative makes connections between past events and the experience that people 'inhabit' in the present; in other words, narrative is accomplished through an ongoing interpretation of past events in the light of what is happening now in actual experience." Narratives are also closely linked to the context in which they are uttered. If a narrative is taken out of its context then large parts of its meaning disappear.

Particularly during change there are often many different narrations circling in the organization which provide different versions of reality—e.g. resistance, positive or negative aspects of change, earlier change experiences—which together form a collective representation of the change. When these change discussions take place the situation is in flux and people find uncomfortable the ambiguous situation created by the announcement of the change.

In such situations people's perceptions, feelings and attitudes towards change are in part co-created during conversations. It is through the exchange of utterance that: a) we begin to understand what and why others think and act in a certain way in regards to the change; and b) at the same time we form an opinion about what we ourselves think about the change and how we should now act upon it (Jabri 2010).

The different stories that surround a change are in a way different plausible futures. These narratives as such compete with each other for dominance. There is no "one true story of the change," but only different versions of reality that are constantly being contested, negotiated and renegotiated through ongoing conversations. For example, some leaders try to legitimize and create a buy-in for the version of the narrative that is aligned with the organization and formal change program. At the same time others try to destabilize these narratives with their own concept of reality by telling their version of the change (Brown et al. 2008). A simple example of this are the different allegations, "truths," and "counter-truths" that circulate in the hyped circumstances of a US election.

Because sensemaking is highly influenced by narratives, leaders' ability to "tap into" and become an active part of the flow of narration becomes important. For leaders it is essential to be willing to listen to different narratives. Every stakeholder speaks with "their voice" through "their narrative," and as Jabri (2012) points out, leaders can gain advantage from listening to these different stories instead of being preoccupied with, for example, "hard data," numbers and "facts" from surveys and their own passionate version of the change. If they avoid paying attention and acting upon the different narratives that circulate, then they risk making the change illegitimate in the eyes of others, and the risk of failure becomes immediate.

One of the most recent and growing developments within narration studies of sensemaking is the concept of antenarrative (Boje 2008, 2011; Vaara and Tienari 2011; Weick 2012). Boje, who is the concept's originator, defines antenarrative as "fragmented, non-linear, incoherent, collective, unplotted, and pre-narrative speculation, a bet" (Boje 2001: 1). Antenarrative is a form of "pre-story" that consists of fragments and unstructured organizational discourses that has not yet formed into a grand narrative. Because the narrative has not yet taken shape, the antenarrative is not only without a proper plot and sequence (beginning–middle–end), but is also rich in multiple interpretations.

Antenarrative literally means before the narrative, or pre-story. Because of this temporal aspect of the concept, it can be used in analyses of prospective sensemaking. By looking at the narratives before they actually become fully fledged and cemented stories, we can gain understanding of how different interpretations of reality are mobilized by different actors. This game of legitimization ultimately amounts to a winner that transforms itself into one grand narrative (Vaara and Tienari 2011).

Since this chapter only provides a brief overview of some of the sources of sensemaking cues, we will end every section with suggestions for further reading.

Suggestions for further reading

Boje, D.M. (2011) *Storytelling and the Future of Organizations: An Antenarrative Handbook.* New York: Routledge.

Jabri, M. (2012) *Managing Organizational Change: Process, Social Construction and Dialogue.* Basingstoke: Palgrave Macmillan

Change conversations

One of the most powerful ways for leaders to perform sensegiving is through their intended conversations. As both Weick (2001) and Schein (1993) argue, one of the greatest influences on sensemaking takes place when you discover in the middle of a conversation that somebody interprets a concept or an idea in a totally different way than you do. As such, conversation is central to sensemaking and a corner-stone in managing change (Barrett et al. 1995; Ford and Ford 2009; Quinn 1996).

In fact, in most cases a pattern can be detected in conversation, as Ford and Ford (1995: 560) note: "The macrocomplexity of organizations is generated, and chan-ges emerge, through the diversity and interconnectedness of many microconversa-tions, each of which follows relatively simple rules" (also noted by Weick 2001). This section provides some of these "rules."

So what is a good conversation that has the potential to enable sensemaking processes? A straightforward answer to this question is provided by Quinn (1996: 382–383) (building on the works of Bird 1990), who says that a good conversation includes the characteristics of being vocal, reciprocating, issue oriented, rational, imaginative and honest:

- "Good conversations are vocal in that people are encouraged to speak up and to challenge received wisdom."
- "Good conversations are reciprocating in that all sides have a right to partici-pate, and all sides have a right not only to be listened to but to expect their views to have influence on the other parties to the conversation."
- "Good conversations are issues-oriented in that they focus on specific problems and alternative courses of action rather than expressions of personal sentiment."
- "Good conversations are rational in that they are 'intelligible, reasonable and well-argued'."
- "Good conversations are imaginative in that they invite the parties involved to consider unexplored avenues; they do not invite merely assent or dissent."
- "Good conversations are honest."

A little bit more depth on the nature of change conversation is provided by Ford and Ford (2008, 1995). They illustrate how conversation lies at the heart of change and they suggest that intentional change unfolds through four different types of conversation: initiative, understanding, performance and closure. They argue that managed in an adequate way, these four forms of conversation can propel a change process forward: "Producing intentional change, then, is a matter of deliberately bringing into existence, through communication, a new reality or set of social structures" (Ford and Ford 1995: 542). However, if these types of conversation are not properly managed, they can cause a fundamental breakdown of the change process. We will first explore the four different types of conversation and then move on to explain the different breakdowns.

Initiative

The focus of this first type of conversation is on starting the change. It is used to suggest new ideas, goals, visions, futures and direction, and is used to create attention on what is or should be done. The aim is to get people's attention and initiate a conversation about the need for and urgency of change. One simple and illustrative example is John F. Kennedy's speech to the US Congress in 1961: "landing a man on the moon and returning him safely to the earth."

Understanding

In this type of conversation you try to generate an understanding and enhance exploration of a proposed change. The base of the conversation can be, for example, an event, proposal or plan. Here you want to open up for questioning and analysis, and challenge underlying reasons and assumptions of issues. You also want to trigger dialogue and deep reflective conversation about the change. One of the outcomes, it is hoped, is to achieve a more common meaning, language and shared context about the change. Another outcome is increased confidence about the availability of new opportunities and courses of action, as well as to "sell the idea" and get people to like it. A common rationale for upcoming action.

Performance

The third type of conversation is called conversation for performance, and focuses on getting to action and establishing accountability. This usually consists of a manager wanting people to achieve something and therefore making different types of requests by referring to aspects such as deadlines, time, quality and cost. In return, the listener makes promises and there is an agreement for action. The final outcome is that things get done since people have clarity and answers about who, what, when and where-related questions.

Closure

The fourth and final type is conversation for closure, which is "intended to complete or close the loop on any requests or promises still open, actions taken (or not), or results produced (or not)" (Ford and Ford 2008: 448). This is about completing the change. This type of conversation includes acknowledgement and celebration of what has been achieved and a declaration that the change has formally come to an end. It summarizes what has been done and apologizes for what has not been accomplished, such as after-action reviews. One aim of closure conversations is for people to realize that it is time to "let go" of the past. Another aim is to make people move forward by acting on the new opportunities and possibilities that did not exist before.

Overall, these four different types of conversation are often present in everyday talk about change. They also occur in a dynamic fashion since change conversations "jump around" from one type to another. Ford and Ford (1995: 556) note that "a change that has advanced to the level of performance conversations, for example, can be slowed by someone who shifts from making requests and promises into giving explanations and justifications (a conversation for understanding)." Ford and Ford further argue that change leaders need to be trained in change conversation and understand how different utterances enable or disable the change process. They also claim that there are common breakdowns in conversations that can be avoided given the right leadership skills. We will turn to explaining these.

Breakdown in initiative

The first breakdown happens when the conversation of initiative fails to continue to the conversation of understanding and there is a standstill. This happens when the conversation is targeted towards the wrong people, for example if the conversation is conveyed to people who are not in a position (or do not perceive themselves so) to have a role or the power to accomplish anything connected to the change. They are simply not in a position where they see themselves as having the skills, power or authority to move things forward. Another reason for this breakdown is when earlier attempts of change have been ignored or dismissed, or when people feel that they will be ridiculed if they buy into the change.

Breakdown in understanding

Another common breakdown is when managers do not spend enough time on conversation for understanding; they underestimate the importance of creating an understanding of the change. This happens when, for example, managers jump to the conclusion that people will almost automatically interpret the change and its underlying aspects as they themselves are interpreting and viewing it. This amounts to a lack of common understanding and unclear structure and roles: people do not know what must be done, why it must be done, when to do it, how to do it and by whom. In this way there is an unclear statement about conditions for satisfaction of the change. One of the outcomes of such failure is that change resistance can emerge because people are confused and have not vented, discussed and shared their feelings, and ultimately cannot make sense of the situation.

Breakdown in performance

If change has been initiated and a common understanding has been established, a change can still fail because there has not been a conversation about the performance that signifies who is accountable for what. This is a kind of breakdown that occurs because people spend too much time creating a shared meaning but without any clear structure of the requests and what actions should be taken (i.e. the outcome of conversation of performance). "Agreement and understanding must be accompanied by requests and promises in order to produce the coordinated action implied in an intentional change" (Ford and Ford 1995: 558). Leaders fail to ask explicitly and invite people to take action because they take for granted that they already know this. Deadlines, intentions and tasks are not discussed in detail and there is no clear interplay between requests and promises, so things, at best, just move along slowly without any concrete, immediate action. If, instead, people are asked to do something and then respond accordingly, then the likelihood for action is higher.

Breakdown in closure

The final breakdown occurs when leaders fail to acknowledge and reward the closure of the change: "without acknowledgment of what has been accomplished, what has been contributed by the participants, or what has happened in the organization or the environment since the effort began, people may feel their contributions were unappreciated, of no value, or made no difference to the organization" (Ford and Ford 1995: 559). One outcome of such a lack of conversation of closure fosters cynicism and change resistance which often surfaces much later, when a new change is proposed.

Suggestions for further reading

Ford, J.D. & Ford, L.W. (1995) The role of conversations in producing intentional organisational change. *Academy of Management Review*, 20(3): 541–570.

Ford, J.D & Ford, L.W. (2009) *The Four Conversations: Daily Communication that Gets Results*. San Francisco, CA: Berrett-Koehler Publishers.

Quinn, J.J. (1996) The role of 'good conversation' in strategic control. *Journal of Management Studies*, 33(3): 381–394.

The different elements in change messages

One important aspect when it comes to communication and sensemaking is to understand conversations and exchange of meaning from the perspective of employees and other stakeholders (Bartunek et al. 2006). What is it that people are mainly concerned about in a discussion about change, and what is it that they are trying to make sense of when change is discussed? The research of Armenakis and his colleagues focuses particularly on this subject and according to them there is a pattern in stakeholders' meaning making of change messages (Armenakis and Harris 2002; Armenakis et al. 1993). They have summarized their research into "the change readiness framework," consisting of five different elements that they argue are the key aspects that employees try to make sense of in different forms of communication about the change message.

As Table 4.1 shows, the change readiness framework comprises: discrepancy, which is about the difference between the present situation and the desired future, and is essentially about explaining and discussing whether change is needed. Appropriateness addresses the question of whether the proposed change will fix the current problems that the organization faces. Self-efficacy is concerned with people's confidence and what it takes to execute change. Principal support focuses on the extent to which the suggested change has top management support, and if higher management is willing to allocate the required resources that the change demands. Finally, the essence of personal valence is captured in the phrase, "what's in it for me?"

The rationale of the framework, according to Armenakis et al., is that if leaders adequately and consistently address these different elements in their ongoing communication, it can influence the effectiveness of the change. In other words, and by using the ideas that we presented in the first chapter, if the change readiness framework is skillfully deployed it has the potential to shorten the time from making sense of where we are now, towards gaining awareness, and then understanding, to arrive finally at creating the willpower to execute the change.

Of course, the framework has its shortcomings and there are also other factors that influence the outcome of the communication that need to be considered, such as the trustworthiness of the communicator (Ahmad et al. 2013; Bernerth 2004; By 2007). What is also crucial is the contextualization of the message—the language

TABLE 4.1 The change readiness framework

Dimension	Explanation	Key concern for employee
Discrepancy	The gap between where we are today and where we want to be	Is this change really necessary? Why should we change?
Appropriateness	The possibility and appropriateness for the change to fix the current problems and move the organization from where we are today towards where we want to be	Why this change? Will this particular change work and will it fix the problem and get us to where we want to be?
Self-efficacy	Instilling confidence in employees and groups, and making them understand that they have what it takes to cope, manage and drive the change forward	Do I have what it takes? Will I be able to execute my part of the change successfully?
Principal support	The extent to which the management and leaders of the organization are engaged with and fully support the change	Do we have top management support? Is the management serious about this change and do they "walk the talk"? Do the leaders believe in this?
Personal valence	Clarifying and explaining the different extrinsic and intrinsic benefits of the change	What's in it for me and what does this mean for me? How will I benefit from this?

Source: Adapted from Armenakis and Harris 2002; Bernerth 2004: 41.

use, tone, words and phrases have to fit and resonate with the culture and audience (we will return to this below). Overall, the framework is not a panacea—just ticking off all five components in a change message will not do the trick. *If I just make sure that I include all these aspects in my speech, this should surely be okay?* Instead, the framework should be considered as a template that provides some guidelines on the different underlying aspects that will most likely recur during the change journey but will come into being in different ways.

Further, depending on who you talk to and depending on the situation, some elements will be more important than others. A skilful change leader knows what and when certain aspects should be emphasized and has different ways to address the same underlying questions. Finally, communication will most likely be altered during the course of the change. For example, certain answers to some of the question in column three in Table 4.1 will be different depending on if the change is just starting, is half-way through or nearing its end. Therefore a dynamic approach is advisable which includes continuously looking closely at what is going on and what stakeholders are trying to make sense of, and then updates and alters the communication about the change accordingly.

Suggestions for further reading

Armenakis, A.A., Harris, S.G. & Mossholder, K.W. (1993) Creating readiness for organizational change. *Human Relations*, 46(6): 681–703.

Bernerth, J. (2004) Expanding our understanding of the change message. *Human Resource Development Review*, 3(1): 36–52.

By, R.T. (2007) Ready or not … *Journal of Change Management*, 7(1): 3–11.

Roles in conversation and social interaction

So far in this chapter the main focus has been on what is being uttered in the conversation—the content of the discussion. Another way to analyze and improve conversations is to look at the different roles we play during discussions and social interactions. Here the systems psychologist and family therapist David Kantor has made a contribution by developing the four-player model (Kantor 2012; Kantor and Lehr 1977). This model suggests that when we discuss things we often do so by using several roles: move, follow, oppose or bystand. By analyzing conversations through the four-player model, we can uncover the cues and meanings that flow in everyday conversation which together make up some aspects of how we make sense of a discussion. See Table 4.2 for an overview.

All four roles are necessary for a fruitful and productive discussion. For example, without movers, a conversation does not progress and there is no direction; the absence of followers leads to a lack of impetus and energy; a lack of opposition results in a loss of critical thinking and ultimately no improvement; and finally, without bystanders there is no room for reflection, learning and ideas, and deadlock is preserved.

TABLE 4.2 The four-player model

Role	Explanation	Example
Mover	Driving things forward by providing action and direction or by initiating ideas	Let's start with the most critical point on our agenda
Follower	Validating, completing and supporting what is said and happening	Yes, let's do this. I am ready to go
Opposer	Challenging, questioning or correcting what is being said	I do not agree with you because I believe that we should abolish the new training program altogether
Bystander	Giving a perspective on what is going on and trying to resolve competing ideas and opinions	George thinks that the formal change should be announced earlier and Lisa thinks we should keep our earlier time agreement. What do you think?

The four roles are not mainly about the content of what is being uttered. Instead, the type of speech act is to a large extent determined by less explicit aspects, such as tone, wording, emphasis and rhythm. For example, as Kantor (2012: 26) explains, an enthusiastic "'Oh, sure!' is a follow, whereas a sarcastic 'Oh, sure!' is an obvious oppose." Also, the speech acts are dynamic, meaning that the same person usually moves between different speech acts in one conversation. Kantor further argues that a productive conversation requires a balance between the four roles. A skilled leader knows when to use different roles and how this creates concrete action:

> So if you're dealing with fierce opposers, you don't start off by opposing them. You bystand first. "I see how concerned you are about this decision, and it's having an effect on the group." Then you follow. "I think you have reason to be concerned." Only then do you move. "It seems to me that we've got to change our decision and address your concerns, but we can't lose the momentum of the original plan either." Three different actions: bystand, follow, move.
>
> *(Kleiner 2013: 3)*

In this way, a skilled leader can not only distinguish the different roles of the people in the conversation but also analyze them and actively shift between the four different roles during an ongoing conversation. Kantor talks about the skilled leader who can walk straight into a tense team meeting and "read the room" and immediately make sense of the shifts between different roles that make up the negative conversation. The leader can then, with just a few words, restore the balance in the room and in the conversation and get the team back on track. For some leaders this sensemaking ability is natural, while for others it can be learned by cues filtered through the four-player model.[3]

Suggestions for further reading

Kantor, D. (2012) *Reading the Room: Group Dynamics for Coaches and Leaders*. Hoboken, NJ: John Wiley & Sons.
Kantor, D. & Lehr, W. (1977) *Inside the Family*. San Francisco, CA: Jossey-Bass.
Kleiner, A. (2013) The thought leader interview: David Kantor. *strategy+business*, Summer (71): 1–5.

Dialogue

Dialogue[4] is another source of cues for sensemaking. Dialogue can be seen as a higher-level type of discussion that should, according to many (Barge and Little 2002; Isaacs 1993; Jabri 2004), be distinguished from ordinary conversation. When you converse, you often do so by having a predetermined outcome in mind and you consciously or unconsciously want others to agree with you (Jabri 2012). This was, for example, the underlying structure of what we earlier covered in the section about change conversation. In this way, most conversation can be seen as different flows of subliminal persuasion between different people. Dialogue, on the other hand, is essentially about the exploration of different meanings and ideas among a group of people with the purpose of exchanging ideas and uncovering underlying patterns of a subject—but without persuasion and without surrendering to a final point. In other words, dialogue is the meeting of minds where you suspend your defensive stand, and by doing so you gradually realize the many different meanings that people ascribe to a given subject (Isaacs 1993; Jabri 2012).

One of the proponents of dialogue is William Isaacs. He defines dialogue as an act of thinking together and he has developed guidelines and models for attaining dialogue by extending the aforementioned work of Kantor. For Isaacs, the essence of dialogue is about balancing *inquiry* (i.e. seeking to understand) and *advocacy* (i.e. trying to be understood):

> To advocate well, you must move and oppose well; to inquire, you must bystand and follow. Yet again, the absence of any of the elements hinders interaction. For instance, someone who opposes, but fails to also say what he wants (i.e., moves) is likely to be less effective as an advocate. Similarly, someone who follows what others say ("tell me more") but never provides perspective may draw out more information but never deepen the inquiry.
>
> *(Isaacs 1999a: 3–4)*

In many cases, dialogue fails to emerge because people are trained in advocacy as they want to express their opinion as fast as possible, or as Isaacs puts it: "People do not listen, they reload" (Isaacs 1999a: 3). By using the idea of a balance between "seeking to understand" and "trying to be understood," Isaacs has developed four key principles that can foster dialogue: voicing, listening, respecting and suspending judgment (illustrated in Figure 4.1).

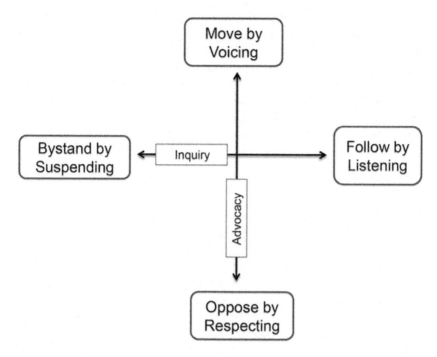

FIGURE 4.1 Four key principles for fostering dialogue
Source: Adapted from Isaacs 1999a: 4.

Voicing

This is essentially to speak one's own opinion, and in doing so we are "revealing what is true for each of us, regardless of all the other influences that might be brought to bear on us" (Isaacs 1999a: 5). This is about bringing forth your own genuine voice in the discussion. Voicing is also about putting forth what you believe in the wholeness of the flow of the discussion and speaking out about what is currently unfolding and emerging out of the interaction between the participants. Voicing renders question such as: What needs to be expressed here based on you, others and the whole dialogue? What is my own opinion and have I shared my own feelings, doubts and ideas? What is actually surfacing in the interaction between us that needs to be "put on the table"?

Listening

When we listen on a daily basis, we often do so on a shallow level and to a large extent impose our thoughts and ideas on what we are hearing. By listening, Isaacs refers to deep listening where we slow things down and actively reflect on the "music" of the conversation and the respective "meanings" and "truths" of those we are talking with (Isaacs 1999a). In short, mindfulness in listening. This requires not only listening to what "they" are saying but also to what "I" am saying: we have to learn to listen to ourselves before we can really understand others (Schein 1993). One of the aims is to see the world as they are seeing it and to understand others' point of view. The result is a shared emergence of a collective meaning where things are obvious and clear because "we are talking about the same thing." Such flow of listening is, however, rare. Active and deep listening renders questions such as: What is the meaning in what they are trying to convey? How are they feeling? What is their "truth"? What voices are downgraded and marginalized?

Respecting

This is a stance that requires a humble approach where you acknowledge that people often have different viewpoints and show mutual respect for one another. When dialogue is in motion, respect means that you should view others' opinions with the same legitimacy as your own, even if you do not agree with them (Isaacs 1999a). There is an acknowledgement that you are among equals, honoring all those who participate in the dialogue, and avoiding blaming, disputing and dismissing others. Respect affords reflective questions (Isaacs 1999b), like: What is at stake in this situation? How can we conduct a candid dialogue that will engage everybody? Am I showing awareness and respect for others' opinions?

Suspending judgment

When we are listening we are prone either to agree or disagree, and in so doing form a judgment and opinion about what is being said. Isaac argues that in a dialogue we should strive to suspend our judgment because such an act enables us to explore the underlying assumptions and rationale in what is being said. In this way, we should try to avoid an early "lock-in" of forming an opinion. This guideline puts forth questions such as: What is the most fundamental question underlying this formal question or issue? Why am I comprehending or judging the issue in the way that I am? What kinds of patterns or connections can I identify in what is being said? Can the issue be understood and comprehended in a different way, and if so, what is it?

Suggestions for further reading

Barge, J.K. & Little, M. (2002) Dialogical wisdom, communicative practice, and organizational life. *Communication Theory*, 12(4): 375–397.

Isaacs, W. (1999) *Dialogue and the Art of Thinking Together: A Pioneering Approach to Communicating in Business and in Life*. New York: Currency, cop.

Schein, E.H. (1993) On dialogue, culture, and organizational learning. *Organizational Dynamics*, 22(2): 40–51.

Storytelling

One way for leaders to contribute to the narrative processes and discussions that go on during organizational change is by the sensegiving activity of storytelling (Boje 1991, 1995; Brown et al. 2009; Gabriel 2000; Maclean et al. 2012). Storytelling is an activity that leaders—consciously or unconsciously—perform on a daily basis when they are posed with questions from stakeholders, like "What is the real story behind this change?" In such situations they have to craft a story that makes sense and supplies comfort for the unknown, explains prior actions and decisions, and makes efforts to align coming behavior.

In this way, the ability to tell stories is an integral part of the sensemaking process, as Weick (1995: 61) notes:

> A good story holds disparate elements together long enough to energize and guide action, plausibly enough to allow people to make retrospective sense of whatever happens, and engagingly enough that others will contribute their own inputs in the interest of sensemaking [...] And a good story, like a workable cause map, shows patterns that may already exist in the puzzles an actor now faces, or patterns that could be created anew in the interest of more order and sense in the future. The stories are templates. They are products of previous efforts at sensemaking.

Weick continues to explain that storytelling has strong explanatory power because the sensegiving stories that leaders can provide explain what is going on, why prior decisions and acts have been made, and by doing so reducing anxiety and feelings of uncertainty. However, the power of storytelling lies not only in this retrospective aspect but also in the way it can energize people to go forward and guide their trajectory.

What is a good story? The short and enduring answer from Aristotle is that it has a beginning, a middle and an end (Ibarra and Lineback 2005). Other components of a good story include characters, sequencing, plots and elements of surprise (Boje 1995). A powerful story also conveys an emotional message that engages the listener. McKee, for example—one of the world's best screenwriting lecturers—argues that there are too many stories using conventional rhetoric based on, for example, analytical SWOT analyses (strengths, weaknesses, opportunities, threats), and statistical data presented in too many PowerPoint presentations (McKee and Fryer 2003). His message is that leaders should simply skip these kinds of presentations with their adjacent orthodox rhetoric. Conventional and rational rhetoric are problematic because even if the leader manages to convince people and inspire them, they will only be, at best, intellectually convinced. Since sensegiving processes are often more powerful if they contain emotional elements (Maitlis et al. 2013), stories that reach the heart of the audience are therefore often the most effective. McKee (1997) offers several ways in which to do this for screenwriting, and Burke (2008: 241) has used these ideas as a template and translated them into the context of organizational change (see Table 4.3).

TABLE 4.3 Elements of a good story

Elements of a good story in screenwriting	Elements of a good story in organizational change (Burke)
What does my protagonist want in order to restore balance in his or her life? Desire is the blood of a story. Desire is not a shopping list but a core need that, if satisfied, would stop the story in its tracks	What must be done to restore balance?
What is keeping my protagonist from achieving his or her desire? Forces within? Doubt? Fear? Confusion? Personal conflicts with friends, family, lovers?	What is keeping us from doing this?
How would my protagonist decide to act in order to achieve his or her desire in the face of these antagonistic forces? It's in the answer to that question that storytellers discover the truth of their characters, because the heart of a human being is revealed in the choices he or she makes under pressure	How should we act to achieve this desire for restored and renewed balance?
The storyteller leans back from the design of events he or she has created and asks, "Do I believe this? Is it neither an exaggeration nor a soft-soaping of the struggle? Is this an honest telling, though heaven may fall?"	Do I, as the leader and storyteller, believe this? Is it truthful? Is it believable and not just hype? Can I come across with integrity?

Source: McKee 1997; Burke 2008: 241.

However, just providing "a good story" is not a panacea, as Maitlis and Lawrence (2007: 79) underline: "they must tell sensible stories (drawing on relevant expertise) at the right time and place (opportunity) and occupy a social position that leads others to listen (legitimacy)." In other words, a good story is highly contextually sensitive and situated in both time and space. What is also important to bear in mind is that there is the difference between a narrative and a story (Jabri 2012). A story must contain some sort of theme and key message or lesson, as well as having a clear closure and ending. Narratives, on the other hand, are more continuous, often lack clear closure and are more about daily conversations and utterances that people have by the coffee machine, during lunch and in the corridor.[5]

Another important feature of stories is that they often have multiple meanings (Boje 1991). They can be interpreted in different ways, depending on the storyteller's own version of what has transpired and its context. A leader can tell their story of the change, but at the same time a stakeholder who is negatively affected by the change will most likely provide an immediate counter-story. In fact, all events contain multiple meanings that can be interpreted in multiple ways which ultimately leads to multiple stories that can even be incompatible. Indeed, as Jabri (2012: 86) underlines, "A single (coherent) story that links all processes does not exist [and] people chase different stories and explore different plots (counter-stories) as they seek to make sense of their unfolding experience."

Despite the notion that storytelling can be dangerous because of asymmetrical and disparate interpretation, it still has a powerful role to play in communicating the need for change. Stories serve us the rationale for change and in doing so trigger change readiness. Without compelling stories it would be considerably more difficult to get out of crisis situations, to get a stagnated organization moving, to change from A to B—all in all, to survive in the long term would be highly problematic. If stories are well crafted they have the potential to create a common ground among stakeholders which enables them to make choices and perform activities aligned with the proposed change (Iveroth 2010a, 2011). More simply put, good stories explain the past and by doing so they also energize for action in the future.

Suggestions for further reading

Boje, D.M. (2008) *Storytelling Organizations*. London: Sage.
Ibarra, H. & Lineback, K. (2005) What's your story? *Harvard Business Review*, 83(1): 64–71.
McKee, R. (1997) *Substance, Structure, Style, and the Principles of Screenwriting*. New York: HarperCollins.

Symbolism

In their sensegiving efforts leaders may also use different symbols in their communication to make people, as well as themselves, comprehend and understand change (Cornelissen 2012; Cornelissen et al. 2011; Gioia et al. 1994; Hill and Levenhagen 1995). This can take many forms and be embedded within, for example, individual language, clothes and behavior, or in organizational systems, routines and rituals (Johnson 1990). Symbolism, as such, is "basic to the process of sensemaking ... because [its] inherent ambiguity provides a bridge between the familiar and the strange, thus fostering a sense of continuity while simultaneously facilitating change" (Gioia et al. 1994: 365). Indeed, symbolism is powerful because it can communicate underlying and tacit meanings which aids the collective construction of meaning in a group of people.

By using symbolic language a leader tries to comprehend the change situation themselves. They also try to create a buy-in, legitimize the change and frame it in a certain way for different stakeholders. Symbolic language can also be used to explain the current critical situation that the organization is facing or using in a vision about a future state that the organization aspires to attain. Leaders' use of symbols is sometimes done spontaneously such as during an ongoing conversation with a group of employees during a workshop. Or it can be planned and strategically crafted as a way to influence the meaning making of others in a desired way, or to invoke a feeling of familiarity.

One of most basic components of symbolic communication is the metaphor. The metaphor's role in sensemaking processes can be described as the relationship between the cue and the frame, going back to our discussion in Chapter 3. The Merriam-Webster dictionary defines metaphor as "one thing that is used to refer to another thing in order to show or suggest that they are similar." As such, metaphors serve two purposes: first, they compress and structure the change into an understandable format (Cornelissen 2012). Leaders try to make the unfamiliar more familiar and reduce feelings of ambiguity, anxiety and uncertainty (Gioia et al. 1994). Second, metaphors can be used to validate or discredit actions and decisions (Cornelissen 2012). They are used to legitimize and socially justify why some actions and decisions have been taken and at the same time pre-empt and discredit why other actions and decisions were not valid.

The more aggregated concept of symbols—which can be seen as the "theme" of many metaphors—manifests itself in many ways and can be embedded in any kind of communication vehicle. According to Balogun and Hailey (2008), symbolic communication can specifically be used in change by leaders in:

- Challenge to the status quo: raise the awareness for change, legitimize questioning of "the way we do things around here," illustrate a break with the past and create change readiness for the future.
- Expectation: communicate symbols that convey what is expected by employees in the new situation and environment.
- Identity: illustrate and aid the construction of new and unified identity through symbols.

As such, symbols can be grouped into six different categories (based on Johnson et al. 2011): rituals, physical and material aspects, organizational systems and processes, behavior, stories, and language.

First, symbolic sensemaking can be performed through different types of rituals (Trice and Beyer 1984). These can be strategically crafted as a way of communicating change or less preplanned and an activity that has emerged during the change process. These rituals can be of different types (Johnson et al. 2011; Trice and Beyer 1984), as illustrated in Table 4.4.

Second, physical and material aspects can provide cues for sensemaking such as artifacts, logotypes and dress codes. The symbolic content in these types of sensegiving activities are in many cases very clear (but without a guarantee for sensemaking that the leaders wish for). An example of physical and material symbolic sensegiving activities is geographically placing a department closer to headquarters.

Third, organizational systems and processes carry with them symbolic messages. These systems are often in the form of organizational structure, a rewards system, control system and recruitment system, and embody values and meanings. For example, the way a control system rewards and punishes behavior is a way of showing what is liked and disliked by the organization.

Fourth, one powerful sensegiver is the behavior that leaders show. For example, a leader trying to reinforce the need for change and the alarming financial situation by applying different kinds of behavior: announcing that the leader is selling the

TABLE 4.4 Different types of rituals in symbolic communication

Type of ritual	Explanation	Examples
Passage	Confirms and aids individuals' transition to another role. Promotes new roles and interaction	• Induction programs • Training programs
Degradation	Weakens social roles and their political power	• Visibly acknowledging problems • Firing certain people • Dissolving groups or redrawing group boundaries • Publicly praising some employees and at the same time discrediting others
Enhancement	Increases social roles and their political power	• Publicly acknowledging individual accomplishment to motivate others • Awards and promotion • Spreading the good news
Renewal	Conducts structural changes to improve functioning. Changes or creates management attention on certain issues	• Employing a consultant • Increasing focus on certain issues and away from others • Reassuring that the organization is dealing with the problems • Formally engaging in organizational change
Conflict reduction	Reduces conflict and aggression	• Collective bargaining through negotiating committees • Slow consensus driven decision making processes
Integration	Encourages feelings of commonality, common values and binds people together	• Regular beverages after work on Friday afternoons • Christmas party • Uniforms
Challenge	Challenges the status quo and a desire for changing "the way things are done around here"	• The CEO having new clothes • Visibly displaying different behavior • Reducing conformity and increasing critical thinking through asking people for their opinion, and consistently questioning salient behavior as well a yes-yes attitude
Counter-challenge	Confirms the status quo and a desire for "things to stay as they are"	• Sticking to rules, standards and common practices • Displaying change resistance by not attending meetings concerning the change and sabotaging change efforts • Anti-change talks and conversations

Source: Adapted from Trice and Beyer 1984; Johnson et al. 2011.

company car that he uses, starting to use public transport, changing his salary to £1, and so forth.

Fifth, stories, according to Johnson and his colleagues (2011), are also a powerful way of communicating a symbolic message. We have illustrated this already in the section about storytelling above, but here story means not only the stories that leaders tell, but also the more mundane stories people share with each other. Johnson et al. provide a telling example of one CEO who wanted to communicate certain issues. He did so by having his secretary leave a memo in the photocopier with the text "strictly confidential" written on it. The storytelling and the gossip in the organization was intensive and immediate after the memo was found.

Finally, language plays a key role in symbolic sensemaking. Sometimes leaders and change agents communicate a symbolic message without knowing it and without realizing the energizing effect that their choice of words has. At other times they consciously try to kick-start and stimulate change with phrases like, "*We have a match to play and we must win it,*" and other sports metaphors.

However, using symbols as sensegiving is associated with risk, as it can backfire when people interpret them in unintended ways. Knowing and controlling how people make sense of symbolic communication is hard but there are some guidelines that can aid such efforts. To start with, symbolic communication should be crafted in a systematic way and not be treated as a one-off intervention (Balogun and Hailey 2008). Symbolic communication is most likely to be effective if different kinds are strategically planned throughout the change process.

Another important aspect is to identify and eliminate any kind of symbol that carries the message to uphold the status quo and continue "to do things as we have always done." It is not that hard to think out and execute a way to communicate the change in a symbolic way. It is much more complex to do this while conducting a critical examination and elimination of the stories, power structures, organizational structures, control system, rituals and routines that carry a symbolic message that upholds the status quo.

A further issue of importance is the extent to which the symbolic act is aligned with the context and culture of the organization. A powerful symbol or metaphor used in a private organization in the USA in the 1950s would most likely be less effective when used now in Sweden. Why? Because it is out of context. For a symbolic act to be as effective as possible, it should be congruent with what people feel and think in a particular organization at a particular point in time. Therefore the effectiveness of using symbols and metaphors as sensegivers by managers is connected to a leader's ability to "tap into" and get a feeling and a sense of the culture and what is going on in an organization (we will explore this aspect in greater detail in Chapter 5).

A final point is that symbolic communication can be significantly more powerful if it is communicated in a variety of ways that together are aligned. Or, as Gardner (2004: 16) explains: "A change of mind becomes convincing to the extent that it lends itself to representation in a number of different forms, with these forms reinforcing one another." For example, the same message can be told using as many forms as possible of the above types of symbolic acts: ritual (as many as eight different types), organizational systems and processes, physical and material aspects, behavior, stories, and language. Likewise, the way one receives the message can also vary: discussing the change during a coffee break, reading about the alarming situation within your organization in the tabloids, hearing about the bad circumstances of your market niche on the global news, talking about it with your friends on a night out in town, discussing it with your partner over the weekend, reading about the need for change in a research report, and so forth.

Suggestions for further reading

Cornelissen, J.P., Holt, R. & Zundel, M. (2011) The role of analogy and metaphor in the framing and legitimization of strategic change. *Organization Studies*, 32(12): 1701–1716.

Gioia, D.A., Thomas, J.B., Clark, S.M. & Chittipeddi, K. (1994) Symbolism and strategic change in academia: the dynamics of sensemaking and influence. *Organization Science*, 5(3): 363–383.

Johnson, G. (1990) Managing strategic change; the role of symbolic action. *British Journal of Management*, 1(4): 183–200.

Trice, H.M. & Beyer, J.M. (1984) Studying organizational cultures through rites and ceremonials. *Academy of Management Review*, 9(4): 653–669.

Embodied sensemaking

Most of the research conducted in the area of organizational sensemaking tends to focus on, to some extent, imperceptible and invisible practices connected to cognition and language—such as most of the aspects that we have covered so far in this chapter. However, sensemaking research has been criticized for paying too much attention to such intangible aspects and too little to how sensemaking is embedded and embodied in physical bodies and artifacts (Cunliffe and Coupland 2012; Maitlis and Christianson 2014; Sandberg and Tsoukas 2014; Stigliani and Ravasi 2012; Whiteman and Cooper 2011; Yakhlef and Essén 2012). The idea is that we not only make sense of the world through, for example, the conversation we have with the people around us, but also through the feelings of our body and the physical artifacts that we use in our daily lives. As a response, there is a growing stream of research looking at how the body, material and physical "things" can provide cues for sensemaking through the symbols and meaning that they carry. Since this can be considered one of the leads of sensemaking research, we will spend some time explaining this area here and below. We will also at the end of this chapter provide you with a real-life example from the field which illustrates how embodiment can be used in a simple workshop exercise to enhance sensemaking.

The first example of this type of sensemaking research is a stream that looks at how we make sense through feelings of our physical body (Cunliffe and Coupland 2012; Yakhlef and Essén 2012). Here the work of Cunliffe and Coupland is illustrative. Cunliffe and Coupland (2012: 66, 64) postulate that not only do we "make sense of our experience through narratives, stories or drama," but more importantly "whether we are aware of it or not, we make our lives and ourselves 'sensible' through embodied (bodily) interpretations in our ongoing everyday interactions." They illustrate their point by showing a sudden event in a rugby match and how the body language, facial expressions, rhythm of the body and position of the different players influenced sensemaking processes.

Cunliffe and Coupland demonstrate how sensemaking can be embodied in our body but there is also research on how sensemaking is embodied in material and physical artifacts that are incorporated into strategic practices. For example, Heracleous and Jacobs (2008) show how LEGO bricks can be used in crafting strategy. Through different types of workshops, the participants of the study used LEGO bricks to debate different strategic challenges. Heracleous and Jacobs argue that LEGO bricks can embody sensemaking metaphors that enable them to tap into underlying assumptions during discussions. This can then amount into a shift in the mindsets of the strategists. They summarize some of the managerial implications for strategists:

- By crafting embodied metaphors, strategy teams can surface and critically reflect on their current mode of strategizing and envision alternative modes.
- This practice can capture intangible and collective dimensions of organizational identity that cannot be as vividly or tangibly captured through the tools most commonly used in strategy.
- Crafting and decoding embodied metaphors can deliver insights and potential shifts in managers' mind-sets that would have been difficult to gain in more conventional, numbers driven, board-meeting style sessions.

(Heracleous and Jacobs 2008: 322)

Similar research has been conducted on a variety of other material artifacts used in strategy practices. For example, Stigliani and Ravasi (2012) have demonstrated how the materiality of process models within a consulting firm stimulates verbal exchange and cognitive process in collective sensemaking. Other studies have examined, for example, the use of PowerPoint (Kaplan 2011), process maps (Fenton 2007) and numbers (Denis et al. 2006).

What is common to many of these studies is not only that they are concerned with crafting of strategy (Whittington 2006), but more importantly that they examine prospective sensemaking. In other words, the artifacts provide cues for sensemaking and sensegiving which influence future events, decisions and actions. Different strategy tools in different forms such as process maps, PowerPoint presentations, flipcharts, figures, LEGO bricks, all afford forward-looking thinking. They stimulate structuring and help devise different future organizational trajectories.

Suggestions for further reading

Cunliffe, A. & Coupland, C. (2012) From hero to villain to hero: making experience sensible through embodied narrative sensemaking. *Human Relations*, 65(1): 63–88.

Heracleous, L. & Jacobs, C.D. (2008) Crafting strategy: the role of embodied metaphors. *Long Range Planning*, 41(3): 309–325.

Stigliani, I. & Ravasi, D. (2012) Organizing thoughts and connecting brains: material practices and the transition from individual to group-level prospective sensemaking. *Academy of Management Journal*, 55(5): 1232–1259.

Sociomateriality and information technology

Another research stream closely connected to the area of embodied sensemaking is the study of sociomateriality and IT. The underlying theoretical notion is to view IT not as a simple functional tool but as a device that can have social implications because it is deeply ingrained in our daily practice (Leonardi 2013; Orlikowski and Scott 2008). For instance, sociomaterial informed study of an information system implementation is concerned not only with the functionality of the technology (material), but also how the information system enables its users to make sense of the new practices that the technology introduces (socio) (Iveroth 2010b). In the perspective of sensemaking, sociomaterial informed studies are concerned with how IT is embodied with symbols and metaphors and how this influences sensemaking and sensegiving processes.

In this area there is a range of studies focusing on various aspects of technology (Griffith 1999; Korica and Molloy 2010; Leonardi 2009; Orlikowski 2000), and the work of Iveroth serves here as an illustrative example of studies of sociomateriality (Iveroth 2010a, 2011, 2012; Iveroth and Bengtsson 2014). He has demonstrated in two longitudinal research projects how sensemaking is pivotal to the implementation of large-scale information systems. The first research project concerned a global implementation of an enterprise resource planning (ERP) system within the multinational telecommunications company Ericsson (Iveroth 2010a, 2011). This work illustrates that when a change is complex—such as a large-scale ERP implementation—then change recipients will begin to make sense of the change differently. They start having divergent interpretations of what the new IT (and the adjustments that it brings) truly means for their daily practice. In other words, there is a lack of common meaning because people are making sense of the technology in different ways. As a result, recipients will have incompatible meaning structures and will interpret and use the new IT differently. In turn, the initiative will take off in different directions and the change will ultimately fail.

Iveroth further demonstrates that this development can be avoided by change leaders' sensegiving activities consisting of acts of translation that aim to surmount incompatible meaning structures among recipients through reflection and learning. That is, the sensegiving activities are focused on reducing divergent sensemaking processes connected to the new technology. In practice, Ericsson performed such activities through numerous activities such as workshops, seminars, one-to-one communication and by having change managers with key skills such as two-way communications, experience-based knowledge, and know-how and people-management skills (as they termed it). The aim of these activities was to respond to recipients' feelings of ambiguity and equivalence by trying to translate the local implications of the ERP system, how daily practice would be altered and how they would perform their work in future.

The second research project was concerned with the question of how to change individuals' behavior towards more sustainable practices using IT (Iveroth and Bengtsson 2014). To answer this research question, Iveroth and Bengtsson examined the implementation of an IT system for sustainable transport logistics and procurement in Uppsala, a small municipality of Sweden. The purpose of the IT project was to attain a more sustainable transportation flow between goods deliverers and recipients within larger parts of the municipality. The overarching goal of the project was to aid the municipality to be more sustainable by developing new practices. In the aftermath the envisioned goals were in most cases realized based on triple bottom line measures: economical, environmental and social sustainability (Elkington 1997).

The results are similar to the research project at Ericsson in that they show how the successful change towards sustainable practices is an entanglement of both social and technical-structural elements over time. In this process, structures such as IT are the enablers, and the actors and their social activities are the tipping-point factors that ultimately determine the success of changing individuals' behavior in a more sustainable direction.

The main point is that the research shows that it is not the technology per se, with its functionality, that is the strongest driving force in changing people's behavior to more sustainable practices. Neither is it the adjacent structures such as plans, policies, rules, procurement routines, frameworks, plans for sustainability. Instead, it was the sensemaking and sensegiving activities that played the pivotal role in changing behavior. For example, one of the perceived smaller parts of the IT project was the implementation of a sustainability reporting system. This was a kind of decision support system that supported the triple bottom line perspective and ensured the attainment of long-term sustainability goals. When the recipients used this system, it prompted learning and reflection about the meaning of sustainability among peers at the local level. Through collective sensemaking that grew out of using the sustainability reporting system, they became aware that sustainable issue of logistics is more complicated than just saving fuel. In this way, the success of the project was due to, in many respects, unintentional sensemaking and sensegiving activities that surrounded the IT project.

The work of Iveroth demonstrates that IT affords more than just its functionality, since it is intertwined with social aspects (Orlikowski and Scott 2008; Zammuto et al. 2007). In fact, symbolic meaning can be embodied in different ways and by doing so can be considered as having sensegiving properties. They give something to talk about, to reflect upon and to discuss with others which together reduce feelings of equivalence as well as provide energy to move forward.

Suggestions for further reading

Iveroth, E. & Bengtsson, F. (2014) Changing behavior towards sustainable practices using information technology. *Journal of Environmental Management*, 139(June): 59–68.

Leonardi, P.M. (2009) Why do people reject new technologies and stymie organizational changes of which they are in favor? Exploring misalignments between social interactions and materiality. *Human Communication Research*, 35(3): 407–441.

Leonardi, P.M. (2013) Theoretical foundations for the study of sociomateriality. *Information and Organization*, 23(2): 59–76.

Sensemaking exercises from the field

In this section we will present three short real-world examples of how workshop exercises based on symbolism, change conversations and embodiment can enhance sensemaking. The purpose is to show how these three aspects, covered earlier, can be used and implemented to enhance sensemaking. By doing so, we also want to convey that in many respects sensemaking does not have to be complicated in practice. These exercises are basic; however, it takes a bit of structure, courage and ability to facilitate them.

We will look closer at the following aspects:

- How symbols can be used to trigger sensemaking about the current state and the need for change.
- How change conversations facilitate sensemaking about a desired future state and the change journey of getting there.
- How bodily movements combined with conversations create understanding of culture and core values.

For every example we will give a short introduction combined with some broad instructions, and then we will finish with a vignette from a live change assignment. The vignettes are taken from one of our change projects. The main character is the change leader, Eva. In September 2012, she becomes IT director at a Swedish public authority. Eva's change mission, coming straight from the director-general, is to re-engineer the whole IT department which has been poorly managed for many years. Eva recollects her feelings from the start in the fall of 2012: "*About 70 employees and 50 consultants worked in the department and we had a dreadful situation. Poor leadership, inefficient processes, no strategy, no common goals, no customer orientation and on top of everything else a culture that was killing us. It was really bad.*"

The general reason for this assignment is an efficiency problem but the root could be described as a cultural problem in the shape of an absence of service orientation. When Eva is assigned to take on this challenge, she starts with an initial analysis which results in a range of change projects sorted into the following five streams:

- Culture and values
- Management and control
- Cooperation
- Resource allocation
- Professional supplier

The projects were finalized in December 2014 and led to a significant increase in internal customer satisfaction, apart from the deployment of new processes and IT solutions. Eva, who is an empathic leader sincerely interested in the "people side" of change, used the following three exercises (among others) to enhance sensemaking during the initial stages of the transformation.

Exercise: the symbol

This is a simple exercise with symbols that can be used to stimulate sensemaking about the current state and the need for change. It can also be a way to set off a discussion connected to individual and organizational identity and hopes for the future. Moreover, it can communicate underlying and tacit meanings which can fuel a collective construction of meaning in a group of people. The exercise can be embedded in large meetings consisting of at least 20 people. The outcome is usually a more common understanding of the current situation and change challenges.

Preparation

- Decide what context or subject you want to be symbolized. For example, if it is a change process it could be the current and future state and the vision of what the change is going to achieve.
- Approximately a week before the meeting, ask everyone involved to choose "a thing" that symbolizes the current state and/or future state (either from their home and private life or from the office).
- Formulate the task in simple words, avoiding being too specific and allow the task to be open ended.

During the exercise

- Ask the participants to present their symbols
- Mix the group into five to six people
- Tell them to get together in separate rooms or tables and ask them to account for their symbols and openly discuss them (without interference of the workshop facilitator)
- Ask the groups to pick some good examples from the group discussions
- Share and discuss these examples in the large forum consisting of all the small groups
- Summarize by reflecting on what can be learned from this
- Afterwards take pictures and publish good examples on the intranet, notice boards and other communication channels

A vignette from the field

It is November 2012 and the first time we gather the whole IT department for a whole-day workshop about the upcoming change initiative. Eva has set the scene and presented the background to her assignment from the director-general. The aim now is to start to discuss strengths and weaknesses in the current state and the gap between the present and the future. As a "warm-up," the crowd is asked to start by sharing the results of the individual homework prior to this day: to find and bring a symbol of the IT department. Chairs scrape against the floor as groups form small circles. Initially, people are a little hesitant, but very soon the energy increases. This turns out to be a real success, as people have brought the most hilarious things. Within the small groups, almost everyone has taken the exercise seriously and they share things, thoughts and feelings. We end the session by asking for good examples.

One woman stands up and presents a wad of tangled yarn with raisins in the loose ends. She explains: "*This is symbolizing our department. Right now it feels like everything is tangled, but if we sort it out we will find good things in the loose ends.*" People cheer. Right now the workdays are fussy and the direction unclear, but the raisins symbolize a good future, which will be reached if they untangle the situation.

Another woman has brought a wooden Burr Puzzle—an interlocking puzzle consisting of six notched sticks, combined to make one three-dimensional symmetrical knot. She explains: "*This knot consists of six pieces. It is tricky to put together, but once assembled it is as strong as hell. The loose pieces symbolize our current state. Our future state should be the tight knot.*" People nod thoughtfully. Today the teams work separately, the department does not operate as a unit; however, with cooperation and unity, they will grow strong.

A man has brought a pack of powder for chocolate pudding. He is called up on the stage to elaborate on his choice: "*Well, the powder doesn't look like much but if you add some water and energy it evolves to something really yummy.*" More laughs, nodding heads and applause. The chocolate pudding shows that insignificant things can evolve into something good if you add energy.

We finish the exercise in good spirits. The stories (and many more from others in the room) together symbolize a common notion that the current state is problematic but can be solved—a better future can be discerned. Besides energy, laughs and a plethora of symbolic objects, the whole exercise strengthens the understanding of the need for change and the gap between today and the future. "*They have just summarized my own analysis,*" notes Eva, pleased.

Exercise: the gap text

The exercise illustrates how change conversations about a possible desired future can be triggered by using a "gap text" (see below for an example). The participants are asked to fill in the blanks and then to discuss their text with others. By doing so, they share their feelings of equivocality and uncertainty about an upcoming change and the journey ahead. In this process they also explore different plausible meanings about the change and its possible outcomes. The result is a common frame of "a story of the future," things achieved and very often a lot of laughs. The exercise is in most cases embedded in large meetings consisting of at least 20 people but can also be performed in smaller groups. The preparation and structure are as follows:

Preparation

- Prepare a template with a gap text about a future scenario. The recommendation is that this "future" is three to five years away, as it helps people to free themselves from the current state. The text can be general or tailored to an organization's specific requirements (see example below).
- Ask the participants to fill in individually the gaps in the text. This can be done either during the event or as preparation before the meeting. The instructions should be open: "*Imagine a day at work in five years' time. Fill in the template and bring it to the meeting.*"

During the exercise

- Mix the group into small groups of five to six people (we recommend multifunctional groups, preferably with individuals who do not know each other well)
- Ask everyone to present their completed texts in the small groups
- Ask the small groups to agree on a joint text
- Reconvene in the large group and share the joint texts
- Reflect on common patterns, similarities and differences

Example of gap text template

It's Tuesday, 26 April 2017 and I am _____ years old. In my bag I carry _____. As I walk through the entrance to the office, I feel _____.

To be honest, I never thought we'd make it this far with the change, but we have accomplished both _____ and _____. Even _____ seems quite happy.

Unlike back in 2012, we are now _____ and have stopped _____, but we have also managed to preserve our _____. Today we are characterized by _____ and _____. In the long run, I hope we _____.

When I look back on our journey since 2012, I am especially pleased with _____. I think something that was crucial for all of us in order to get this far in recent years was _____ and I realize now how much I have contributed by _____.

And wait, here comes Eva again and she says that we must _____. Some things never change!

A vignette from the field

This is the second department workshop in April 2013 and the first item on the agenda is a group exercise around the future state of the IT department. People are asked to fill in individually the gaps in a prepared text about "a day in the IT department in 2017." This exercise triggers an outburst of activity. People spread out in the room and in the nearby lobby and start scribbling on their worksheets. After ten minutes, each team leader gathers their team and a new iteration begins. Now they are asked to share their texts and then merge them into one team version. Per (the man with the chocolate pudding) reads his creation:

> It's Tuesday, 26 April 2017 and I am 45 years old. In my bag I carry *the latest e-reader*. As I walk through the entrance of the office, I feel *proud*.
>
> To be honest, I never thought we'd make it this far with the change, but we have accomplished both *better efficiency* and *a nicer workplace*. Even *the director-general* seems quite happy.
>
> Unlike back in 2012, we are now *one unit* and have stopped *all bullshit*, but we have also managed to preserve our *good laughs*. Today we are characterized by *service* and *quality*. In the long run, I hope we *survive*.
>
> When I look back on our journey since 2012, I am especially pleased with *our improved service level*. I think something that was crucial for all of us in order to get this far in recent years was *a new team spirit* and I realize now how much I have contributed by *serving chocolate pudding every Friday*.
>
> And wait, here comes Eva again and she says that we must *stop hanging out at the coffee machine*. Some things never change!

The energy level peaks as the building fills with giggles and guffaws. Eva grins; this burst of activity is somewhat unexpected. We stand aside and listen to the noise. Eva reflects: "*I think we have a pent-up need for open discussions. Apparently, they have been nonexistent in the past. As I understand it, my predecessor was not interested in these kinds of events. He was more of a technician.*" Afterwards we gather in the big room and share the many different stories of the future, in a nice mix of playfulness and seriousness. The text above and other samples are read out loud. The loudest explosion of laughter comes when someone says "*Here comes Eva again and she still looks like a hamster in a washing machine.*" When Eva protests at that description, the man excuses himself and says that it is meant as a compliment. "*There are so many projects in the air and you often run around like hell. We just hope that you will keep your energy and stand out in this turmoil.*" The gap texts send a consistent signal: people want to strive for unity, efficiency and a new team spirit. The solid result is a good foundation for the following discussions about long-term objectives.

Exercise: the body of culture

The purpose of the exercise is to enhance sensemaking by bodily movements combined with conversations which together create and increase understanding of culture and core values. It shows how we make sense through the feeling of our physical body and the movement of others, and not only from our experience through narratives, stories or intellectual drama. More importantly, we make our lives and ourselves sensible through embodied interpretations in our ongoing everyday interactions, whether we are aware of it or not. This exercise shows how such sensemaking can be enhanced. It works best for large numbers of people. There should be a distinct sense of "a crowd" in the room and not just a group of individuals. We will start by giving details about the twofold structure of this workshop, followed by a larger vignette from our real-world example.

Step 1

- Prepare a list of watchwords that signifies different types of values
- Form groups of four to five people, preferably with colleagues who do not work together every day
- Ask the participants each to select three to five values from the list
- Instruct the groups to agree on three core values that they believe should characterize the organization (or the aspect that is the focus of the workshop). Tell them to write the chosen values on three post-it notes and explain how the values contribute to the vision and goal of the organization
- Tell the participants to put the post-it notes on a big wall
- The facilitator clusters the notes by theme (if this has not occurred naturally)
- Participants comment on and briefly discuss these

Step 2

- The facilitator puts a large figure 1 in one corner of the room and in the opposite corner places the figure 6
- Ask all the participants to stand up
- Instruct the participants to assess the extent to which the organization lives up to these chosen values and watchwords by taking a deliberate physical position in the room. Ask them to place themselves somewhere between the number 1 and number 6, where 1 stands for the values not being deployed and 6 stands for them being fully deployed in the organization
- Give time for people to reflect and then ask individuals to comment on their physical position in the room
- While standing up, instruct everyone to examine themselves and how well they live up to these values. Ask them again to position themselves in the room according to this
- Give people time to reflect and then ask individuals to comment on their physical position in the room
- Summarize and comment on the outcome

A vignette from the field

Yet another workshop is aimed to address the core values of the IT department. It starts with Eva distributing a worksheet with a list of 150 possible value watchwords such as: commercial, active, responsible, efficient, thoughtful, flexible, creative, helpful and so forth from our database from earlier similar assignments. People are asked to form groups of four to five people, preferably with colleagues with whom they do not work every day. I give the following instructions: *Start individually: select three to five values from the list. Within the group, agree on three core values that you believe should characterize all decisions and behaviors of the IT department. Write these on post-it notes and discuss how your chosen values contribute to our vision and goals.*

Eva is a little bit worried here. She fears that "wrong" things will come up, things contrary to the chosen direction. *"What if they come up with weird stuff?"* However, when the groups put their notes on a big whiteboard, affinity patterns emerge and she can see that the process has been working. Three distinct areas stand out. There is a cluster of notes evolving around customer focus, another one around engagement and a third around professionalism—all aspects that Eva has been communicating since she started.

We then do something a little bit outside everybody's comfort zone. In one corner of the room we have put the figure 1 on the wall and in the opposite corner we have put the figure 6. I ask the crowd: *"Please stand up"* (silence) *"You should now assess the current state of these values in your organization by taking a deliberate position in the room. 1 stands for not deployed and 6 stands for fully deployed. Please move."* The crowd begins to move slowly like a viscous liquid. The only sound is a quiet hum and chairs scraping against the floor. Not surprisingly, the group dynamics form a normal distribution, and after a short while a majority is crowded in the middle, perhaps with a tilt towards the lower figures.

I take command again: *"Okay, look around you … this is the result of the group assessment of the values of your department. Comments?"* Dead silence. People begin to sense their surroundings. A few individuals have actually placed themselves in the 1 corner (i.e. not deployed). I approach them and ask frankly: *"Okay, why did you choose to stand here?"* Awkward silence—we are out of the comfort zone now. I wait. Finally, a man in his thirties clears his throat and says: *"Well … personally I think we don't live these values at all. Our current values suck. That's why I'm standing here."* He looks rebellious. Some move a little, some giggle nervously. *"Thank you for your openness,"* I reply and let the comment sink in a little. I turn back to the man in the corner: *"Okay, how do you feel about this discussion?"* He replies, *"Well … they are good. But we have a long way to go …"*

I nod, thank him again and move on to the few on the opposite side where the number 6 is located, where one of the team leaders stands and almost apologetically says: *"Well, perhaps we don't live these values every day but I sincerely think that we are customer focused, engaged and professional,"* followed by scattered cheers and applause from the people around him. Voices from the big crowd in the middle fill in and say things such as, *"We have started but we are not there yet,"* *"We are on the move,"* *"it will be good,"* and so forth. I then ask Eva to comment on the scene. *"I think this outcome actually is a pretty good reflection of our current state. That is why it is crucial to continuously monitor and discuss our values. I also want to thank you for your honesty and openness. These matters are really important to me. I guess you know that by now."*

In a split second, all is quiet and still. I decide to push this a little bit further. *"Okay, before we break up. Look around again. This is the current state for the whole department. Now I want you to examine yourselves: how well do YOU live up to these values? Please position yourself."* New movement in the room ... the crowd slides slowly towards the 6 corner (i.e. fully deployed). This is really challenging. I decide to keep a low profile. When people realize what has just happened, it becomes dead quiet.

"Okay, I can see a higher score now. What can we conclude from that?" Now everybody slowly begins to scan the room. Making sense of their own physical position and of where all the others are standing. They begin to realize the obvious: they think that they as individuals are customer focused, engaged and professional ... but not the group as a whole. No one says anything. Finally a female voice in the crowd: *"Apparently we all think we are better than everyone else."* Embarrassed but liberating laughter follows.

We return to our seats, a little shaken. I glance at Eva. She looks concentrated. The reality has been almost painfully visualized. As a final reflection, I urge them to talk in trios about what we have just experienced and what it says about our culture and values. *"We have a lot to do,"* is the most common comment. Eva wraps up elegantly: *"Wow, what a session. We have together pinpointed our most important values and I think we all feel that the current state is far from good. In order to achieve our aspirations we need to live our values every day. Apparently, we feel that we do so individually. That is fine, but we also must feel it as a whole. I can assure you that I will do my utmost to make this happen."*

Summary

In this chapter we have explored the sources of cues that people draw upon to make their world more sensible, meaningful and workable. In doing so, we have also limited the proximity between leadership and sensemaking by showing different research-based models and approaches that leaders may use to their advantage. In the next chapter we will increase this focus on leadership and sensemaking by reviewing some of the research that goes more directly to the point and by developing eight guidelines for leading sensemaking.

Notes

1 The focus in this chapter is primarily on different aspects that trigger organizational sensemaking. However, there is also a considerable amount of research on sensemaking that is triggered by more profound changes such as environmental jolts, organizational crisis, threats to identity and disasters. For an overview, see Maitlis and Sonenshein 2010; Maitlis and Christianson 2014; and Sandberg and Tsoukas 2014.

2 An extreme example is authoritarian regimes that try to control the sensemaking of citizens through different types of propaganda and media control strategies.

3 The four different roles of move, follow, oppose or bystand presented here are just one of several dimensions of this complex model (the others being operating systems of closed, open and random, and communication domains of affect, meaning and power). In its

most sophisticated form, the model provides guidelines for the cues and meanings that flow in everyday conversations. See Kantor (2012) for more information.

4 Overall there are two strands of research with two different types of departure (Barge and Little 2002). One strand of research (Jabri 2004, 2010) departs from the work of Bakhtin (1981), and another (Argyris 1993a, 1993b; Isaacs 1999b; Senge 1993) focuses on the work of Bohm (1980). We do not wish to make a stand or contribute to this particular debate. Here we use the work of Isaacs since it is illustrative and pedagogical for some of the aspects of dialogue.

5 As Jabri (2012) points out, there are, however, some who interpret story and narrative as the same thing. See e.g. Ricoeur 1988.

Bibliography

Abolafia, M.Y. (2010) Narrative construction as sensemaking: how a central bank thinks. *Organization Studies*, 31(3): 349–367.

Ahmad, R., Ferlie, E. & Atun, R. (2013) How trustworthiness is assessed in health care: a sensemaking perspective. *Journal of Change Management*, 13(2): 159–178.

Argyris, C. (1993) *On Organizational Learning*. Cambridge, MA: Blackwell.

Armenakis, A. & Harris, S. (2002) Crafting a change message to create transformational readiness. *Journal of Organizational Change Management*, 15(2): 169–183.

Armenakis, A.A., Harris, S.G. & Mossholder, K.W. (1993) Creating readiness for organizational change. *Human Relations*, 46(6): 681–703.

Bakhtin, M.M. (1981) *The Dialogic Imagination: Four Essays*. Austin: University of Texas Press.

Balogun, J. & Hailey, V. (2008) *Exploring Strategic Change*. Harlow: Prentice Hall.

Barge, J.K. & Little, M. (2002) Dialogical wisdom, communicative practice, and organizational life. *Communication Theory*, 12(4): 375–397.

Barrett, F.J., Thomas, G.F. & Hocevar, S.P. (1995) The central role of discourse in large-scale change: a social construction perspective. *The Journal of Applied Behavioral Science*, 31(3): 352–372.

Bartunek, J.M., Rousseau, D.M., Rudolph, J.W. & Depalma, J.A. (2006) On the receiving end: sensemaking, emotion, and assessments of an organizational change initiated by others. *Journal of Applied Behavioral Science*, 42(2): 182–206.

Bernerth, J. (2004) Expanding our understanding of the change message. *Human Resource Development Review*, 3(1): 36–52.

Bird, F. (1990) "The role of 'good conversation' in business ethics." In *Proceedings of the First Annual James A. Waters Colloquium on Ethics in Practice*. Chestnut Hill, MA: The Wallace E. Carroll School of Management, Boston College.

Bohm, D. (1980) *Wholeness and the Implicate Order*. London: Routledge.

Boje, D.M. (1991) The storytelling organization: a study of story performance in an office-supply firm. *Administrative Science Quarterly*: 106–126.

Boje, D.M. (1995) Stories of the storytelling organization: a postmodern analysis of Disney as 'Tamara-Land'. *Academy of Management Journal*, 38(4): 997–1035.

Boje, D.M. (2001) *Narrative Methods for Organizational & Communication Research*. London: Sage.

Boje, D.M. (2008) *Storytelling Organizations*. London: Sage.

Boje, D.M. (2011) *Storytelling and the Future of Organizations: An Antenarrative Handbook*. New York: Routledge.

Brown, A.D., Gabriel, Y. & Gherardi, S. (2009) Storytelling and change: an unfolding story. *Organization*, 16(3): 323–333.

Brown, A.D. & Humphreys, M. (2003) Epic and tragic tales: making sense of change. *The Journal of Applied Behavioral Science*, 39(2): 121–144.

Brown, A.D., Stacey, P. & Nandhakumar, J. (2008) Making sense of sensemaking narratives. *Human Relations*, 61(8): 1035–1062.

Burke, W.W. (2008) *Organization Change: Theory and Practice*. Thousand Oaks, CA: Sage.

By, R.T. (2007) Ready or not ... *Journal of Change Management*, 7(1): 3–11.

Cornelissen, J.P. (2012) Sensemaking under pressure: the influence of professional roles and social accountability on the creation of sense. *Organization Science*, 23(1): 118–137.

Cornelissen, J.P., Holt, R. & Zundel, M. (2011) The role of analogy and metaphor in the framing and legitimization of strategic change. *Organization Studies*, 32(12): 1701–1716.

Cunliffe, A. & Coupland, C. (2012) From hero to villain to hero: making experience sensible through embodied narrative sensemaking. *Human Relations*, 65(1): 63–88.

Denis, J.-L., Langley, A. & Rouleau, L. (2006) The power of numbers in strategizing. *Strategic Organization*, 4(4): 349–377.

Elkington, J. (1997) *Cannibals with Forks*. Oxford: Capstone.

Fenton, E.M. (2007) Visualising strategic change: the role and impact of process maps as boundary objects in reorganisation. *European Management Journal*, 25(2): 104–117.

Ford, J.D. & Ford, L.W. (1995) The role of conversations in producing intentional organisational change. *Academy of Management Review*, 20(3): 541–570.

Ford, J.D. & Ford, L.W. (2009) *The Four Conversations: Daily Communication that Gets Results*. San Francisco, CA: Berrett-Koehler Publishers.

Ford, J. & Ford, L. (2008) Conversational profiles: a tool for altering the conversational patterns of change managers. *Journal of Applied Behavioral Science*, 44(4): 445–467.

Gabriel, Y. (2000) *Storytelling in Organizations: Facts, Fictions, and Fantasies: Facts, Fictions, and Fantasies*. Oxford: Oxford University Press.

Gardner, H. (2004) *Changing Minds: The Art and Science of Changing our Own and Other People's Minds*. Boston, MA: Harvard Business School Press.

Gioia, D.A., Thomas, J.B., Clark, S.M. & Chittipeddi, K. (1994) Symbolism and strategic change in academia: the dynamics of sensemaking and influence. *Organization Science*, 5(3): 363–383.

Griffith, T.L. (1999) Technology features as triggers for sensemaking. *Academy of Management Review*, 24(3): 472–488.

Heracleous, L. & Jacobs, C.D. (2008) Crafting strategy: the role of embodied metaphors. *Long Range Planning*, 41(3): 309–325.

Hill, R.C. & Levenhagen, M. (1995) Metaphors and mental models: sensemaking and sensegiving in innovative and entrepreneurial activities. *Journal of Management*, 21(6): 1057–1074.

Ibarra, H. & Lineback, K. (2005) What's your story? *Harvard Business Review*, 83(1): 64–71.

Isaacs, W.N. (1993) Taking flight: dialogue, collective thinking, and organizational learning. *Organizational Dynamics*, 22(2): 24–39.

Isaacs, W. (1999a) Dialogic leadership. *The Systems Thinker*, 10(1): 1–5.

Isaacs, W. (1999b) *Dialogue and the Art of Thinking Together: A Pioneering Approach to Communicating in Business and in Life*. New York: Currency, cop.

Iveroth, E. (2010a) Inside Ericsson: a framework for the practice of leading global IT-enabled change. *California Management Review*, 53(1): 136–153.

Iveroth, E. (2010b) *Leading IT-enabled Change inside Ericsson: A Transformation into a Global Network of Shared Service Centres*. Doctoral thesis no. 146. Uppsala: Uppsala University, Department of Business Studies.

Iveroth, E. (2011) The sociomaterial practice of IT-enabled change. *Journal of Change Management*, 11(3): 375–395.

Iveroth, E. (2012) Leading IT-enabled change across cultures. *European Management Journal*, 4(3): 340–351.

Iveroth, E. & Bengtsson, F. (2014) Changing behavior towards sustainable practices using information technology. *Journal of Environmental Management*, 139(June): 59–68.

Jabri, M. (2004) Change as shifting identities: a dialogic perspective. *Journal of Organizational Change Management*, 17(6): 566–577.

Jabri, M. (2010) Utterance as a tool for change agents: implications based on Bakhtin. *Journal of Management Development*, 29(6): 535–544.

Jabri, M. (2012) *Managing Organizational Change: Process, Social Construction and Dialogue*. Basingstoke: Palgrave Macmillan.

Johnson, G. (1990) Managing strategic change: the role of symbolic action. *British Journal of Management*, 1(4): 183–200.

Johnson, G., Whittington, R., Scholes, K. & Pyle, S. (2011) *Exploring Strategy: Text & Cases*. Harlow: Financial Times Prentice Hall.

Kantor, D. (2012) *Reading the Room: Group Dynamics for Coaches and Leaders*. Hoboken, NJ: John Wiley & Sons.

Kantor, D. & Lehr, W. (1977) *Inside the Family*. San Francisco, CA: Jossey-Bass.

Kaplan, S. (2011) Strategy and PowerPoint: an inquiry into the epistemic culture and machinery of strategy making. *Organization Science*, 22(2): 320–346.

Kleiner, A. (2013) The thought leader interview: David Kantor. *strategy+business*, Summer (71): 1–5.

Korica, M. & Molloy, E. (2010) Making sense of professional identities: stories of medical professionals and new technologies. *Human Relations*, 63(12): 1879–1901.

Leonardi, P.M. (2009) Why do people reject new technologies and stymie organizational changes of which they are in favor? Exploring misalignments between social interactions and materiality. *Human Communication Research*, 35(3): 407–441.

Leonardi, P.M. (2013) Theoretical foundations for the study of sociomateriality. *Information and Organization*, 23(2): 59–76.

Maclean, M., Harvey, C. & Chia, R. (2012) Sensemaking, storytelling and the legitimization of elite business careers. *Human Relations*, 65(1): 17–40.

Maitlis, S. (2005) The social processes of organizational sensemaking. *Academy of Management Journal*, 48(1): 21–49.

Maitlis, S. & Christianson, M. (2014) Sensemaking in organizations: taking stock and moving forward. *The Academy of Management Annals*, 8(1): 57–125.

Maitlis, S. & Lawrence, T.B. (2007) Triggers and enablers of sensegiving in organizations. *Academy of Management Journal*, 50(1): 57–84.

Maitlis, S. & Sonenshein, S. (2010) Sensemaking in crisis and change: inspiration and insights from Weick. *Journal of Management Studies*, 47(3): 551–580.

Maitlis, S., Vogus, T.J. & Lawrence, T.B. (2013) Sensemaking and emotion in organizations. *Organizational Psychology Review*, 3(3): 222–247.

McKee, R. (1997) *Substance, Structure, Style, and the Principles of Screenwriting*. New York: HarperCollins.

McKee, R. & Fryer, B. (2003) Storytelling that moves people. *Harvard Business Review*, 81(6): 51–55.

Orlikowski, W.J. (2000) Using technology and constituting structures: a practice lens for studying technology in organizations. *Organization Science*, 11(4): 404–428.

Orlikowski, W. & Scott, S. (2008) Chapter 10: Sociomateriality: challenging the separation of technology, work and organization. *The Academy of Management Annals*, 2(1): 433–474.

Quinn, J.J. (1996) The role of 'good conversation' in strategic control. *Journal of Management Studies*, 33(3): 381–394.

Ricoeur, P. (1988) *Time and Narrative. Vol. 3*. Chicago, IL: University of Chicago Press.

Sandberg, J. & Tsoukas, H. (2014) Making sense of the sensemaking perspective: its constituents, limitations, and opportunities for further development. *Journal of Organizational Behavior*, 36(1): 6–32.

Schein, E.H. (1993) On dialogue, culture, and organizational learning. *Organizational Dynamics*, 22(2): 40–51.

Senge, P.M. (1993) *The Fifth Discipline: The Art and Practice of the Learning Organization*. London: Century Business.

Stigliani, I. & Ravasi, D. (2012) Organizing thoughts and connecting brains: material practices and the transition from individual to group-level prospective sensemaking. *Academy of Management Journal*, 55(5): 1232–1259.

Trice, H.M. & Beyer, J.M. (1984) Studying organizational cultures through rites and ceremonials. *Academy of Management Review*, 9(4): 653–669.

Vaara, E. & Tienari, J. (2011) On the narrative construction of multinational corporations: an antenarrative analysis of legitimation and resistance in a cross-border merger. *Organization Science*, 22(2): 370–390.

Weick, K.E. (1995) *Sensemaking in Organizations*. Thousand Oaks, CA: Sage.

Weick, K.E. (2001) *Making Sense of the Organization*. Oxford: Blackwell Business.

Weick, K.E. (2012) Organized sensemaking: a commentary on processes of interpretive work. *Human Relations*, 65(1): 141–153.

Whiteman, G. & Cooper, W.H. (2011) Ecological sensemaking. *Academy of Management Journal*, 54(5): 889–911.

Whittington, R. (2006) Completing the practice turn in strategy research. *Organization Studies*, 27(5): 613–634.

Yakhlef, A. & Essén, A. (2012) Practice innovation as bodily skills: the example of elderly home care service delivery. *Organization*, 20(6): 881–903.

Zammuto, R.F., Griffith, T.L., Majchrzak, A., Dougherty, D.J. & Faraj, S. (2007) Information technology and the changing fabric of organization. *Organization Science*, 18(5): 749–762.

5

LEADERSHIP AND SENSEMAKING

The purpose of this chapter is to show the relationship between leadership and sensemaking, and to illustrate how leaders can influence such a process. We start by looking at some research on the role of leaders as sensemakers. Then we explore some of Weick's (2000: 235) own opinions on the issue which includes what he refers to as the "four bare-bones conditions required for successful sensemaking." We then extend these bare bones with four additional conditions, amounting to eight guidelines for leading sensemaking. After we have covered these activities of sensemakers, we finish by explaining what the process and trajectory of sensemaking look like and comparing them to other perspectives.

Leaders as sensemakers

Research has recurrently demonstrated how people having a leadership role aid stakeholders' sensemaking processes through different kinds of sensemaking activities (Gioia and Chittipeddi 1991; Gioia et al. 1994; Lüscher and Lewis 2008; Maitlis and Lawrence 2007; Rouleau 2005; Rouleau and Balogun 2011). These and other studies alike underline that leaders do indeed have a great influence on people's ability to make sense of events, information and experiences and common understanding in the organization.

One illustrative study of leaders' sensegiving capabilities is by Rouleau and Balogun (2011), who show how middle managers contribute to the formation and implementation of strategic sensemaking. Their conclusion is that there are two distinct activities paramount for middle managers' sensemaking: "performing a conversation," and "setting the scene." "Performing a conversation" is just what it sounds like, as it refers to managers' ability to create interest in the change through their social and daily verbal interaction. It is about formal and informal daily conversation with the various stakeholders during a change process which aims to legitimize and create a buy-in for the change. This includes, for example, knowing what to say to each stakeholder, using the right phrases and words, using the right social rules, and relating to others by using first names and putting people at ease by asking for advice. In a way, "performing a conversation" is about mastering many of the aspects that were presented in Chapter 4.

"Setting the scene" is more structurally oriented and refers to the manager's ability to construct a context and background for the conversation, to make it effective. It includes making sure that the right people are there, and future-oriented activities such as building a positive image of oneself as a spokesperson for the change. For example, a manager who is good at setting the scene knows who to target, who to use for influence, building networks for the future, what communication vehicle works best for a certain stakeholder, when to deliver the message, and so forth. However, the manager's ability to "perform a conversation" and "set the scene" hinges on the extent to which the conversation and actions are aligned and correspond with the organizational history, context, culture and symbols. More simply put, it is vital for managers to know the organization and its history as well as being able to "read" and "tap into" the culture and current "feelings" of different stakeholders. Sensegiving activities are context specific and have to resonate with the audience.

Leaders can also have an effect on how people think, and help them escape from ingrained ways of thinking. In so doing, the leader acts as a facilitator and tries to alter the frames and knowledge structures that people draw upon in their sensemaking processes. For example, Lüscher and Lewis (2008) have demonstrated this in their action research of managerial sensemaking during a strategic restructuring at the Danish LEGO Company. The study focused on reflecting and "sparring" sessions where they tried to deeply examine the problems and issues connected to the organizational change. The aim was to provide space and time for managers to express their concerns and explore alternative meanings of problems. During the sessions they tried jointly to reframe their current problems and seek alternative ways and perspectives to think about and interpret their problem. These alternative ways of making sense of the change were done by means such as energized reflection, provoking unconventional thought, and promoting conversation and dialogue.

The result of their study (Lüscher and Lewis 2008: 235) extends earlier research (e.g. Argyris 1993) by showing that a facilitator plays a crucial role in sensemaking, "by provoking discussions that disrupt ingrained modes of thinking," and that "a facilitator may help actors break out of single-loop learning into double-loop reframing, particularly during major organizational change." In other words, a leader with the role of facilitator can make people question, reflect on and ultimately change the underlying assumptions, mental models or governing systems and principles of a certain issue (i.e. double-loop learning that is about "doing things differently/doing different things" and thinking outside the box, compared with single-loop learning that is inside-the-box thinking, "doing things better"). Altogether, Lüscher and Lewis have provided evidence that not only do leaders have the possibility to influence the sensemaking process of others by acting as facilitator, but when they do so, it is most effective when it is performed in intensive social interaction.

On a bigger scale, the connection between leaders' sensemaking can also be illustrated by the concept of "mythcycles" (Hedberg and Jönsson 1978). The Scandinavian management thinker Nils-Göran Olve (1985) explains that the concept refers to the common belief/myth that what the company and its people are doing is actually the main reason for its success (and by doing so, disregarding any other reasons). People on a daily basis seek confirmation of this myth. In many cases they are right and the myth does in fact describe some true reasons for success. However, since the myth is ingrained in their way of thinking, it guides their sensemaking and in turn their action. For example, during the Middle Ages most of the people believed in the myth of the world being flat and therefore European sailors avoided going too far west on the Atlantic ocean. In fact, this myth most likely influenced the sensemaking of sailors to such an extent that it made them see monsters and giant waterfalls on murky days at sea. There are numerous examples of mythcycles in business. The most commonly known are disruptive innovations such as Kodak which was stuck in the mythcycle of chemical photography and realized too late the disruptive innovation of digital photography. Other examples in history include, for instance, rail and horse transportation vs. automobiles, the telegraph vs. telephones, mechanical vs. electronic calculators.

Mythcycles are, however, a necessity as they help us make sense of what we are doing and make things workable and understandable. Otherwise we would not be doing what we are doing. What the concept of mythcycles underlines is that there are seldom any single and complete truths. The awareness of mythcycles makes us understand that one day our "superior technology"—what we believe is the main reason for an organization's success—will sooner or later fall apart because customers will be more attracted to a new technology from a totally different field or a more novel design. When such things happen, the organization begins to move in a downward spiral: it loses customers, suppliers go elsewhere or want to renegotiate contracts, employees start seeking other, more attractive jobs in competing organizations, and on downwards. Possibly the organization can transform and survive the technological shift, and if they do so, they begin to believe in another mythcycle.

The role of leaders is, of course, to guide people's sensemaking in such a situation. Leaders need to re-learn and try to understand why the way they are managing their business is not working. They must clearly and truthfully acknowledge the crisis situation, discuss and seek a new solution, and minimize compliance during their ongoing discussions. They must learn from their mistakes, deeply question what they are doing and the value they deliver to their customers.

In doing so, they modify their "sense" of the world and in turn they redesign the organizational strategy aligned with their reinterpretation of reality. It is a challenge for leaders to do this for themselves, but it is considerably more complex and difficult to guide others' sensemaking in a similar way: to re-learn together.

Suggestions for further reading

Lüscher, L.S. & Lewis, M.W. (2008) Organizational change and managerial sensemaking: working through paradox. *Academy of Management Journal*, 51(2): 221–240.

Rouleau, L. (2005) Micro-practices of strategic sensemaking and sensegiving: how middle managers interpret and sell change every day. *Journal of Management Studies*, 42(7): 1413–1441.

Rouleau, L. & Balogun, J. (2011) Middle managers, strategic sensemaking, and discursive competence. *Journal of Management Studies*, 48(5): 953–983.

The four bare bones of sensemaking

The relationship between leadership and sensemaking can also be discussed in relation to the ideas of Weick. A good way to start such a discussion is to recite a poem by Holub (1977: 118). This poem is a well-used reference in the explanation of the nature of sensemaking and leadership. Weick in particular uses the reference in various places in his writing, but has often chosen to tailor the poem to his own story. We choose to use the original:

> Albert Szent-Gyorgyi, who knew a lot about maps
> according to which life is on its way somewhere or other,
> told us this story from the war
> due to which history is on its way somewhere or other:
>
> The young lieutenant of a small Hungarian detachment in the Alps
> sent a reconnaissance unit out into the icy wasteland.
> It began to snow
> immediately, snowed for two days and the unit
> did not return. The lieutenant suffered: he had dispatched
> his own people to death.
>
> But the third day the unit came back.
> Where had they been? How had they made their way?
> Yes, they said, we considered ourselves
> lost and waited for the end. And then one of us
> found a map in his pocket. That calmed us down.
> We pitched camp, lasted out the snowstorm and then with the map
> we discovered our bearings.
> And here we are.
>
> The lieutenant borrowed this remarkable map
> and had a good look at it. It was not a map of the Alps
> but of the Pyrenees.
>
> Goodbye now

The moral of the story is that when you consider yourself lost, almost any map will do (Weick 1995: 54). To some extent it does not matter which map you have, as long as it is a map and as long as you can, with the help of the map, instill some confidence in your people, decrease confusion, and most importantly use the object for taking swift action. The crucial point is that the map provides some pattern and reason to go from anguish to action: "Maps are pragmatic images that provide temporary guides for action" (Weick 2001: 11). Weick (1995: 55) further explains: "Managers keep forgetting that it is what they do, not what they plan, that explains their success. They keep giving credit to the wrong thing—namely, the plan—and having made this error, they then spend more time planning and less time acting. They are astonished when more planning improves nothing."

Leaders often know that there are several maps to choose from with no exact map that truly captures reality (see the last section in Chapter 3). What a leader must do is: a) choose a useful map that most closely resembles the situation; b) that to some extent captures the complexities of what is being faced; c) that explains these complex things in simple terms; and d) that makes people start working using the same map and encouraging enactment and action from subordinates in that same direction (Colville and Murphy 2006). The map brings order out of chaos and fosters morale, confidence and alignment of where to go next. The good leader will take advantage of this and get everyone moving in the same direction. This action will in turn provide cues for where they were, where they are now, and where they are heading. In this way, the map sets things in motion by functioning as a sensemaking device.

Holub's poem illustrates how sensemaking is a process that occurs between people and not solely within them. The formation of a dominant idea of where the soldiers were, what they should do and where they should go was created collectively through their social interaction. In this way, meaning is created intersubjectively through our constant negotiations, dealings and relations with both people and materiality of the world of which we are a part. In this process leaders play a crucial role because they have the opportunity to influence this meaning-creating process. Of course, leaders are unable to control fully the sensemaking process and such efforts will be contested by peers and stakeholders and other cues from the environment.

So how can leaders influence the sensemaking of others? Through activities such as tapping into the ongoing narratives, by telling strategically crafted stories, by different forms of listening, by engaging in dialogue, by using material artifacts as occasions for sensemaking, by embodying their communication with symbolic content, by acting as facilitators, and so forth. In the same way as for the soldiers in the Alps, there is no perfect roadmap for change. In fact, as Weick (2000: 235) explains, it does not really matter which program an organization chooses to implement: "any old program will do." So it does not matter what contemporary label is given to the change: Six Sigma, Balanced Scorecard, Total Quality Management, Lean, Agile (or any other management hype at any moment). Instead, what is pivotal is that the map (or program) is used by the leader as a reason to:

- Make people stay in motion: animate people, jump-start them, get them to act on hunches rather than being hesitant, make them experiment and, above all, keep them moving ahead.
- Provide direction: induce confidence in people, decrease confusion, show where to go by using symbols and maps.
- Update often: pay close attention to what is happening, encourage everybody to stay informed, improve situational awareness, reassess the situation on a continuous basis, avoid early and premature conclusions.
- Facilitate respectful interaction: base conversations on mutual trust and self-respect, make people discuss and engage in dialogue, allow people to exchange honest opinions of what they face, be open to multiple understandings and interpretations of what is going on.

In fact, these four aspects are what Weick (2000: 235) refers to as the "four bare-bones conditions required for successful sensemaking." This is the heart of the connection between leadership and sensemaking. Weick argues (as also illustrated in Chapter 2) that both planned and emergent change exists, and that both can be used to influence these four factors. However, at the same time, Weick proclaims that since these four factors are what occur in the trenches and on the front line of change, it is mainly emergent change activities that will be most effective: "Whether the chosen program involves economic value added, or total quality or the creation of a learning organization, or transformation, or teachable points of view, or action learning or culture change or whatever, effectiveness will improve or decline depending on whether the program engages or blocks the four components of sensemaking" (Weick 2000: 236).

Suggestions for further reading

Colville, I.D. & Murphy, A.J. (2006) Leadership as the enabler of strategizing and organizing. *Long Range Planning*, 39(6): 663–677.
Weick, K.E. (2000) "Emergent change as a universal in organizations." In M. Beer & N. Nohria (eds), *Breaking the Code of Change*. Boston, MA: Harvard Business School, pp. 223–241.

Eight guidelines for leading sensemaking

Besides the four bare bones, Weick provides in his writings additional aspects to what leaders in practice can do to facilitate sensemaking processes. The underlying notion of these aspects are recurrent in his writings and comprise: improvisation, learning, translation, and logic of attraction.

Improvisation

Improvisation is important because it narrows the time gap between planning and implementing in such a way that the composition of change (i.e. planning) converges with the execution of the change (i.e. implementation) (Miner et al. 2001; Moorman and Miner 1998). Crudely put, improvisation has the potential to influence the effectiveness of change by narrowing the time between planning and execution.

In practice, improvisation has to do with avoiding being too tied up with following plans, routines and blueprints in favor of acting in real time and using whatever resources and tools are at hand. In such an environment people should not be afraid of minimal structures or to build on what others have produced and have self-reliance to deal with non-routine events. Actions are carried out here and now without too much distraction from memories and anticipation, and the pace and tempo are attuned to others nearby (Weick 1998).

In fact, if you think about it, improvisation is much like playing in a jazz orchestra. This is why there are sensemaking researchers who have examined jazz musicians (Hatch 1999; Humphreys et al. 2012; Meyer et al. 1998). Maitlis and Christianson (2014: 78) help to explain why the connection between sensemaking and jazz is a powerful one:

> Jazz orchestras are a classic example of mutually constructed meaning: members must listen closely to each other, take turns leading and following, and respond together in real-time to novel or unexpected performance [...] Yet, even in more top-down processes, when organizational leaders engage in sensegiving, organizational members are not simply passive recipients of meaning but instead engage in their own sensemaking and adopt, alter, resist, or reject the sense they have been given [...] Likewise, "framing contests" can develop between peers as they attempt to persuade each other to adopt their perspective and, eventually, one viewpoint emerges as dominant.

Learning

Another important aspect of sensemaking leadership is to foster learning. Here the main idea is that learning is crucial in sensemaking because it enables the alteration of the shared mental model. In turn, this alteration changes the skills and knowledge of the people of the organization which in the long run changes the organization's response repertoire. Weick and Quinn (1999: 377) note that one of the main ideas of learning is "that it is a range of skills and knowledge that is altered rather than a specific action, as well as the idea that a change is not just substitution but could also include strengthening existing skills. A change in repertoire is also a change in the potential for action, which means action may not be manifest at the time of learning."

In the last section of this chapter we will show how change in many cases comes about as a downward and upward spiral. One of the key aspects that determine the trajectory and the speed of the loop is the extent to which people learn. If you are unable to learn from your mistakes you are less likely to move forward—you are stuck in the same position in the change spiral, or worse, you are moving backwards, regressing. On the contrary, if you are able to learn from your experiments and actions, you are more likely to speed up the change process and have a steeper, upward loop. Hopefully, you also have a leader to guide you. This exemplifies why learning is essential for effective organizational change through sensemaking.

Leaders play a pivotal role in the learning process by promoting double-loop learning—as we saw at the beginning of this chapter, where we examined the action research by Lüscher and Lewis of the strategic restructuring at LEGO. Ordinary learning often takes place within a given frame and existing system. We call this single-loop learning, and it is about "doing things better." Double-loop learning is more profound and is learning that takes place outside one's frame of reference: "doing things differently" or "doing different things." The aim of such learning is to question, reflect and ultimately change the underlying assumptions, mental models or governing system and principles. The leader has the ability to influence this process.

Translation

Translation is a vital ingredient in what leaders do when they perform sensemaking and sensegiving processes (Teulier and Rouleau 2013; Whittle et al. 2010). Here the main idea is that leaders translate by adopting and editing all the ideas that travel through the organization in such a way that it becomes manageable and sensible for people. They make ideas fit with the current and immediate circumstances and purposes at hand. In other words, leaders take the ideas from the "machine of planned change" and make them local, workable and understandable.

The translation that takes place at the forefront of change is significant because without it, change becomes less "socially acceptable and credible" (Weick 1995: 61). Indeed, without translations people become much less prone to accept the change, the buy-in is significantly lower and the implementation becomes less smooth. For example, Whittle and her colleagues (2010) show that when leaders are too wedded to the original framing of the idea of the change and less prone to translate it into local and understandable terms, then the chances for creating buy-in are very low. In many ways, translation is at the very heart of sensemaking because, as we saw in Chapter 3, sensemaking seeks plausibility rather than accuracy. To make things more plausible, more workable and more sensible, we have to translate and adjust it to local circumstances. It is only when this translation has been performed that action is possible: filtered information breeds action (Starbuck and Milliken 1988).

However, for leaders to translate a change message they need to be very aware of local circumstances such as the history of the people and the department, people's concerns, what they are working with, current issues, how things are done, conflicts, local politics and so forth. Roughly speaking, they have to have good knowledge of "the way we do things around here" and "what makes people tick." At the same time they also need to have an aggregated and more strategic perspective of the change and what it means for the organization and the business as a whole. By being knowledgeable about both local practices and culture as well as more global and strategic aspects of the change, they are more equipped to translate and redirect the change.

Logic of attraction

A final characteristic that we believe is important is the concept of logic of attraction. Here the main idea is that change can only be effective if it starts right at the top with the leaders transforming themselves before requiring others to change. Then after they have experienced and gone through change, they can let others be attracted and inspired by it. In this way, leaders act as role models and try to show that change is not going to happen while you are sitting down, relaxing, and that everybody has to be willing to change to make this work. Change goes from being something that goes on "out there" and instead becomes something that exists "in here" in which all employees partake.

Logic of attraction can be compared with "logic of replacement," which is the dominant idea in planned change. The rationale behind this kind of thinking is that one thing is replaced and substituted by another thing. For example, a functional organization is replaced by a matrix organization. One separate thing is removed, replaced or destroyed before another separate thing is installed and constructed. Ford and Ford (1994: 775) explain that with such an approach the "change process becomes a sequence of events in which a person (a) determines or defines what currently exists (what is A), (b) determines or defines its replacement (Not-A), (c) engages in action to remove what is currently there, and (d) implants its replacement."

With this perspective change becomes an either/or thinking, where change is something that someone with authority enforces on someone with less authority. Needless to say, logic of replacement is seldom effective. Weick and Quinn (1999: 380) summarize this by arguing that change can only truly be led by letting people be attracted to it: "To manage change is to tell people what to do (a logic of replacement), but to lead change is to show people how to be (a logic of attraction)."

Now, if we boil down what we have learned from earlier chapters and take out the most important aspects so far of this chapter—such as the different schools of change, the wisdom from the story of the soldiers in the Alps, Weick's bare bones and other recurring themes—we get a list of eight intertwined guidelines for leading change through sensemaking:

- Stay in motion
- Provide a direction
- Look closely and update
- Converse candidly
- Unblock improvisation
- Facilitate learning
- Translate
- Change through logic of attraction

We will return to these guidelines in more detail in the next chapter, but before we do so, let's take a look at the process of sensemaking.

The spiral of sensemaking

With the eight guidelines for leading sensemaking from the earlier section we get a little bit closer to answering the key question of this book: What is it that managers actually do when they lead change through sensemaking? However, the picture is still unclear, as we have not yet explored the process of sensemaking. How does the sensemaking process—from a leadership perspective—emerge, develop, grow or terminate over time? Before we answer this question, let's do a short recap of what earlier research has offered on how change comes about. As you will recall from our discussion in Chapter 2, there are two different answers, depicted to the left and the far right in Figure 5.1.[1]

On the one hand, we have the standpoint of planned change which argues that change resembles a progressive movement from one stable state to another. Change as such follows a linear trajectory towards a specific end state that is defined by a vision (i.e. at the end of the arrow). From this perspective, change is rational and moves across different steps such as explore, plan, action and integrate. On the other hand, if we now look to the far right in Figure 5.1, we have the other extreme of emergent change which suggests that change proceeds in a circular trajectory. In this sense, change is a cycle of stages in the development or growth of something (Van de Ven and Poole 1995). In Chapter 2 we provided examples from continuous change processes and feedback loops (plan–do–check–act; plan–implement–assess–modify), and from the stages of team development (form, storm, norm, perform, deform).

These two standpoints can be considered as two extremes, and as we discussed in Chapter 2, both actually depict some of the realities of change. Both draw up some of the true colors and realities on the canvas of change but in different ways. In this sense, both types of trajectory tell us something about the nature of change, but with their own respective significant drawbacks that are not properly addressed. We believe that in reality, and with the lens of leading sensemaking, change should instead be portrayed as a spiral that moves upward, as depicted in the middle of Figure 5.1.[2] The idea is that sensemaking emerges in a spiral motion that is energized by our sensemaking or, as Weick and Quinn (1999: 373) note, "change is not a linear movement through the four stages but a spiral pattern of contemplation,

FIGURE 5.1 Three different trajectories of change

action, and relapse and then successive returns to contemplation, action, and relapse before entering the maintenance and then termination stages." We now explain this sensemaking trajectory of change from an individual and leadership perspective, and then we finish by explaining how this perspective addresses some of the shortcomings of the arrow trajectory of planned change and the cyclical trajectory of emergent change.

For an individual the spiral is composed of a constant interplay between your sensemaking and the actions you perform as a result of the sensemaking. The growing sense and answers to the question "what's the story?" build up into an understanding that informs and guides your future action. This very action then provides you with fuel for more sensemaking which enables you to act yet again, and so forth. The effectiveness of your own individual spiral—the extent to which you move upward or downward—is governed by the properties of sensemaking that we discussed in Chapter 3.

Here follows a crude example of such a process: Jim is not happy in his current job and he has set a personal goal of trying to get a new job. One morning he discovers that a new job has been announced in a new department within his company. Now his decision and proceeding action of what to do is in part determined by the sensemaking that grows out of: a) the discussion about the job that he conducts with his colleagues and friends (i.e. property of social context), as well as b) the extent to which the job fits his identity (i.e. property of identity construction). He is trying to make sense of this new job and if he should apply or not. After this there are three different likely scenarios.

Scenario one: Jim decides not to apply for the job because his colleagues tell him that the job is boring, together with the fact that the role and responsibility of the job do not really fit well with Jim as a person. In this case Jim relapses in his sensemaking spiral and moves around in the same loop at the same level of the spiral.

Scenario two: after a fruitful conversation with his colleagues, he begins to understand that this is a truly interesting job and that it fits well with what he wants to become. He therefore decides to take the job and therefore moves up in his sensemaking spiral.

Scenario three: Jim decides not to take the job because he has understood through reading about it and conversations with peers that it is highly challenging. In fact, this event weighs heavily on his mind, he begins to question his current job, he starts seeing all the dull aspects of what he does, he wonders if there will ever be a job that fits him, he gets depressed and he goes downward in his spiral of sensemaking.

Now to elevate this to an organizational level and show the consequences for the change leader. To start with, the question of if you are able to move the whole of an organizational change process upward or downward in the spiral hinges on the effectiveness of organizational sensemaking. More specifically, the effectiveness of the movement up the spiral is governed by a leader's skill in deploying the eight guidelines of sensemaking presented above, as well as using the different types of cues that we presented in Chapter 4. For example, if you can provide a direction for your people, instill confidence and show where to go, then the chances are higher that the spiral will move upward. Likewise, if you can encourage improvisation and people are allowed to test things out against reality and learn from doing so, they might be able to move higher in the spiral. Of course, this improvisation and experimentation of ideas could lead nowhere, with people "going round in circles" and relapsing in the same loop. This relapsing is actually precisely what happens when there is a strong mythcycle in the organization (see above) which in the long run can amount to a downward spiral. When such a situation is apparent, the leaders play a pivotal role in navigating people beyond the mythcycle and upward in the spiral. There is also a risk that you underestimate the complexity of the change, that you fail to translate the change to create buy-in, that you spend too little time taking part in the narratives and change conversations, and that you do not lead by example. In these cases the spiral goes downwards.

We could provide example after example, but these are just simple illustrations of activities pertaining to the eight guidelines of change—quick snapshots. Such illustrations avoid explaining the whole process of organizational sensemaking—what really goes on inside the spiral. In fact, examining the spiral from within is a concept in itself and deserves its own chapter. We call this concept "landscaping," and this is the core subject of the next chapter. However, before we turn to landscaping, let us discuss some of the drawbacks of the trajectory of planned and emergent change, and how the spiral of sensemaking addresses them.

If we compare the trajectory of planned change to show how change occurs outside the textbook—out in the real world—several problems emerge. To start with, notice that the arrow in Figure 5.1 starts out of nowhere and comes "out of the blue," with little or no consideration of what is before the arrow begins. That is, there is no consideration of the past and the history of the organization. Planned change is ahistoric (a common critique of the planned perspective). As we know, however—and as we explored in the story of the five monkeys in Chapter 2—history plays a vital role in change. The spiral acknowledges the importance of history and its role in current change. This is so because the spiral is very long with an unknown beginning. What is being done, here and now, is always to some extent influenced by what has already transpired (i.e. the retrospective nature of sensemaking). The sensemaking of good and bad experiences of change from the distant past makes people react in a certain way which influences the direction of the spiral (i.e. path dependency of change). Another way to put it is that the current position of the spiral and how it moves forward, the aim, is in part determined by the lower parts of the spiral.

Another problematic aspect of the trajectory of planned change is that the arrow ends abruptly when it comes to its clear end state. This is also far from reality. During change, the so-called end state is always renegotiated and altered; it is a moving target. In addition, change actually never ends. Instead, it reaches different goals and there is always another change around the corner which starts when the earlier change project has formally reached its last milestone, one change continuing where the earlier one left off. The spiral signifies this limitless aspect of change as it endlessly continues upward (or downward) without end. It might for a moment move more slowly, or it might relapse in the same loop, but sooner or later it continues on its constant journey. As we noted in the property of "ongoing" in Chapter 3, sensemaking never stops, nor does it start clean, as it is a continuous process, a constant, ongoing flow.

Yet another problematic aspect of planned change is that it is highly rational and has a linear trajectory. For example, the phases of planned change are divided into very clear ending and beginning and move forward without friction. Therefore the perspective disregards the messiness of everyday life, or as Burke elegantly encapsulates it:

> when planning organization change, the process is usually linear, that is, Step 1 or Phase 1, then Step 2, 3, and so on. And although an attempt is made in the implementation of change to follow these steps or phases, what actually occurs is anything but linear. The implementation process is messy: Things don't proceed exactly as planned; people do things their own way, not always according to the plan; some people resist or even sabotage the process; and some people who would be predicted to support or resist the plan actually behave in just the opposite way. In short, unanticipated consequences occur. Leaders of change often say something like "For every step forward we take, we seem to fall back two steps; something always needs fixing to get us back on track."
>
> *(Burke 2008: 12; see also Balogun 2006)*

The spiral addresses this shortcoming because it recognizes the "messiness of the real world" and that change is sometimes frictionless and rational (with clear movement upward), but can also sometimes (and often rightly so) be composed of unanticipated events, experiments and improvisation over time. Some of these aspects make the spiral go upward toward a goal because they turn out to be successful; some do not result in anything which makes the change relapse in the loop of the spiral; some have disastrous consequences that make the spiral go downward.

The circular trajectory of emergent change also has problems when compared with our lived experience of change which are addressed by the spiral trajectory of sensemaking. First, the change follows a cyclical course that seems to have the same focal point without any movement forward. The change process as such becomes merely a journey through different stages which after going full circle are revisited. When this happens, the stages are hopefully altered as a consequence of going through the process. For example, after you have gone through the stages of plan-do-check-act, it is hoped that you will be enriched by your earlier experience and plan with higher quality when you perform the stages the second time round. The spiral, on the other hand, has a movement forward and upward (or downward). In doing so, this aspect of the spiral illustrates that change is always related to a bigger frame or context and there is in most cases some sort of feeling that we are moving. We try to struggle forward toward some sort of goal, milestone, idea, dream or vision which "pulls" the spiral in a certain direction.

Furthermore, a change following a cyclical trajectory can be considered as imprisonment by its very nature, because the process follows a "prefigured program" or a "code" which forces the development to progress or regress in a certain specific way. As such, the process can never escape its "cage." For example, there is no room for new stages to appear in the cyclical process because it follows the laws of a certain number of stages that are prefigured. Another way to illustrate this is that the rationale of the cyclical trajectory limits the possibility for innovation and sudden breakthrough. Van de Ven and Poole (1995: 515) summarize this "caged" aspect by saying that the cyclical trajectory: "has within it an underlying form, logic, program, or code that regulates the process of change and moves the entity from a given point of departure toward a subsequent end that is prefigured in the present state." Not even the environment in which the change is situated can alter the circumstances: "External environmental events and processes can influence how the entity expresses itself, but they are always mediated by the immanent logic, rules, or programs that govern the entity's development." In this sense, an entity going through a development can never break free from its past and its prefigured program.

However, the spiral is free to go in any direction and at any speed. This is also why it is portrayed as being a little bit messy, with some loops intensive and circling almost around the same focal point, some loops less concentrated and moving quickly upward, some loops larger and some smaller. This unevenness in different dimensions signifies the different degrees (or absence) of sensemaking that take place during change. For example, when the change is cumbersome the loop is large, and when the sensemaking is effective the loop is smaller. From a broader perspective, this aspect of portraying change gives degrees of freedom to new ideas and innovation which lie outside common ways of thinking and doing and outside any form of "prefigured program" or "code." The spiral of sensemaking allows us to explain many of the sudden breakthroughs of the human species that have amounted to sudden jumps in its development process: stone tools, making fire, agricultural practices and so forth. Similarly, the spiral of sensemaking acknowledges disruptive innovations such as the printing press, personal computers and innovations connected to digitization.

Summary

In this chapter we have finally begun to pin down and explain what it is that leaders actually do when they lead sensemaking processes. We have done so by exploring the role of the leader in such processes, examining the activities that the leader executes which amount to the eight guidelines for leading sensemaking, and finally describing briefly the process as a spiral and comparing it to the dominant perspectives and trajectory of planned and emergent change. We will continue this exploration in the next chapter, where we will show you what it is like inside the spiral of organizational sensemaking.

Notes

1 This book covers the most common process theories of organizational change that underlies emergent change (life cycle) and planned change (teleology). However, there are also other change process theories. Please see Van de Ven and Poole (1995) for an overview.
2 See Lindvall and Iveroth (2011) for an in-depth, empirical illustration of the sensemaking spiral.

Bibliography

Argyris, C. (1993) *Knowledge for Action: A Guide to Overcoming Barriers to Organizational Change*. San Francisco, CA: Jossey-Bass.

Balogun, J. (2006) Managing change: steering a course between intended strategies and unanticipated outcomes. *Long Range Planning*, 39(1): 29–49.

Colville, I.D. & Murphy, A.J. (2006) Leadership as the enabler of strategizing and organizing. *Long Range Planning*, 39(6): 663–677.

Ford, J.D. & Ford, L.W. (1994) Logics of identity, contradiction, and attraction in change. *Academy of Management Review*, 19(4): 756–785.

Gioia, D. & Chittipeddi, K. (1991) Sensemaking and sensegiving in strategic change initiation. *Strategic Management Journal*, 12(6): 433–448.

Gioia, D.A., Thomas, J.B., Clark, S.M. & Chittipeddi, K. (1994) Symbolism and strategic change in academia: the dynamics of sensemaking and influence. *Organization Science*, 5(3): 363–383.

Hatch, M.J. (1999) Exploring the empty spaces of organizing: how improvisational jazz helps redescribe organizational structure. *Organization Studies (Walter de Gruyter GmbH & Co. KG.)*, 20(1): 75–100.

Hedberg, B. & Jönsson, S. (1978) Designing semi-confusing information systems for organizations in changing environments. *Accounting, Organizations and Society*, 3(1): 47–64.

Holub, M. (1977) Brief thoughts on maps. *Times Literary Supplement*, 4(February): 118.

Humphreys, M., Ucbasaran, D. & Lockett, A. (2012) Sensemaking and sensegiving stories of jazz leadership. *Human Relations*, 65(1): 41–62.

Lindvall, J. & Iveroth, E. (2011) Creating a global network of shared service centres for accounting. *Journal of Accounting & Organizational Change*, 7(3): 278–305.

Lüscher, L.S. & Lewis, M.W. (2008) Organizational change and managerial sensemaking: working through paradox. *Academy of Management Journal*, 51(2): 221–240.

Maitlis, S. & Christianson, M. (2014) Sensemaking in organizations: taking stock and moving forward. *The Academy of Management Annals*, 8(1): 57–125.

Maitlis, S. & Lawrence, T.B. (2007) Triggers and enablers of sensegiving in organizations. *Academy of Management Journal*, 50(1): 57–84.

Meyer, A., Frost, P.J. & Weick, K.E. (1998) The Organization Science Jazz Festival: improvisation as a metaphor for organizing—overture. *Organization Science*, 9(5): 540–542.

Miner, A.S., Bassoff, P. & Moorman, C. (2001) Organizational improvisation and learning: a field study. *Administrative Science Quarterly*, 46(2): 304–337.

Moorman, C. & Miner, A.S. (1998) Organizational improvisation and organizational memory. *Academy of Management Review*, 23(4): 698–723.

Olve, N.-G. (1985) *Beslutsfattande: en tänkebok om rationella och intuitiva beslut*. Malmö: Liber Förlag.

Rouleau, L. (2005) Micro-practices of strategic sensemaking and sensegiving: how middle managers interpret and sell change every day. *Journal of Management Studies*, 42(7): 1413–1441.

Rouleau, L. & Balogun, J. (2011) Middle managers, strategic sensemaking, and discursive competence. *Journal of Management Studies*, 48(5): 953–983.

Starbuck, W.H. & Milliken, F.J. (1988) "Executives' perceptual filters: what they notice and how they make sense." In D. Hambrick (ed.), *The Executive Effect: Concepts and Methods for Studying Top Managers*. Greenwich, CT: JAI Press, pp. 35–65.

Teulier, R. & Rouleau, L. (2013) Middle managers' sensemaking and interorganizational change initiation: translation spaces and editing practices. *Journal of Change Management*, 13(3): 308–337.

Van de Ven, A.H. & Poole, M.S. (1995) Explaining development and change in organizations. *Academy of Management Review*, 20(3): 510–540.

Weick, K.E. (1995) *Sensemaking in Organizations*. Thousand Oaks, CA: Sage.

Weick, K.E. (1998) Improvisation as a mindset for organizational analysis. *Organization Science*, 9(5): 543–555.

Weick, K.E. (2000) "Emergent change as a universal in organizations." In M. Beer & N. Nohria (eds), *Breaking the Code of Change*. Boston, MA: Harvard Business School, pp. 223–241.

Weick, K.E. (2001) *Making Sense of the Organization*. Oxford: Blackwell Business.

Weick, K.E. & Quinn, R.E. (1999) Organizational change and development. *Annual Review of Psychology*, 50(1): 361–386.

Whittle, A., Suhomlinova, O. & Mueller, F. (2010) Funnel of interests: the discursive translation of organizational change. *Journal of Applied Behavioral Science*, 46(1): 16–37.

PART II
Practice

6

LANDSCAPING

Leading through sensemaking

The concept of landscaping

In this chapter we will present landscaping, which is our way of conceptualizing sensemaking and visualizing how a proactive change leader can guide people through four different imaginary landscapes of meaning: comfort, inertia, transformation and consolidation. We will also explain the connection between the landscaping metaphor and the spiral of sensemaking that we presented earlier, as well as how the eight guidelines for sensemaking drive such a spiral forward. In doing so, we are getting under the skin of the process of leading sensemaking.

A prominent leader once said to us:

> Well, I don't care that much about theories, textbooks and such. Over the years, it has been obvious to me that academic theories and management models are one thing while the actual realization of these is another. You academic guys introduce various models, concepts and ideas in a clean and simplified manner but reality is always less clear cut. All these predesigned maps simply don't work in a blurry reality. The landscape will always surprise you. I pretty much follow my own path.[1]

This statement could be true for many leaders we have met over the years. Our own research also shows that predesigned models and "how-to" textbooks are seldom used in real life (Hallencreutz 2012). There is a gap between theory and practice and between knowing and doing (Van de Ven 2007). For sure, leaders frequently read management literature (otherwise, what's the point in writing this book?), but far too seldom do the theories come to work in practice. From a manager's point of view, one might dismiss the diversity of descriptions in management handbooks and academic literature as being too theoretical with no meaning in practice, just like our executive friend quoted above.

Of course, management theories may diverge, but a similar diversity is observed in real life. Based on a survey among Swedish production managers, Poksinska et al. (2010) have illustrated that the application of a specific management model differed significantly between organizations as well. Thus, managing change gives rise to a contextualization challenge. While the descriptions in the literature may seem appealing, they are not directly applicable without some adaptation. We notice in our everyday life as theorists and practitioners that a variant of Weick's cartographer metaphor is often used by frustrated leaders battling with complicated change processes: "*There seems to be a gap between the map and the terrain*" (please revisit the "Sensemaking and cartography" section in Chapter 3).

To close this gap between theories, models and plans ("the map") and the social systems on the ground ("the terrain"), our conclusion is that change leaders must improve their ability to lead sensemaking processes. Bluntly: managers must help people become aware of, understand and find meaning in new things. When leading through sensemaking, change is not just about following predesigned change-management models. It is about acknowledging local, emerging interpretations and constructions of meaning through a series of dialogues. This approach to effective organizational change emphasizes the diffusion and translation of ideas, rather than just executing a set of activities. A spiral sensemaking approach to organizational change requires a deeper understanding of the social systems. Specifically, change leaders need to understand how people in a social system create for themselves systems of meaning of their world (Geertz 1973; Weick 1995). These meanings are the foundation on which social life proceeds.

How can these fluffy and tacit matters be made more understandable and manageable? One metaphor has suggested itself in a powerful way in the last decades of social theory; the metaphor of "field." This insight has inspired us to look further into other domains than the traditional management literature. During these excursions we have found works by the American sociologist Isaac Reed, who uses yet another metaphor to decode social systems and suggests that we should extend the field metaphor to include a whole landscape (Reed 2011). Social systems, according to Reed, are "landscapes of meaning." Reed visualizes this metaphor by using the famous painting *The Harvesters* by Pieter Brueghel (1565). As in many of his paintings, the focus is on peasants and their work—a depiction of both production and consumption of food. On this vast and varied landscape, there are a variety of human actors, motivated to do a variety of activities. Some of the peasants are shown eating while others are harvesting wheat. Pears can be seen on the white cloth in front of the upright sitting woman who eats bread and cheese, while a figure in the tree to the far right rear can be seen picking pears. A sense of distance is conveyed by the workers carrying sheaves of wheat through the clearing, the people bathing in the pond, the children playing and the ships far away.

Looking closer at the painting we also see that various hard structures arise: trees, houses, churches and a village in the distance. We observe results from interactions

FIGURE 6.1 *The Harvesters* by Pieter Brueghel the Elder
Source: The Metropolitan Museum of Art, Rogers Fund, 1919 (19.164).

between people with certain tools and capacities, such as sheaves of grain from the harvest. In these interactions people also activate certain larger processes and mechanisms (such as harvesting the whole field).

This Brueghel painting shows the instantiation of meanings made by humans in a rural landscape, through which humans must act and interact. Moreover, as the actors place themselves in different locations in a given landscape, they take up different positions and thus have different views. *"The world looks different from the bell tower than it does from the fields"* (Reed 2011: 110). People see, interpret and understand things in different ways depending on what they do, where they are positioned, their skills, hierarchical positions and background. The very same variation is also true for people in an organization. Thus the landscape metaphor can capture the variety of ways in which meaning and processes of communication provide the basis and ground for various actors' different intentions and actions. The organizational landscape is in this way the accumulation of all actors' individual preferences and meanings, and if we zoom out and look at the whole (if we take a step back and consider the entire painting) we will be able to see different characteristics that together form a larger pattern or canvas.

However, while a painting of a landscape is static, reality is not. Let us therefore burden you with yet another metaphorical story about terrains and fields just to show that landscapes can actually be deliberately changed. We are talking about landscaping. This is a profession dealing with both visible features of an area of land, including living elements, such as flora or fauna and natural elements such as landforms, topography or bodies of water. A landscaper also handles abstract elements such as the weather, lighting conditions and concrete human elements such as structures, buildings, fences or other material objects. A landscaping project may span large areas of land (for instance during large infrastructural projects) or small gardens. In other words, a landscaper could change more or less every aspect covered in the Brueghel painting. The experienced landscaper Vagn Ekeroth summarizes the most important steps when changing a landscape:[2]

> Let planning take time. The planning phase is crucial. To create a landscape is not so much about taming nature as approaching it. It is always important to think about how the surroundings look when you start to plan. If you have a site map, enlarge it so that a meter is a centimeter and make a detailed sketch. Let the sketch develop in the future, make it in multiple layers, or let sketches of different parts of the landscape be more detailed. Late winter is ideal for sketches and measurements, but do not imagine that you for instance should create a perfect garden this first season. To fix everything in a single season is both expensive and often quite difficult, because much will have to be repeated next year. Landscaping takes time. The very creation of the landscape might also be stressful. It often looks like chaos, with mounds of earth and stones, plants helter-skelter and machines processing the land. If it is a private piece of land, the owner might get really nervous in this phase. Will this mud hole ever become a beautiful landscape? The key here is ongoing communication with the client and adjustments to the site map as we proceed. It never fails.

We find the landscaping metaphor striking. Landscapes can be changed and the same features are valid for change leaders trying to mold the landscapes of meaning within an organization. It is not a hopeless task, but effective organizational change through sensemaking requires a deep interest in and understanding of social processes in these landscapes, just as the landscaper needs to learn about nature. It also requires an organizational climate of trust and empowerment together with engaged leadership. The key approach is sensemaking. And a map is needed.

We all navigate in different landscapes of meaning. Leaders frequently seek to find detailed maps to guide the way forward. Often they get lost in the woods. Here, we can resume the moral of the story outlined in Chapter 5: when you are lost, almost any map will do. As long as it can instill some confidence in your people, decrease confusion and, most importantly, be used to take swift action. The point is that the map provides one reason for going from anguish to action. However, getting lost is seldom a successful change strategy. Instead, we suggest another, more proactive approach. By doing so, we are aware that we also run the risk of introducing yet another model that does not work in reality, but we are prepared to face that challenge.

A model can be described as a set of related concepts, describing the context we want to understand in a simplified manner. Models can be generally seen as partial representations or maps of theories (Van de Ven 2007). In practice, leaders at all levels often know that there are several maps to choose from, with no exact map that truly captures reality. We argue that leaders, instead of searching for prede-signed maps (i.e. off-the-shelf change-management models), should be inspired by theory but sketch and adjust their own maps as they go along—just as the land-scaper does when shaping the land. We call this management approach landscaping, inspired both by the above-mentioned American sociologist Isaac Reed and our good friend the Swedish landscaper Vagn Ekeroth. Our strong belief is that leading through landscaping is important to achieve effective organizational change and avoid many of the pitfalls associated with predesigned change models. The key is enhanced sensemaking.

In short, landscaping during a change process is about guiding a population on a journey through four imaginary landscapes. The trip is not the most direct route, but rather a spiral pattern with a distinct sense of going upwards through a series of trial, action and relapse—just as we discussed in the previous chapter. The four landscapes are composed of comfort, inertia, transformation and consolidation. These are graphically displayed in Figure 6.2 and are summarized in Table 6.1.

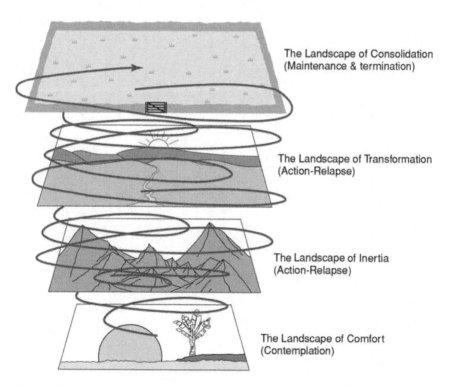

FIGURE 6.2 An upward sensemaking spiral through four different landscapes of meaning

TABLE 6.1 Summary of the four landscapes

	Stage 1: the landscape of comfort	Stage 2: the landscape of inertia	Stage 3: the landscape of transformation	Stage 4: the landscape of consolidation
Characteristics	The topography is flat and comfortable. Visibility is good. Nature is usually stable, open, friendly and characterized by habitual patterns, contemplation and complacency. People go about and do their thing. The climate is usually calm, mild and easy to forecast	The topography is hilly and rocky. Nature is thick, difficult to overlook and often characterized by inactivity, resistance and sometimes turmoil. People await and search for guidance. The climate can shift rapidly between hailstorms and sunshine	The topography is hilly, but easier to navigate. Nature is volatile and characterized by renewal and confusion, bursts of activity, trials, learning loops and fallback plans. People alternate between action and relapse. The climate is slowly stabilizing but is still unreliable and rapidly changing	The topography is leveling out to new plains. Nature is characterized by enactment, maintenance of new patterns and a sense of contentment. People are terminating change processes and adjusting to the "new normal." The climate is stabilizing and the wind calming
Role of the leader	Strategic, problem orientation. Gain understanding of the social context. Produce a useful roadmap. Articulate an inspiring vision and direction. Bring the right people together. Enable trustworthy dialogue about the need for change. Use symbols and metaphors to get people's attention. Spread the word about "the *why*." Challenge old habits and truths. Discuss and sell "the problem," not the solution. Obtain supplies and equip the organization for worse climate	Tactical, facilitative orientation. Take the lead and be a forerunner. Provide direction through close-up navigation. Facilitate respectful interactions. Repeat "the why," the vision, objectives and plans. Meet people candidly in their context. Tell people what you know and what you do not know. Listen respectfully and avoid persuasion. Look for early adopters. Dress for bad weather	Tactical, problem-solving orientation. Keep up the pace and provide energy. Stick to the plan but be prepared to redesign it. Secure motion and help people navigate and take decisions. Confront losses and gains. Translate abstractions, symbols and metaphors. Enhance improvisation, experiments and testing. Highlight good efforts. Spread the news. Provide space for both celebration and relapse	Strategic, follow-up orientation. Following the route all the way. Secure resilience and new behavioral patterns. Control and follow up results. Allow people to remember the past. Allow feelings of grief and loss. Visualize the achievements and reward and celebrate. Spread lessons learned. Keep on talking. Provide on-the-job training. Anchor the new state in symbols and artifacts. Scan the new landscape and forecast the next change

	Stage 1: the landscape of comfort	Stage 2: the landscape of inertia	Stage 3: the landscape of transformation	Stage 4: the landscape of consolidation
The most critical guideline for leading sensemaking	Change through logic of attraction. Provide direction. Translate. Converse candidly	Stay in motion. Observe closely and update. Converse candidly	Stay in motion. Observe closely and update. Unblock improvisation	Facilitate learning
Example of sensemaking triggers	Vision, goals, direction? Today's problems and challenges? Why is it necessary to leave the current situation? What will happen if we remain in the current situation? How does it feel?	Direction and motion? What will it be like when we get there? In what ways will things be better? What are the problems and difficulties? How? Who? When?	What do we win? What do we lose? What are the drivers? What prevents us? How can we help? What more is needed? How long? What if? Try this?	Are we through? How does it feel? Has anything or anyone been forgotten? Did we succeed? Are we ready for the next journey?
Signs of motion towards the next landscape	Broad-based conversations about *why*. Signs of trials, movement and action. Growing awareness and understanding. Cues signaling uneasiness and questioning. Defending current state	Bursts of problem-solving activity in parts of the organization. Individuals demonstrating tiredness of whining and nagging. Cues of upcoming flow and motion. Traces of early wins	Significant behavioral changes in parts of the organization. Measurable impact. Conversations about "the new" instead of "the past." Late adopters and resisters abide or leave	A feeling of comfort, reduced energy and lower speed. Impatience among key stakeholders. Control systems signal new needs for change
Signs of being lost	Endless discussions in top management. Sluggish analysis and demand for facts and figures. Rigorous planning procedures. Silence and low energy. Reluctant middle managers. Widespread "no change needed" signals	Management focus on resistance and contemplation. Absence of decisions. Conversations and cues downplaying the need for change. Too much symbolism and abstraction. No signs of motion	Reluctance to take necessary decisions. Mixed signals from key stakeholders. Parallel versions of maps, plans and directions. Illusions of progress, but no signs of sustainable change. Leaders checking out	Management declares victory and abandons targets and objectives. Things relapse into old structures and behaviors. Passivity and indifference allowed to take over

The leader adopting landscaping is aided by eight guidelines of sensemaking that we theoretically described in the earlier chapter. Below we revisit these with a short summary and examples of how they can play out in practice. All these guidelines are critical to successful sensemaking, but instead of just proclaiming that "all are equally important all the time" we sort them in order of magnitude. Thus, this enumeration of guidelines could be seen as a checklist for change leaders to assess critically before hurtling into new change initiatives.

1 Change through logic of attraction

The importance of trustworthy and persistent leadership is a recurring pattern in most research on organizational change. Successful change initiatives start at the top, with a committed and well-aligned group of leaders strongly supported by the chief executive. Employees will believe real change is occurring only when they see it happening at the top of the organization. Or as one senior manager put it: "*When I lead others in change, I always start with the change in myself because you cannot tell others what to do without doing it yourself.*"

In practice …

- Start changing yourself first, and then let people be attracted, drawn and inspired by your transformation.
- Lead by example.
- Make all leaders understand that change does not automatically happen "out there." The starting point is in themselves.
- Show in detail how change is done and let people mimic and copy it.

2 Provide a direction

Without strategic clarity and direction any change initiative is bound to fail. The alignment of the change leaders is crucial and cannot be taken for granted. Strategic work of alignment and congruence must be done in advance, as well as reassessment along the way to ensure that everyone agrees about the direction of the change and the particulars for implementing it. Clear and aligned direction is needed to instill confidence in people, decrease confusion and, most importantly, to take swift action. Without a map you will get lost.

In practice …

- Create awareness and understanding of the need for change and the consequences of not changing.
- Use visions, symbols or maps that provide cues and enable people to move ahead in a common direction.
- Instill confidence in your people, decrease confusion and show the way. Visualize a desired future state.

- Encourage people to look for cues in their everyday environment so that they can understand where they are and where they should go.

3 Translate

Change leaders' ability to translate strategic abstractions into concrete messages and action plans is crucial. Visions and long-term strategies must be made local, workable and understandable. In addition, front-line people tend to have rich repositories of knowledge about where potential problems may occur, what technical and logistical issues need to be addressed, and how customers may react to changes. Thus, enabling translation at all levels will strengthen the engagement of people and smooth the way for complex change initiatives. Filtered information breeds action.

In practice ...

- Translate vision and strategy into a concrete plan of action.
- Decode complexity and help people decide what to do and where to go.
- Enable the translation, adoption and editing of ideas so that they fit the purpose at hand.
- Make sure that all leaders have local and experience-based knowledge that increases the quality of the translation.

4 Stay in motion

Change initiatives often tend to get stuck in excessively tedious analyses and discussions. Change leaders should instead make major, visible decisions in days instead of weeks or months. Initiatives on the ground should be promoted. People respond to calls to action that engage their hearts as well as their minds, making them feel as if they are part of something consequential.

In practice ...

- Generate activities, praise early interventions, and ban excessively tedious analyses and discussions that do not result in action.
- Make sure that policies and processes do not hinder people but instead encourage action and animate them.
- Get people to move ahead and inspire deeds and performance.
- Enable people to act on hunches rather than being hesitant.

5 Look closely and update

Change leaders should visibly be "out there" and assess in real time the evolving situation on the ground and pick up cues from the front line: "What is the story here?" The path of rolling out change is much smoother if leaders are updated on the situation, when people have situational awareness, and when uninformed and premature conclusions are avoided. Close-up examination and reassessment of the situation pave the way for complex change initiatives.

In practice …

- Leave the conference rooms and reassess the situation on the ground.
- Follow up and rewrite plans on a regular basis based on new senses of the situation, and take swift action to secure motion in the right direction.
- Improve people's situational awareness and make sure that they pay attention to the current and evolving situation.
- Suspend judgment, avoid early and premature conclusions, and resist normalization.

6 Converse candidly

Change leaders often imagine that if they convey a strong message of change at the start of an initiative, it will make sense and people will understand what to do. They could not be more wrong. Powerful and sustained change requires constant and candid communication, throughout the whole change process. Change leaders' ability to facilitate respectful interaction and make people engage in dialogue and exchange honest opinions of what they face is key to effective organizational change.

In practice …

- Make people talk.
- Get out in the everyday environment and facilitate respectful interaction.
- Strive to make conversations vocal, reciprocative, issue oriented, imaginative and honest.
- Listen deeply to what people are saying and try to understand other people's "meanings" and "truths."

7 Unblock improvisation

A leadership challenge is to narrow the gap between planning and execution. This can be done by allowing early adopters to be forerunners and improvise and test ideas. This energy can be released if the change leaders avoid being too tied up with following plans, routines and formalities in favor of acting in real time, using whatever resources and tools are at hand. The unblocking of improvisation is also about staying in motion. It signals "work in progress" and strengthens commitment, since people tend to support what they co-create.

In practice …

- Get rid of organizational obstacles that hamper improvisation.
- Enable people to conduct experiments and test ideas.

- Encourage yourself and others to forego planning, work without plans and deviate from routines.
- Stimulate people to work with material at hand and pay attention to what others are doing so that they can build on it.

8 Facilitate learning

Leaders play a pivotal role in facilitating different forms of learning, especially double-loop learning. Interpretations and learning emerge in a circular motion between our current understanding and our encounters with new experiences and ideas, which lead to new understandings and in turn will guide future interpretations and actions. Leaders have the possibility to aid this process and this is needed in order for people to alter their range of skills and knowledge aligned with the new situation, as well as to make them more resilient to change. Formal training is also important as it plays the role of making change stick and making sure that the new pattern of behavior becomes cemented and part of the social structure of the organization.

In practice …

- Provide space for reflection and discussion of what people have recently experienced and been through.
- Provoke outside-the-box thinking and make people question existing frames, models and ways of doing things (i.e. double-loop learning), allowing them to explore alternatives.
- Avoid punishing mistakes and failure; instead, view such instances as an opportunity for learning.
- Cement new behavior through formal education, training, workshops, and reinforce the behavior through feedback and reward.

The landscape of comfort

When a change leader is about to embark on a change journey, the departure will most likely take place from the landscape of comfort. This is a really sweet place. If we were to look at a painting of this landscape, we would see a place where the topography is flat and comfortable. It could be rural fields, a beach, an archipelago or perhaps just a calm sea. The whole environment is open and friendly. The sky is blue, perhaps garnished with some nice cumulus clouds. Visibility is good. The climate is usually calm, mild and easy to forecast. Nature is lush and green, perfect for picnics and relaxation. People go about and do their thing. Activity seems to be characterized by habitual patterns, contemplation and sometimes also complacency. No one is hurrying and there is always room for yet another discussion in the shade.

When a change process is introduced to a social system within an organization the current landscape can often be described in these metaphorical terms. Senses of contemplation, comfort, calmness and stability are often present in early stages of a change process. This does not necessarily mean that every individual is happy and content, but the landscape of meaning as such holds these characteristics. The actors and activities that constitute this state are driven mostly by habitual patterns. You do what you do. The prevailing mindset is to look back and consolidate the current situation rather than to change and develop: "If it ain't broke, don't fix it." A low level of energy, conflict and resistance can be observed within the social system and decision-making processes often seek consensus. Even if dread clouds are gathering over the horizon, there is no widespread awareness of any need to change.

As a change leader the first challenge at this stage is to get people's attention and start a sensemaking process to create understanding of the need for change. It is equally important to stress the consequences of not changing. In theory there might be many stakeholders to take into consideration but in practice the change leader needs to start this process in the management team. In this early stage the leaders need to take time to understand the landscape about to be changed. Reflexive questions to ask in the management team are: Do we fully understand the rationale behind this change initiative? What kind of change is it? Is it fine tuning (build or improve) or are we facing a major transformation (release and recreate) of structures, processes and people? Is it adaption (react and preserve) or a new direction (relocate and regenerate)? (See Figure 2.2 in Chapter 2.)

In the landscaping process the leader studies the landscape from various angles and thinks about what he wants to make more visible or to hide. He walks the distance, gets a picture of how different change designs might look and learns about different climates. Because each landscape is unique, the leader should really stay in place and get to know the context before producing a useful map that resembles the situation the most and at least to some extent captures the complexities of what the organization is facing. This initial map should answer the fundamental questions: Why? Who? When? What? How?

After sketching the map, the change leader must set the scene by articulating an inspiring vision and direction *or* whip up a sense of crisis and urgency. Or a little bit of both, depending on the type of change the organization is facing. The aim of this sensemaking process is to inject an awareness of the need for change. Through narratives, storytelling and dialogue, the background, purpose, objectives and plans are disseminated through the current landscape of meaning (see Chapter 4). The mission is to "sell and discuss the problem," not the solution, and to give people space to digest the cues of information and impressions. This can be done in different manners. The constant flow of sensemaking can, for instance, be enhanced and interrupted by a shock: "The reality of flows becomes most apparent when that flow is interrupted. An interruption to a flow typically induces an emotional response, which then paves way for emotion to influence sense making" (Weick 1995: 45).

Shaking up people might be needed to create awareness and urgency, but the most critical approach is to organize dialogue—people must be reached in all arenas available. Signs of progress are broad-based conversations about *the why* and signs of trials, movement and action. A growing awareness and understanding should also be observed: *"Okay, we realize that something has to be done, but what?!"* Most likely, there will be cues signaling unease and questioning: *"Aha, but can we really trust these figures? How do we know that this is the right strategy?"* Quite often elements of current-state defense occur: *"This is a stable process that has been operational for years … you simply don't know how well it works."*

The change leader should avoid negative sensemaking activities such as endless discussions with top management about details, methodologies and demand for facts and figures. Since the landscape of comfort is nice and cozy, it might also be tempting to spend too much time on rigorous planning procedures and dis-proportionate analysis. A scattered management team viewing the landscape from too many different angles will most likely provide diverging communication and reluctant middle managers. General silence and low energy are other warning signs. However, the greatest threat to organizations stuck in the landscape of comfort is widespread "No change needed" signals.

However, by providing direction and space for candid conversation, these obstacles can be dismantled, and suddenly one morning the feeling of a weather change will be in the air: a nervous gust of wind, dark clouds, falling temperature. It is impossible to forecast exactly when it will happen, but the proactive change leader has already obtained supplies and equipped the organization for worsening climate. Signs of a shift are an urge to move forward, but also growing unease and resistance within the population. It is time to move on.

The landscape of inertia

The spiral will strive to ascend and eventually dismantle the existing frames and mindsets in the landscape of comfort. People will be guided from the pleasant environment to the rougher landscape of inertia. This is a totally different setting, more like a cut from Mordor in J.R.R. Tolkien's *Lord of the Rings*. The virtual topography is now hilly and rocky, with steep ascents and dangerous ravines. Nature seems frantic and nervous. Vegetation is thick, impenetrable and difficult to overlook. The climate shifts rapidly between hailstorms and sunshine. The living seek cover and the whole environment is characterized by inactivity, although sometimes interrupted by bursts of noise and turmoil. All seem to be waiting for something better.

When the change process really starts to "work" on a social system, uncertainty and resistance are likely to occur. People might still not understand the need for change, will question motives and seek rational answers. There might be structures, processes, hierarchies and incentives attracting people to remain in the old land-scape. Moreover, there might be social resistance and conflicts of interest such as loyalties, relations, duties linked to social networks representing "the old." There will also be psychological resistance: people seek predictable and stable environments, and change tends to trigger uncertainty. All these features will most certainly be encountered on the long and winding road through the landscape of inertia.

A major success factor when leading change is how well the leaders handle the phase of inertia, uncertainty and resistance. As a change leader, the challenge is really to take the lead, provide direction and maintain motion through attentive navigation. Unprepared leaders are in great danger of getting lost in this difficult and frightening terrain. Individual defense mechanisms and an urge to turn back have to be overcome. These feelings can be handled and possibly avoided if the change leader continuously and firmly repeats the vision and direction by meeting people candidly in their current situation.

This is a stage of action and relapse—always seeking ways forward through the woods. The change leader should facilitate interaction and enhance sensemaking by organizing dialogue around the ever-present "why, what, how, who and when" questions, especially now, when the weather is rough. This is not the time to try to persuade people to feel differently. A key to success at this stage is information transparency: Tell people what you know—and what you do not know. Repeat "the why" at all levels and locations. As resistance might grow, it is even more important to get people to talk and acknowledge people's feelings of chaos, loss and anger. It is even more important to look for early adopters, emphasize good examples and opportunities and sustainably drive the change through this demanding landscape. The sensemaking processes will eventually help people to let go of the past and start looking forward and search for the outline of a new landscape. Motion and activity are crucial. Phenomena indicating that this landscape is about to evolve into something new can be bursts of problem-solving activity in parts of the organization, individuals who clearly demonstrate that they are tired of whining and nagging, and a general sense of flow and movement.

This landscape can really be a tough one. Warning signs are absence of necessary decisions, too much management focus on resistance and contemplation, as well as too much symbolism and abstraction instead of clarity and action, and conversations and cues downplaying the need for change or questioning the direction. This is in line with our discussion about mythcycles in Chapter 5. History is full of examples of organizations that failed to find a path through the landscape of inertia (see Box 6.1 for two of these).

BOX 6.1 TWO EXAMPLES OF FAILED ATTEMPTS TO GET THROUGH THE LANDSCAPE OF INERTIA

In Sweden, the downfall of Facit AB is a well-used example. During the 1960s this company was a global player in mechanical office machines, such as calculators and typewriters. In 1970, the company was at its height with 14,000 employees, offices in 140 countries and a turnover of nearly SEK 1 billion. Two years later the company was insolvent. How could that happen?

By the mid-1960s, electronic calculators from Japan were slowly taking market share from mechanical ones. In 1965, 4,000 electronic calculators were sold in the world. In the following year, sales totaled 25,000. In 1967, 15 percent of the market was digital. Electronic calculators from Japan were smoother, faster and cheaper. However, the management of Facit could not overcome old habits and truths.

Another striking example is Eastman Kodak, once one of the world's most well-known brands, held in high esteem. Although Kodak's engineers developed a digital camera in 1975 (actually the first of its kind), the product was dropped as it would threaten the company's photographic film business. The company was successful for another two decades, but in the late 1990s Kodak began to struggle financially as a direct result of the decline in sales of photographic film and the company's inability to transition to digital photography, despite having invented the core technology used in digital cameras. In January 2012, Kodak filed for Chapter 11 bankruptcy protection and has not yet recovered.

With stubborn leadership, strategic clarity and focus on the people side of change, the expedition will find a way through this uncongenial landscape, and—probably when it feels endlessly dark, cold and hopeless—a bird will start to sing and a sudden breath of fresh air will caress tired faces. As with all game changes, it is impossible to tell exactly when this will happen, but the proactive change leader will already have taken action, noticed small changes in the landscape and thus foreseen the next phase.

The landscape of transformation

Systematic sensemaking will continue to mold the landscape, as the change process proceeds. The challenging landscape of inertia will be reshaped into the landscape of transformation. Here, the topography is hilly but easier to get through. Imagine scenes from the Scottish Highlands or the Norwegian Fjords. The climate is slowly stabilizing even if the weather is unpredictable—the fluctuations are no longer as violent; it is also a little warmer and generally friendlier. However, nature is still volatile and life is characterized by bursts of activity, trial, learning loops and fall-back plans. People alternate between action and relapse, renewal and confusion, while seeking solutions and ways forward. Some have chosen to leave, others are still searching for motivation. Some feel misplaced and unhappy in this new environment, still remembering the good old days in the landscape of comfort before the new management spoiled everything.

When the change process "comes out of the dark" it meets a new landscape flavored by renewal, hope and belief in things to come. As before, this does not necessarily mean that every individual awaits a bright future, but the landscape of meaning as such holds these characteristics. The actors and activities that constitute this state are driven mostly by curiosity and learning. People seek new solutions. Even if "the new" is chaotic and unstructured, the mindset is to look forward: "*Okay, let's try this new stuff.*" A high level of energy, conflicting interests and the remnants of resistance can be observed within the social system of this landscape.

At this stage the spiral spins in multiple iterations of action, relapse and contemplation. For the change leader, this is typically a period of confusion and transition, and a feeling of "one step forward, two steps back."

A short illustration of this came from a senior manager in one of our research projects (Lindvall and Iveroth 2011), who told us the following, when describing his foremost advice on managing large-scale organizational change:

> When you recognize that you are sitting on a dead horse you had better get off immediately. When you discover that the things you are doing are in a deadlock, when you are in a blind alley, then don't be afraid to get off and change direction [...] We have turned around many times and we still do this when we discover that a certain idea is not good enough. We simply try something else—one should not be afraid of this.

Decision-making processes should now help people decide and confront losses and gains. As a change leader the challenge at this stage is not to declare victory too soon. The journey is not completed and there is still an obvious demand for active leadership. The leaders need to stick to the chosen direction and keep up the pace, by highlighting good efforts and enhancing trials and testing. At this stage, the executive change leader might want to sit down and rest, but that is risky. Energy needs to be provided since new processes and working procedures are not in place. Securing motion and helping people through are still crucial.

The sensemaking processes in this stage encourage reflection and collaboration and give people space to find their own solutions. Navigation is still needed, since the nature can surprise you—suddenly a cleft can emerge and hurl the crowd back into turmoil and resistance. Chaos might still be a salient feeling and there might be multiple iterations in the borderland between inertia and transformation. Therefore directions must be crisp and concrete. Too much abstraction and fluffy talk should be avoided. It is also important to get people's attention and remind them of the need for change. It is equally important to stress the consequences of slowing down and sliding back.

At this stage the leaders need to spend time on monitoring within context, as each landscape is unique. The fundamental questions—Why? Who? When? What? How?—will probably have to be answered again and again. Other questions to follow up at this stage are: What do we win? What do we lose? What are the drivers? What prevents us? How can we help each other? What more is needed? How long? The map might also need some adjustment, as people are aware that the old frames are being challenged but do not yet have a clear picture as to what the organization is replacing them with. As the change process proceeds, the leader needs to allow both freedom and direction. Sensemaking at this stage guides people to look forward, make choices, see new solutions and leave old stuff behind.

Signs of progress are significant behavioral changes in critical parts of the organization. In the landscape of transformation, measurable impact from partial change initiatives should be presented. Broad-based conversations around coffee machines and lunch tables should by now be about "the new" instead of "the past." Late adopters and resisters make up their minds to abide by the new, or leave. The most critical warning sign in this phase is if illusions of progress are allowed to spread, while no tangible signs of sustainable change are observed. The change leader must also avoid negative sensemaking cues such as different, parallel versions of maps, plans and directions or mixed signals from key stakeholders. The change leader might sometimes have to intervene and "shock" the organization to avoid total stoppage and people checking out. However, there might also emerge new change signals from internal or external stakeholders, calling for new initiatives or projects. Here, the change leader needs to be agile and listen to demands and expectations from "the world outside." Sometimes there is not time for final adjustments.

Many change leaders find it difficult to leave this third landscape. Instead of pushing ahead, the organization gets stuck in a never-ending loop of action and relapse—see Box 6.2 for a short example. This will blur the long-term direction and replace it with reactive, short-term activities with poor outcomes. As a consequence, the organization gets overstrained and will eventually run down, as the spiral will backfire and run downwards. This will cause change exhaustion which is just as dangerous and risky as complacently remaining in the shade under a tree in the landscape of comfort. However, if the change process is carefully governed, the spiral will make a final twist upwards. The expedition, guided by bold and enlightened leaders, will find a way through and meet new plains behind the hills.

BOX 6.2 AN EXAMPLE OF GETTING STUCK IN THE LANDSCAPE OF TRANSFORMATION

Some years ago we had an assignment at a medium-sized Swedish manufacturing company experiencing ongoing problems in *"getting the production people to keep the sales people's promises."* For decades the business had moved on, but now the company was suffering from intensive attacks from new low-cost competitors. The margins were gone. Moreover, there was escalating complaint from several key customers about rigid and slow procedures, old-fashioned pricing and a general lack of customer orientation. The management team was frustrated since they constantly battled with different change initiatives, but these initiatives were never completed. They were stuck in the landscape of transformation.

The sales manager, a young, ambitious woman, was constantly displeased with late deliveries, high production costs and destroyed calculations. She was squeezed between different interests—on one side from the customers' demand for flexibility and value for money, while on the other from the owners' desire for return on capital invested.

The production manager, a senior who had worked for the company for some 30 years, had a totally different viewpoint. According to him, the company had abandoned its genuine focus on supreme product quality. Nowadays, the clients were allowed to make late changes and design adjustments without coordination and very often "free of charge." The sales rep's paperwork was rarely correct.

The communication between sales, the engineering department and procurement was confused despite the ISO 9001-certified quality management system and different attempts with Lean—never fully implemented. The CFO, a loyal clerk and cousin of one of the owners, was disgruntled. He was worried about the new balanced scorecard and the managing director's need for facts, figures and control.

The managing director, a highly skilled man around 40, had also expressed doubts about the future of the company. His mission was to grow the company by all means modern and ready for the competition of the 21st century, combined with strong profitability along the way to keep the owners happy. However, he doubted the ability of his management team as well as the rest of the organization. Everyone—at least in the management team—was fully aware of the need for change, but they were somehow stuck in a loop of change events without a clear direction or outcome. They could not find the way out of the landscape of transformation.

The landscape of consolidation

Weick and Quinn (1999) argue that the spiral pattern eventually ends up in a maintenance and termination stage. This is what we call the landscape of consolidation. In this, the fourth and final landscape, the topography is leveling out to a new plain. The terrain may outwardly be strikingly similar to the landscape of comfort. We could once again visualize a rural field, a beach, an archipelago or a calm sea. However, looking closer at the details we can spot new actors, artifacts and work procedures. The whole environment is opening up and easing off. The sky is blue again, except for some light clouds. The climate is stabilizing and the wind calming. A new mindset is crystallizing and people's sense of comfort is returning to previous levels. Nature is characterized by enactment, maintenance of new patterns and a sense of contentment. People are terminating change processes and adjusting to a new common frame—"the new normal"—which will soon turn into new habitual patterns.

In one way this landscape can be seen as a terminus, but is a change process ever "done" if our ontological assumption is that change is mainly emergent? As we discussed in Chapters 3 and 5, sensemaking never stops, nor does it start clean as it is a continuous process, a constant and ongoing flow. Thus, the actors will go on trying to make sense of things even in the landscape of consolidation. This means that sensemaking evolves over time as there is a constant new flow of cues and experiences during a change process, even when the job is done, the waypoints have been passed and, it is hoped, the organization has achieved its intended objectives. The spiral continues.

A critical question must therefore be: Can you ever slow down in a world in constant motion? The answer is probably "not really," but we advocate that every organization from time to time find space for reflection and recovery, while the new landscape of meaning is set and behaviors reinforced through learning, tools and structures.

Leadership focus should now be on securing resilience and new behavioral patterns. There should also be some room for celebration and reward, as well as allowing people to remember the past. At this stage the change leader should initiate activities to visualize and celebrate successes and goals achieved. People should be encouraged to keep on talking and spread lessons learned, as no sensemaking is performed in isolation and it is always constrained or facilitated by the past landscapes. Questions to follow up are: How does it feel? Are we through? Has anything or anyone been forgotten? Did we succeed? Are we ready for the next journey? By retrospective sensemaking, the new state will be embedded in symbols, artifacts and activities, and as things settle, the leaders need to raise their eyes again and develop new visions and plans based on new conditions. The organization's strategies, structures and people must be prepared for the next change, as the population slowly turns into a new mood of stability and comfort. To strengthen change resilience is a good investment during the stay in this landscape, as this will improve the organization's ability to embark on new change challenges. See Box 6.3 for a short illustration.

BOX 6.3 AN EXAMPLE OF HOW MULTIPLE CHANGES BUILD AGILITY AND RESILIENCE

Agria is a wholly owned subsidiary of the Swedish insurance company Länsförsäkringar AB, and has specialized in the provision of animal and crop insurance. The turnover in 2013 was about €175 million and the market share about 60 percent of the total market in the animal and crop insurance segment in Sweden. In 1992 a new CEO was appointed at Agria. He immediately initiated a comprehensive change program to improve quality, innovation and change resilience. Ten years and many different change initiatives later, the turnover had grown fivefold and the company had received the Swedish National Quality Award twice. According to the CEO, Anders Mellberg, the organization succeeded in building change resilience through a set of core values, a common language, a corporate change culture, and focus on improvement and creativity. However, he also stated "90 percent is about leadership." According to Mellberg (now retired), a major success factor was the integration of a change-management model and the company's business planning process:

> It didn't work well in the beginning. We spent half a year on learning the model. A door-opener was when two consultants told us that we should focus on building a process-based quality management system, which we did in 1996–97. In 1998 we certified our system according to ISO 9000

and also participated in the Swedish Quality Award (SQA) for the first time. We built resilience and agility by applying a multifunctional approach and not just playing around with the concepts in the management team. That gave us a link to day-to-day operations ... We spent much time on dialogue, communication and anchoring. And we were stubborn and focused on the long-term perspective, through every change initiative.

The conversion from the landscape of consolidation to the landscape of comfort is insidious and often not associated with conscious actions. Feelings of saturation, reduced energy and lower speed indicate that the system is falling back into a more passive, vegetative state. The resilient change leader will scan the new landscape and look for patterns forecasting the next change. "*It makes good evolutionary sense to construct an organism that reacts significantly when the world is no longer the way it was*" (Weick 1995: 46). Cues of new change triggers could, for instance, be impatience among key stakeholders, game changers in the world outside or control systems signaling new needs for change, or just new behavioral patterns indicating too much complacency. One day, perhaps sooner than we would like to admit, we find ourselves back in the landscape of comfort. Even if new dread clouds once again gather over the horizon (these days, we can assume that they are there all the time) there is probably no widespread awareness of any new need for change.

Suddenly, one morning the feeling of a weather change will be in the air. A nervous gust of wind, dark clouds, falling temperature. It is impossible to forecast exactly when it will happen, but the proactive change leader has already obtained supplies and equipped the organization for worsening climate. Signs of a shift are an urge to move forward, but also growing unease and resistance within the population. It is time to move on. Again.

In this chapter we have used the landscaping metaphor to visualize how a proactive change leader can, at least to some extent, guide people through four different imaginary landscapes of meaning: comfort, inertia, transformation and consolidation. We have also highlighted that key leadership tools are the eight guidelines of sensemaking. The overall approach is emergent and we suggest that a change process should be seen as a spiral. However, we also dare to argue that models are useful if we ever want to be able to capture, describe, understand and develop a complex contemporary organization. Yes, a change-management model will be a simplification of a complex reality, but it can help organizations understand why change occurs, how it will occur and what will happen. Or in landscaping terms, you cannot find the way and shape a new landscape without some sort of map of the current terrain of the social landscape in which the change takes place.

Another practical question is, of course, how long does it take to navigate through these landscapes? Here, it is tempting to turn instrumental and set exact timeframes, but the honest answer is "it depends." A sensemaking approach will most certainly speed things up. In the case presented in the next chapter it took three years to make the way through. A hint based on our real-life experience and other field studies is that "hard effects" such as lower costs or increased margins can be measured within months, but profound behavioral change throughout a population takes three to five years to achieve if you focus on it. However, if you neglect the behavioral aspects, it will probably take up to ten years or even longer to see any lasting effects, if you ever get through the terrain in the landscapes of inertia and transformation.

In Chapter 2, we concluded from an academic point of view that there seems to be no universal, prescriptive and systematic change-management model to cover the diversified nature of change in organizations. We do not claim to have unraveled the ultimate truth. After all, "The world looks different from the bell tower than it does from the fields" (Reed, 2011: 110). We strongly believe, however, that we have shed some new light on how proactive sensemaking—landscaping—effectively can guide organizations through challenging change processes.

Notes

1 During reflexive conversations with managers over the years we have noticed that metaphors like "the landscape" or "the terrain" are often used to describe fluffy things like social systems and culture.
2 Based on an interview with Vagn Ekeroth, 23 July 2014.

Bibliography

Geertz, C. (1973) *The Interpretation of Cultures: Selected Essays*. New York: Basic Books.

Hallencreutz, J. (2012) *Under the Skin of Change Meanings, Models and Management*. Doctoral thesis. Luleå: Luleå University of Technology.

Lindvall, J. & Iveroth, E. (2011) Creating a global network of shared service centres for accounting. *Journal of Accounting & Organizational Change*, 7(3): 278–305.

Poksinska, B., Pettersen, J., Elg, M., Eklund, J. & Witell, L. (2010) Quality improvement activities in Swedish industry: drivers, approaches, and outcomes. *International Journal of Quality and Service Sciences*, 2(2): 206–216.

Reed, I. (2011) *Interpretation and Social Knowledge*. Chicago, IL: The University of Chicago Press.

Van de Ven, A. (2007) *Engaged Scholarship: A Guide for Organizational and Social Research*. Oxford: Oxford University Press.

Weick, K.E. (1995) *Sensemaking in Organizations*. Thousand Oaks, CA: Sage.

7

EXPLORING LANDSCAPING
IN PRACTICE

Case study background

In the previous chapter we introduced the landscaping metaphor to visualize how proactive change leaders guide people through four different imaginary landscapes of meaning: comfort, inertia, transformation and consolidation. We also highlighted that key leadership tools are the eight guidelines of sensemaking and suggested that behavioral change should be seen as a sensemaking spiral.

In this chapter we will tell a story from the complex reality of organizational change and link it to the concept of landscaping outlined in the previous chapter. The story revolves around aspects of how landscaping can contribute to effective organizational change in practice. It is narrated as a chronological report, based on the triangulation of different types of empirical data that we have collected in our craft of doing action-oriented research and consultancy assignments within the organization.[1]

We will take you on a three-year change journey in a Scandinavian insurance company which covers transformation of organizational structures, business processes, and leadership style and culture. Our story takes place in the consumer claims department in the insurance company.

The insurance business as such is probably more than 2,000 years old. In Europe, fire insurance existed during the early Middle Ages. Around 1350 the Swedish King Magnus Eriksson ("Magnus Ladulås") deployed nationwide terms for this local fire insurance system. By law, all residents of a district or a parish were required to pay a fee to cover costs collectively for the reconstruction of buildings and replacement of certain personal property such as livestock in case of fire. The insurance business grew with increased industrialization. In the 1950s, Sweden had about 1,400 local insurance companies. However, during the 1960s came a period of mergers and today the total number of nationwide insurance companies in Sweden is down to approximately 130.

Insurance companies handle insurance claims. A claim is a formal request to an insurance company asking for a payment based on the terms of the insurance policy. These claims are reviewed for their validity and then paid out to the insured once approved. Insurance claims can cover everything from homes and vehicles to death benefits and accidents.

Our story takes place in a consumer claims department. The main character is Robert,[2] the head of this department. We follow his leadership endeavors during a journey through the four landscapes. The starting point is an organization characterized by low productivity, unwillingness to change and a culture of complacency—in other words, an organization stuck in the landscape of comfort.

The harsh root cause for the change initiative is a cost problem. From a behavioral perspective it could also be described as a cultural problem in the shape of an absence of business orientation. When Robert is assigned to take on this challenge, he starts with an initial diagnosis analysis. This results in the following major change initiatives (headlined "Project Toolbox"):

- A reorganization from specialized subject matter teams to a process-oriented front- and back-office organization.
- The digitization of manual claims-handling processes.
- The implementation of a new control system focusing on individual key performance indicators (KPIs) and follow-up routines.
- A new management team and code of conduct—from administration to development and customer orientation.
- Investment in skills development, training and learning processes.

As we will see as the story unfolds, parallel to these structural and "hard" project activities runs an emergent process of behavioral change catalyzed by sense-making. Besides Robert, other characters in the story are CEO Mats, Eva, who is Robert's boss, team leaders in Robert's management team, and around 100 claims adjusters in the consumer claims department. The change is initiated in spring 2006 and can be considered completed three years later. From an instrumental point of view, this achievement is a success. The transformation that we are about to follow resulted in a 50 percent productivity increase in two years (KPI: claims handled/full-time employees), with a retained level of customer and employee satisfaction according to internal measurements. Through the implementation of a new organizational structure, new leaner digitized processes and a new leadership focusing on efficiency, the number of employees could be reduced by 30 percent, which led to a cost reduction of approximately SEK 25 million/year. Moreover, the shortened lead times made it possible to achieve SEK 40 million in settlement results and SEK 60 million in decreased costs for claims already in 2007. This was accelerated by a landscaping approach.

Initiating change in the landscape of comfort

The departure of this change journey takes place from the landscape of comfort. As depicted in Chapter 6, the climate in such an environment is calm, mild and easy to forecast. People go about and do their thing. Activity is characterized by habitual patterns, contemplation and a friendly, familiar atmosphere. No one is hurrying and there is always room for yet another discussion. Senses of comfort, calmness and stability are salient. The prevailing mindset is to look back and consolidate the current situation rather than to change and develop. A low level of energy, conflict and resistance is observed within the social system and decision-making processes seek consensus. There is no widespread awareness of any need to change. Robert's first challenge at this stage is to assess and understand the current state himself, get people's attention and start a sensemaking process to create a broad-based understanding of the need for change. He will set the scene and outline a new direction by articulating a vision and whipping up a sense of crisis and urgency. By changing his own management behavior, he tries to break up old truths and habits. His mission in this initial stage is to "sell the problem" and provide a strategic direction. Robert also has an ambition to converse and listen, but it turns out to be a tough challenge.

April 2006. The office premises—an anonymous and modest high-rise—is situated in a suburb of Stockholm. On the entrance floor is a lobby and a lunch restaurant, shared with other companies in the business park. I am sitting on a sofa in the lobby, browsing today's paper and waiting for a lunch meeting with Robert, head of the consumer claims department. He is a couple of minutes late. People are coming and going. About 500 people are working here, 100 of them in the claims department. The dress code is casual, the tempo is moderate, and the atmosphere friendly and pleasant. This is not the high street. The insurance company was founded in 1843. Since 1917 it has been part of a nationwide alliance of independent regional insurance companies. The company has been successful and prosperous throughout the years, as well as the rest of the group, and the current situation could be described as one of comfort, calm and stability. Nevertheless, in May 2005, the board decides to change CEO. Mats, the new CEO, recreates his first impressions from that time:

> I came to a sleepy and introverted organization. The company did not have enough bite in the market. It was institutionalized and not customer orientated. My mission from the board was to establish growth and focus on sales and also align the company closer to the federation. It was also some internal fuss. High performers were leaving the company.

The CEO continues describing how he was met with a low level of energy, conflict and unwillingness to change. People stood their ground and defended the current situation rather than change and develop. *"Folks around me said all the right things, but nothing happened."* His approach to the current state was to size-up a new strategy and recruit new leaders:

The analysis on what to do was quite simple. We needed to change from product to customer orientation, and from focus on internal functions to business processes. We also needed a new leadership style, and a more extrovert business culture. I handpicked new leaders to my management team. Our first call was to outline a new strategy and reorganize the company. In December 2005 we had a new structure in place, with a business division and a consumer division.

When we interview him in the process of writing this book he recollects stories, pictures and memories from a social system reminding one of the landscape of comfort. However, this case is not about the CEO as such, but the history of the company, and his comments about the state of the organization at that time contribute to the understanding of the context in which this change process takes place.

My cell phone is buzzing—a text message from Robert: "5 minutes." I switch to another paper. I first met Robert in May 2002, literally in an outdoor hot-tub at a conference center in Sigtuna. Robert was born in the mid-1960s, went to work straight from high school and has built a career in the insurance business both at the front end as a sales representative and manager, and at the back end handling support processes and claims. In the fall of 2002 Robert and I run a short project about mapping business processes in the alliance's life insurance division. Eva, Robert's future boss, is the head of this assignment. We have a couple of meetings. Robert is always eager to go forward but stumbles on methodological issues. *"When I leave our meetings, I think I get the processes … but, hell, you have to explain this once again."* We laugh. Theoretical analysis is not Robert's favorite task. This first assignment ends sometime in 2003. The outcome is mediocre and we lose contact for a couple of years.

Robert shows up, we share a quick meal in the restaurant and take the lift to the floor of the consumer claims department. Around 100 claims adjusters are working here, in an open-plan office. The office environment is bright, the furniture is mostly light wood. In the center of the floor is a coffee room. We grab a cup from the coffee machine and pass by two indoor cabins for smokers, empty right now. Claims adjusters are sitting at their desks, talking on phones, browsing documents or tapping on computers. Robert points at the open office area:

I am sitting right there. I need to be in the middle of things, so I can get a feel of what is going on. I had a separate room at first, but that didn't work. I don't want to be seen as a stiff executive sitting in a fancy office. My style is to be out there in the dirt, talk to clients and handle claims myself. I have to provide a good example if we are ever to bring order to this place. It is much harder to tell others what to do without first doing it yourself.

Here and there are small clusters of people, in quiet discussion. Robert, always neatly dressed in suit and tie, says *"hello"* to everyone we meet. Not all of them answer. One looks down, two are suddenly busy and one just gazes at him silently. Robert doesn't seem to mind:

> Don't worry. Some clerks are really introverts. I am trying to change that by saying "hello" all the time. Listen to this instead. When I started half a year ago I got six or seven emails every day about missing files. And … that was seen as normal! It was a habit to start the day by looking for misplaced documents.

I ask him what he actually did to disrupt this habit. He grins and shows me a 50-square meter conference room, crammed with piles of documents. He shudders:

> Hell, you should have seen the situation a couple of months ago. It was papers all over the place … When I got these emails, I tried to pin down each and every case. I confronted the claims adjuster in charge and together we solved the problems. I called clients myself and asked for missing or lost information. It was tiresome and often quite embarrassing but I felt it was important to signal a new leadership style even if it consumed a ridiculous amount of time. And people picked up this routine. Now we at least have this room. I guess we have about 200,000 claims in here. But the administration is all manual. If someone puts a paper in the wrong place, then it is gone forever. I still get at least one email a day about missing files. It is a little better now, but simply not acceptable.

We move to a small conference room. Robert is frustrated and impatient:

> I have done interviews with all the people in this organization and I am worried. Everyone is whining about all kinds of things, but no one wants to change anything. There is no order. My managers are not in command. They have no track of facts or figures …

He has spent time in understanding the organization about to be changed and presents a slide summarizing the findings of his own preliminary analysis of the current state (see Box 7.1).

BOX 7.1 A SAMPLE OF ROBERT'S FIRST ANALYSIS IN 2006

- 100 companies within the company
- Poor productivity
- Poor focus on process improvement
- Difficulties in managing change
- Focus on the individual customer
- People see themselves as "unique"
- Poor technical competence

- Not seeing the whole
- No individual responsibility—it is the manager's responsibility
- Legally correct but dull approach to the customer
- Managers who are not managers but instead employee representatives
- Major problems between the business department and consumer department

Robert concludes that his organization is in a poor state and needs to be reorganized. The figures look bad. The costs need to be cut: "*We are too many doing too little.*" He wants new managers and a shift in mindset. Eva, his superior, has told him to focus on both the claims adjustment costs and the actual loss ratio. His cell phone beeps. It is his wife. She wants to discuss some child issue. I notice that his voice turns mild and soft, very unlike the firmness he just demonstrated with his colleagues. He ignores me totally. The call ends with a cuddly "*kiss for you.*" He hangs up.

"*Well, what do you want to do?*" I ask. We discuss alternative ways forward and leave the meeting with a sketch of a new assignment called Project Toolbox. The aim is to establish a new organization by the end of 2006 and follow up with process development in 2007.

Project Toolbox starts as a classic restructuring project. In short, the objective is to construct a new organization based on claims type. "Easy" consumer claims and customer service will be handled by a front office and more complicated claims will be handled by a back office. On top of that, new digitized routines will simplify the claims-handling process and speed up the service. Robert's initial analysis also tells him that he needs new management and a sharper control system. The project set-up follows the traditional developmental components of a structural nature: initiation, planning, execution, monitoring and completion.

This is Robert's home ground and he feels safe and confident as long as we fiddle with project details and structural issues. It is fair to say that he is raised in the school of planned change. His ontology is that the world is objective and rational, and that change follows natural steps. According to him, "the world" can be observed, generalized and measured if we just bother to find all the facts and figures. However, he meets greater challenges trying to interact with people and get their attention. "Fluffy stuff" such as social systems, interpretations and constructions of meaning are elusive and abstract and make him nervous.

Robert conducts personal interviews with all employees and holds many meetings but his message seems to pass them by. Very few see a need for change. Or rather, the usual complaint goes the other way around: the department needs *more* resources. The claims adjusters should *not* have to answer the phone. A call center should take care of the clients. Robert tries to explain figures, benchmarks and statistics, but the majority do not see what he sees:

My starting point is that most people get what I get ... Honestly, I don't think of myself as smarter than others. But I guess I just have to change that mindset. Apparently I need to talk about these things in a different language. Not even my team leaders are on board.

It becomes obvious to Robert that another approach to this change challenge is needed. During our first workshops in spring 2006, we spend a lot of time discussing questions such as: *Do people fully understand the rationale behind this change initiative? What kind of change is it? Is "the why" clearly formulated? Who should lead the change? How much time do we have? What are the critical activities? How should we approach the cultural forces?* As we deconstruct his assignment, or—using the Reed metaphor—study the landscape from various angles, Robert realizes that there probably is more to this job than just reorganizing the crowds and structures and giving all the figures a markup. He sees new things. Yes, the assignment is about increased productivity, but as we speak the cultural element grows stronger. We are probably facing a major transformation of structures, processes *and* people. *But how are we to explain, explore and discuss a problem that no one wants to see?*

As a complement to the more instrumental Project Toolbox, Robert realizes that he needs another approach. The first task is to narrate a story about the challenges the department is facing in a way that people understand. We produce slides that explain things in simple terms and translate the strategy to concrete activities. Instead of displaying detailed spreadsheets he uses childlike images of banknotes and money bags in different sizes to explain how the company's income and expenses will look in the years to come. The company's profit margin must increase: *"we need to earn a fiver on every hundred,"* is the simplified message. Instead of talking about high claims-handling costs, he shows a picture of a man in an oversized suit. General terms like "efficiency" and "productivity" are replaced with statements like *"it's not enough to be busy, the question is what you are busy with,"* and *"it's not about doing things right, it's about doing the right things."* He also uses color signals: green is good, red is bad.

As the story begins to come together, Robert also realizes that rather than giving lectures, he has to give people space to digest cues of information and impressions. The mission now is to "sell *and discuss* the problem." However, he finds it difficult to cool down and listen, since he holds all the answers and is eager to move forward. *"What's the point in discussing this with the staff? They are not interested anyway. Their only solution is to hurl in more resources."*

When reflecting about this period retrospectively, Robert admits that he was a poor listener at the beginning:

I was stubborn and decisive at first and didn't think much of my colleagues. I guess I was too frustrated about the total lack of urgency and understanding about the company's situation. We were fat, but not happy. I needed to make a statement and shake things up. Gradually I learned that dialogue was a better way to drive the cultural change. It sort of soaked and softened things and made it easier for people to cope with difficulties. I learned the hard way to become a good listener. For a long time, about half of the staff thought that my very presence at work was the worst thing that had ever happened. Many of them left during the process.

29 May 2006. There are no windows in the conference room—that is why we call it "the bunker." At this meeting, the CEO, the business unit director, Robert and I are about to decide the way forward. As a result of the spring analysis, Robert sees the need to transform his organization drastically. Productivity is too low, costs are too high and the culture is disruptive. Something needs to be done to break habitual patterns. There is tension in the air. Robert presents the setup for Project Toolbox. When CEO Mats says "*Go*," I think this is for real. This is where it all begins.

The CEO recalls:

> We had to cut costs and felt intuitively that something was wrong in the consumer claims department, but we didn't know what. Productivity was low, but everyone seemed very busy. Once I was called to a meeting with the staff in the claims department—they wanted me to explain myself. This was sometime in the middle of 2005. Afterwards, I realized that we had a major management problem. Middle managers saw themselves as mouthpieces for their staff, and not as management representatives. I also realized that we needed someone who knew non-life insurance. That was certainly not my turf, since my background is in banking and life insurance. Robert's predecessor said all the right things, but nothing happened. The situation was not okay. We needed a manager with a documented knowledge about non-life insurance and an ability to execute change. We wanted things to move forward. That's why we chose Robert.

Eva, the business unit director and Robert's superior, fills in:

> I knew Robert from before and was convinced that he would execute the needed changes. So I pretty much handpicked him for this assignment.

21 June 2006. Robert holds a staff meeting in the claims department. Using his new simplified presentation, he wants once again to discuss problems and solutions and give people space to reflect on the information he is about to reveal (see a sample of the slide in Figure 7.1). The aim is to inject awareness and a sense of seriousness and necessity. At the previous meeting, in May, he started to establish the need for change. Now he is about to introduce the way forward. All personnel are attending. They come in small groups, taking coffee and a sandwich and sitting near the back of the room. The mood is cautious, almost reluctant. Robert is concentrated and decisive but also a little nervous behind the smart, stiff facade. A week before, we prepared a slideshow and the message is clear: "We need to

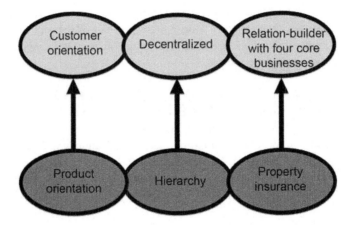

FIGURE 7.1 A slide from Robert's strategy presentation, conducted 21 June 2006

change." The mission is "*to create a modern, efficient and delivering claims organization.*" Robert delivers his presentation. He starts by repeating the translation of the company's overarching "*strategy for profitable growth.*"

He proceeds by repeating "the why": *costs in our department are too high and productivity is too low.* He shows a graph explaining that the company's claims-handling cost is higher compared with the two main competitors. "*If we look at these illustrations, what do they tell you?*" He pauses ... the room is dead silent. To everyone watching it is obvious that the stack of money symbolizing the company's claims-handling cost is the highest. Finally, a senior claims adjuster raises his voice: "*Okay, we get it ... We are too many and too slow.*" Scattered giggles in the room. Robert continues

> Well, it is obvious that our claims-handling cost is too high compared with the competitors at the Stockholm market. We are simply not competitive. This means in practice that we are taking care of too few claims per person—our suit is too big.

Robert shows the man in the oversized suit.
The senior claims adjuster opposes:

> Hold on a little bit ... you are overstating the situation. Our company had a great result in 2005. And we have been around for 150 years. We have seen managers come and go. Do you really think that you can come here and frighten us with statistics? It is obvious that you know very little about claims handling. Quality and service are much more important than speed and quantity.

Robert replies, engaged by the debate:

Yes, we have reported good results over the years but the competition is getting tougher and our profit margin is too low. You are right, quality is important. One could perhaps imagine that the time we spend on each claim pays off in better customer satisfaction and unbeatable service quality, but sorry folks ... there is no such connection.

He shows another slide explaining that the "old truth" about the contraposition of quality and quantity is false. Even the suspicious senior has to admit that Robert has done his homework well.

Robert also presents the vision and plan for Project Toolbox:

My vision is that in three years we are a modern, proactive and cheerful claims organization with excellent key performance indicators that withstand any comparison. We will start in August with 30 interviews and improvement workshops in all teams. I will come back after the summer with more details, but I can already forecast a structural change later in the year. We will look closer at both structures and operating procedures. Some kind of reorganization is most likely needed.

He concludes his presentation with the challenging question: "*Start today by assessing your personal work procedures. It's not enough to be busy. The question is, what are you busy with?*" The last slide holds a variation on an alleged Einstein quote: "*Insanity: doing the same thing over and over again and expecting different results.*"

After the presentation Robert invites the crowd to discuss in trios what they have just heard. A gentle hum of voices fills the room. Robert opens up for questions. Someone in the auditorium raises his hand and asks: "*Well, what if we don't want to change?*" Without hesitation, Robert answers:

You can be sure that the job will change. This will be a really thrilling journey with plenty of opportunities for those who embrace the new. There will be many occasions for everyone to contribute. I foresee new operating procedures, new digitized processes, new customer interfaces and a more extrovert business-oriented culture. Personally, I think it will be great fun. But you are not forced to work here. There are other jobs ...

The crowd is silent and the meeting ends. People look a little shaken. "The problem" is sold. The direction is clear.

Summary

Employee Adam comments on the early stages:

Well, Robert gave the impression of being a good listener and ran around to everyone at the beginning, but that was quite easy to see through. Come on, we have been around for a while and you don't fool us that easily. He wanted to play hardball and had made up his mind quite early. We were too many and too slow. He was not really interested in hearing people's opinions. But ... I must say that I learned to respect him, in a way. At least he was clear, consistent and decisive and showed where to go. It was "my way or the highway." He was stubborn and went on and on about the change he proposed and where it would lead us at almost every meeting ... and he really walked the talk. He was out there with us and gave us attention and confidence. I kind of liked that because it made me feel less confused during the times of turmoil. The direction was clear.

Employee Bertil adds:

Personally, I don't remember much from that time. Robert was anonymous back then. We didn't see him ... No ... I don't recall that I spoke to him at all ...

Employee Carin:

My first impression of Robert was that he really tried to be a good listener even if he was a little stiff at the beginning. I mean, he had an individual meeting with everyone where he wanted to understand our point of view of things. He knew claims and even though he was new at the time, he got into it quickly and understood how we work. Then he drove a little too fast and hard, maybe. We didn't catch up. The attitude was also a bit hard, especially among some of the team leaders. They said things like "take it or leave it," or "there is the door." Many were afraid to speak out. But I personally have always felt that Robert is easy to talk to.

Employee Daisy:

I remember him as a guy I could talk to that could explain things in a simple way and who could keep us focused on what should be done. I remember also that he noticed that I am from Dalarna. You know ... he is married to a Dalecarlian ... Yes, I think it was the first thing we talked about. Another thing that I also recall from that time is that it was a strange staff meeting about business orientation in a sports hall, and that an old colleague described our company like a big pike that would always survive in the lake. Strange ... I don't know why I remember that ... But it said something about our self-image. The company has been around for 150 years and nothing will ever get to us, sort of.

Entering the landscape of inertia

During late summer of 2006 the spiral of change starts to dismantle the existing frames and mindsets in the landscape of comfort, as people are guided by Robert to the rougher landscape of inertia. Now the change process really starts to "work" on the social system and uncertainty and resistance occur. During this phase Robert really takes the lead, provides direction and ensures that the crowd stays in motion through close navigation. He has to handle his own defense mechanism and an urge to turn back has to be overcome. He facilitates interaction and organizes dialogue around the ever present "why, what, how, who and when" questions.

This is a stage of action and relapse. Robert is always seeking ways forward through the woods. As we work away, I try to convince him that a key to success at this stage is information transparency: to be honest and open about what he knows and at the same time be open and honest about his uncertainties and provide likely scenarios of what could happen and what could be done. As resistance grows, Robert encourages people to talk and acknowledges people's feelings of chaos, loss and anger. He also looks for early adopters, highlights good examples and opportunities, and stubbornly drives structural transformation. The sensemaking processes will eventually help people to let go of the past and start looking forward.

10–11 August 2006. The day is warm and humid. I am driving in my car bound for a conference center in the Stockholm archipelago. For the first time, I am about to meet Robert's management team. We have planned for a "lunch-to-lunch" (i.e. starting with lunch on the first day and finishing after lunch on the second day—a common way of organizing events in Sweden). I am a little late and nervous and do not know what to expect. Robert is displeased with their performance as a team and he wants me to be tough. "*We need to test them,*" he has said, although he already knows that he will replace some of them.

It is one of those late summer days when the heat turns tropical. I park my car next to Robert's. I notice that it is just as untidy as my own. The team is sitting on the restaurant veranda enjoying the sunshine. I meet a group of middle-aged, casually dressed people. Two women and six men, Robert included. I notice that it is the first time I have seen him without a suit and tie. The atmosphere is calm and a little hesitant, perhaps also a bit complacent.

During the afternoon we discuss the need for change and Robert outlines his vision for the claims department. The discussions lack energy. Before dinner Robert takes me aside: "*Jacob. I would appreciate it if you could stay around and listen to the small talk afterwards. I can't stand these social occasions and will go to bed.*" I do as he says and follow five of the team leaders down to a jetty, where Stefan, one of the most experienced leaders in the group, insists on taking a dip in the Baltic Sea. As the evening turns to night they get more and more outspoken; "*You see Jacob, we are a real team and inspire each other. Don't let Robert spoil that …*" I feel uncomfortable. I do not want to become their mouthpiece. They go on: "*We have had so much fun over the years …*" Politely, I say good night and leave them there on the jetty.

The next day we have prepared a calculation exercise. This is more of an experiment to test the team leaders' ability to analyze figures. Robert challenges them by asking: "*Here is a little warm-up test. How many claims should a claims adjuster be able to handle a day? One? Two? Five? Think individually for a couple of minutes."* The leaders look at each other, troubled. It is obvious to an external observer that they are uncomfortable with the exercise. One of them looks down, another is flushed to the neck and a third starts counting on his fingers. One by one they reveal their estimates. *"Well … I suppose ten a day is a reasonable figure,"* *"Aha … more, I think,"* *"Hard to generalize, the cases are all different."* Robert grins:

> Friends … if your figures are correct we should be able to run this department on less than half of the staff. So … something is wrong with the map and the terrain here. The true figure is not even one case per day.

A heated discussion follows: *"Aw … Robert, you are simplifying,"* *"People have other things to do,"* *"They are all busy, no one is lazy."* Other comments show some insight: *"Shit, is it really that bad?!"* and *"I have had this gut feeling for some time now."*

Robert provides a set of facts and figures about production results, performance indicators and such. He zooms in on the number of adjusted claims per claims adjuster and the average claims cost, and wants his team leaders to understand that the department really suffers from the wrong mindset:

> We need to kill the myth that few claims per person leads to a more thorough adjustment and a lower claims payment. Statistically, there is no such connection. And … this shift in mindset must start with you, the team leaders.

The true figures look really poor, but the team leaders find it difficult to face the truth. We discuss the need for improved business control but no one is more than dutifully interested. Someone asks: *"Why do we have to play around with these figures?"* The exercise fails and Robert is troubled. We talk on the phone on our way home: *"I can't work with these people … how can I work with them if they don't understand the importance of measurement and monitoring?!"* His management team feels lost in the woods and for the first time, Robert himself also shares some uncertainty about the path to take.

September 2006. Two colleagues and I are doing 30 individual semi-structured interviews with members of the staff. This is a vital part of Project Toolbox. Robert wants us to look closely at the change process and give him a second opinion about the organizational design. Even if he is eager to execute it, he wants to avoid hasty conclusions. We conduct the interviews in small, anonymous, windowless meeting rooms on the conference premises of the business park. We also sit in the open office and try to blend with the daily work. The interview follows a standardized formula. It starts with a presentation of the purpose and background to the interview:

> The management team has identified a need to increase the pace of change and efficiency in the claims department in order to reduce claims-handling costs. The task is to analyze existing working practices, and identify areas of

improvement in order to develop concrete action plans. As part of the analysis, we do interviews with some employees.

We then guide the interviewee through the following topics: organization and control; roles and responsibilities; leadership; processes and work procedures; efficiency; culture and values; customer orientation; and need for change.

No one has any objections to the purpose or the questions. Our general impression is that people are easy to talk to, friendly and willing to share their thoughts. The picture that emerges strengthens Robert's own analysis. At the end of September, we present our findings to Robert and Eva. I quote from our report:

- The ambition of top management has been to get involved and listen to employees' views and ideas during the development of the new strategy. The organization has not perceived this effort as genuine (evidenced by both the interviews and employee survey 2006).
- There is an appreciation and understanding of the need for change among the interviewed employees, but no deeper insight into the background, root causes (market position, cost structure, etc.) and consequences.
- There is a concern for the future and what ongoing change projects will lead to. The interviewees suspect that "something will happen" and call for clarity.
- There are gaps in the management of the claims organization, control systems as well as a weak focus on business development.
- The organization has gone through a series of change projects over the years which have not led to any significant change or improvement.
- The prevailing corporate culture does not support management's desired development.
- Organizational learning is limited. There is no overarching structure that dictates how knowledge-sharing within the claims department, the company at large and the federation should be carried out.
- There is a wide spread in claims process efficiency, on both group and individual levels.

We recommend a range of short- and long-term actions, and support Robert's own structural solution with a front office handling "easy" claims and a back office handling "complex" claims. The overarching change initiative implicates a major reorganization of the whole claims department, but to boost continuous improvement and visualize progress we propose that a "Top 100" list of improvements be published.

Robert is pleased with this report. It fuels his ideas and he decides to move forward: *"I need to keep up the pace."* Mats and Eva back him up.

Robert jump-starts the proposed bottom-up process by displaying the Top 100 list on a whiteboard on wheels in the open office. The official launch is at a staff meeting in September: *"Ladies and gentlemen, this is from now on our improvement hub. Here we will keep track of quick wins as well as more complicated assignments."* The whiteboard is divided into four columns: activity, responsibility, deadline and status. Status is marked on the whiteboard with green ("on track"), red ("delayed") or yellow ("needs attention") magnets. Completed tasks will eventually be moved to another space on the whiteboard to visualize progress. To start with, the list is open to almost any kind of suggestion. The idea is to keep it simple and encourage people to contribute. The team leaders are also asked to look for early adopters within their teams and conduct brainstorming workshops to fuel even more ideas to be put on the list.

Soon the list is crammed with ideas. A small taskforce of volunteers take on the challenge to prioritize and implement quick wins. From now on the whiteboard becomes a regular feature at every staff meeting. Robert is very pleased.

9 October 2006. Another conference center. Today is the moment of truth, after months of planning and preparation. Eva and Robert are about to inform Robert's management team that they will be made redundant. Some of them will be offered retirement; others will be reassigned. Two have been handpicked and will stay throughout the change process. *"It should be cool. I have talked to everyone and they pretty much know what to expect,"* says Robert. However, both Eva and Robert are tense, the mood is irritable. They bicker about who should start, which slides to use and where to sit. I stay in the background. When the team leaders arrive, Eva and Robert become focused and we move to our conference room. They launch the news that will be presented to the whole company the day after: a company-spanning retirement plan and a reorganization of the consumer claims department. Eva is cool, she has done this before. Robert is a little keyed up. However, they deliver the message clearly: a new consumer claims organization from 1 January 2007.

Afterwards an awkward silence ... My task is to facilitate the debriefing. I turn to Bernt, a man in his sixties. *"You have heard Eva and Robert. What about your thoughts and feelings right now?"* He shrugs. *"I feel like the Social Democrats—knocked out ... but we will come again."* We all chuckle. In the election a fortnight before, Prime Minister Göran Persson and his Social Democrats were defeated by the right-wingers. The Social Democrats experienced their worst election since 1914. Bernt's comment lightens the mood a little. We talk around the table about losses and opportunities. Some open up, others are more silent. No one seems really surprised or shocked, but rather pleased that a period of rumor and speculation has come to an end. My feeling is that Robert has done his legwork well. Later, Eva, Robert and I review the day in the car park before we part and go home. They are relieved, but they also realize that we just passed the point of no return. I exhale. Tomorrow the change goes public.

10 October 2006. Robert launches his change plan and a long period of pre-paration comes to an end. If they have not before, people become aware of the need for change. The constant flow of sensemaking has once again been interrupted, but the message is perceived in different ways. Employee Bertil recalls his impression:

> I still remember that day. It was a complete shock ... A bomb ... A flash from a clear blue sky. I had no premonition whatsoever. I knew nothing. I was devastated. Suddenly, we were about to reorganize the whole department.

While Bertil was taken by surprise, employee Daisy was fully aware of the need for change:

> I was not surprised. It was obvious to me that something needed to be done. We had too little to do and the figures looked bad ... it was clear for those who bothered to see the reality. There were no secrets.

Employee Adam was indifferent:

> Robert was clear on this from the very beginning. Personally I was not affected. But I felt sorry for my colleagues who were sent to the front office.

Employee Carin decided to be resilient:

> Oh ... it was such a jumble ... but I decided not to go down that road again. I felt so bad during all the changes that took place in 2005 so this time I said to myself: do I want this or not? Then I made up my mind. I ... just refused to turn negative again ... and Robert was clear and transparent, so it was quite easy.

27 October 2006. Robert has invited all employees to what he calls "change breakfast." "*Welcome. From now on we will offer 'change breakfast' every Friday,*" he proclaims. The idea is to offer a cup of coffee, a sandwich and a casual opportunity to meet Robert and the team leaders for informal conversations about the state of the change and the ever present "why, what, how, who and when" questions. He strives to make these occasions open, informal, issue oriented and honest. Robert believes that after a couple of tentative try-outs and testing of change breakfast, the meeting finds its form and soon becomes a natural hub for change conversations.

The agenda is loose but recurring topics are "*What's going on*" (a quick report from Robert) and a "*100 list follow-up*" (the whiteboard is updated) and "*our worst issues*" (where everyone can address problems and shortcomings). Robert is accused by some of brainwashing, but the ambition to facilitate interaction is sincere on his side. He responds:

> Okay, perhaps I appear to be a poor listener, but I really want to hear what people are saying and try to understand your perspective of things and how you see it. I don't have all the answers, there are many possible future scenarios and ways to choose. But the reason for change is clear as well as our vision and direction.

November–December 2006. Robert is busy recruiting new team leaders and preparing the big transformation planned for 1 January 2007. We have a couple of meetings during this period, where he is thriving and radiating self-confidence. He holds breakfast meetings every Friday and small activities such as the adoption of new standardized letter templates are ticked off the 100 list, but there is also growing unease in the organization. The change process has started to affect the social systems within the department, and uncertainty and resistance are disseminated. We notice the emergence of factions and informal subgroups as people seem to choose a side. Some are positive, outspoken and willing to contribute, while others are just as negative. Early adopters are eager to speed up but many still do not understand the need for change and question the motives at almost every meeting. Robert is hard headed about this criticism. He seems to be certain about the direction, even if many of the followers are insecure.

The end of 2006 is a period of execution, when Robert takes the lead. In the course of a month he recruits a new management team (two from the old team and three external), negotiates a new organization and prepares for an internal relocation of the staff. All is set until Christmas. During this period some individuals look forward to the new and engage in workshops and problem-solving activities, while others are cautious and one faction is feeling completely lost and abandoned. Employee Carin chooses to be positive: "*I made a deliberate choice to see the possibilities and like the change.*" Employee Bertil, however, recollects nothing but bad feeling from the last months of 2006:

> Those months were like working in a vacuum. We were waiting to be placed somewhere in a new organization and got no information whatsoever ... Can you imagine that?! We asked our team leaders but they had nothing to say. Everything was governed by Robert and he was not available. Is that how you handle experienced senior claims adjusters?! No one wanted to be put in the new front office. But I was placed there against my will ...

The human resources director states:

> I am impressed that Robert stood up during this period. He made some really tough decisions. But he had a lot of support from Eva and Mats, in the background.

Navigating through the landscape of transformation

As the change process proceeds, the challenging landscape of inertia is slowly reshaped to the landscape of transformation. Here, the topography is rough but a little easier to get through. The climate is slowly stabilizing but nature is still volatile and life is characterized by bursts of activity, trial, learning loops and fallback plans. Robert and his staff alternate between action and relapse, renewal and confusion, while seeking solutions and ways forward. Some people have chosen to leave, others are still searching for motivation. Some feel misplaced and unhappy in the new organization, still remembering the good old days in the landscape of comfort. For Robert, this is a period of restlessness and a feeling of "one step forward, two steps back." His decisions help people confront losses and gains. He injects much of his own energy since new processes and working procedures are not in place. Securing motion and helping people through are still crucial. Although uncertain about the details, Robert has stubbornly followed his own direction, but he will stumble on unexpected changes in the environment. It is still too early to declare victory.

One of the recommendations from the Project Toolbox analysis was to provide management support to the team leaders during this stage of the change process. Robert and Eva have decided to invest in his new management team and we set up a series of six management seminars during 2007. The purpose is twofold: to strengthen the new leadership in the claims department and to keep track closely of the change process. Eva also wants Robert to grind down some of his own edges and focus more on group dynamics and social processes, but Robert is reluctant to take part in all kinds of "soft" stuff. *"No sissy psychological nonsense in velvet pants. I want us to talk about our mission and how we can reach our goals."* So we label the management seminars "Productive Leadership," and I downplay the "soft" exercises for the time being.

24 January 2007. It has been a relatively mild winter and the ground is bare. I am early and go for a quick walk around the premises, a beautiful building on the shore, completed in 1889. The view of the inlet to Stockholm is stunning. Today is the first meeting with Robert's new department management team. He is very pleased with his new colleagues and has high hopes for the year ahead. Only two "oldies" remain. The rest (two women and one man around 30) are newly recruited. Robert has picked talented leaders and not claims specialists. The team members arrive, full of energy. Robert is enthusiastic: *"I am so pleased to have you onboard and have very high hopes for the year to come."* The new organization with a front and back office has just been launched and the day is full of laughter and excitement. We discuss desirable team properties and conclude that the new management team should be characterized by a good blend of personalities, goal orientation, trust, responsibility and innovation. People leave the meeting in good pioneering spirit. The challenges ahead look thrilling and the team has a common direction.

Two weeks after the January meeting my cell phone rings. It is Robert:

> Hey, we need to do some re-planning. I have run into a major drawback. Erik has left after three days. He couldn't stand the pressure. I am really disappointed. I feel betrayed. Can we meet and talk … I need to look at the plan and make some adjustments.

Erik is one of the new young team leaders and one of Robert's favorites: *"The guy is business oriented and someone to build on."* Apparently, he has literally U-turned in the doorway when facing all the challenges at the new claims front office—the map and the terrain did not match at all. For the first time Robert is shaken and lost in this tricky terrain. When we meet some days later he looks tired. He has taken this defection personally and has battled with an urge to give up and turn back. *"I thought I knew this guy … Hell, why didn't he say something?!"*

The original plan needs to be updated, but there is no Plan B and Robert is confused. He has to improvise to resolve the situation. Luckily, the runner-up for the job, Elisabeth, is still willing to take on the challenge. She is not a claims adjuster but a qualified project specialist leading internal projects in the company's development team. She has been on hand in the background as an assigned internal resource in Project Toolbox. Elisabeth remembers these dramatic events:

> I was really mad at Robert when he chose Erik instead of me. I though he made a really bad decision. So I went for a long winter holiday to cool off. When I came back in the beginning of February I got a call from Robert. I thought he wanted to talk about some new project assignment but he told me about Erik's escape and offered me the job as team leader! That was great! I said yes, of course.

The first quarter of 2007 is just rushing past. Robert and his new management team focus on getting the organization started. The old structure with specialized units is dissolved and replaced with a new front office where the majority of customer contacts are made. Employee Bertil describes the situation:

> The new so-called front office was opened in January. Far too early if you ask me. Many came in new and knew nothing about claims. We, the seniors, were looked upon as reactionary old-timers. No one listened to us. We were told by our superiors to adapt and work. I felt really awkward. It didn't fit with the company culture that I was used to. But I bit the bullet and fought on. Never give in, that's not my style.

Employee Carin fills in:

> I came to the back office, where most of us seniors wanted to be. But some were forced into the front office and were very sad. They literally threw people in there. It went too fast and was out of control.

Elisabeth, head of the newly established claims front office and Erik's successor, has nothing but vague memories from this start-up period: "*I wrote a diary of the first five months of 2007. Very monotonous! Eat–work–sleep … [laughs] …*"

    17 April 2007. We had had a second management seminar about very down-to-earth management structures and working procedures on the last day of February, a day marked by an almost epic snowstorm that cripples Stockholm. Now it is time for the third seminar in the series of six, and we immediately abandon the agenda. Team leader Elisabeth feels worn out:

> I have been at these corporate management training sessions where everything is rosy and nice. No one told me that managing people is a mess. I am fed up

with all the whimpering. Everybody is whining about everything! Why can't people just bite the bullet and work?!

We focus on her distress in the middle of the turmoil of the front office, and talk about ways forward. Everyone in the group is letting off steam. Robert is forced to stop and listen. His management team feels lost in a morass of inertia and resistance. Although they all feel that they invest "all the time in the world" in meetings, explanations, cheering-up events, problem solving and client issues, they feel opposed and disliked by their teams.

We talk about the importance of striving upward and that our energy will eventually overcome the resistance and dismantle the existing frames and mindsets. Once again I urge Robert not to try to persuade people to feel differently. As resistance comes and goes it is even more important to get people to continue talking. He needs to listen to and acknowledge people's feelings. It is equally important to emphasize good examples and opportunities and to drive the change sustainably. Activities such as the Friday breakfast meetings will be even more crucial. "*Okay, I guess I must be the pathfinder that leads my followers forward to safe ground,*" he philosophizes. I nod. As a consequence he decides that all upcoming seminars in the management team should hold a "letting off steam" session where everyone is allowed to debrief.

A Friday in May 2007. Another "change breakfast." This Friday morning is calm. About half of the staff is here. Robert is informing everyone about forthcoming training sessions for the front office. He also rolls up the big whiteboard with the 100 list and highlights several activities:

> Friends, I hereby proudly announce that we have installed two new printers, twice as fast as the old ones. We have also deployed a new phone routine at the front office and launched new checklists for adjusting automotive claims.

Robert moves demonstratively about among the magnets on the board and puts up some more green dots. He applauds and the crowd joins in half-heartedly. He also wants to engage more people in small assignments and asks for volunteers (for instance, improving operating procedures or producing new texts for client correspondence). Some of the newcomers raise their hands. On the whole, the setting is quiet and tuned, but it is turning messy behind the scenes. The change process spins fast around multiple iterations of progress and setbacks.

For Robert this is a period of restless confusion and an awkward feeling of walking in mud. People are aware that the old systems are being challenged but do not have a clear picture as to what the organization is replacing them with yet. Robert is struggling with the balance between allowing freedom and being instructive, but chaos might still be a salient feeling. He tries to guide people to look forward, make choices, see new solutions and leave old stuff behind, for instance by encouraging everyone to settle more claims by phone instead of routinely asking the client to send in a lot of documents. During the hectic start-up period of the new front office established in January, Robert handles claims and answers phone calls from clients himself.

12 June 2007. The series of management seminars proceeds. This afternoon's seminar is by Robert, headlined "*To be in the shit.*" He explains:

> It is brutal out there. We really need to strengthen the team leaders and address how to balance the handling of people that obstruct, but at the same time praise all the good stuff. It is equally important to highlight that things move in the right direction.

I have prepared some slides about change communication and handling inertia and resistance, but once again the agenda is overridden by an urgent matter. The emergent reality is playing tricks again and—once again—plans need to be adjusted. The day before, Robert informed me about a fraud investigation in one of the teams in his department. Employees held in high esteem are suspected. Now the ground is really shaking. He informs his management team about the investigation and urges them to be strictly confidential. There might be arrests and police interventions to come. Two weeks later the following is published in one of the morning papers:

> An employee at the insurance company [XX] is suspected of committing economic crimes in the service. The man was taken from his home on Tuesday and was arrested for gross breach of trust. Elsewhere in the Stockholm area a businessman was arrested on suspicion of serious fraud—criminal charges against the men are linked and related to six figures, said prosecutor N.N. at the National Unit against Corruption.
>
> *(26 June 2007)*

"*Jacob, is it worth it?*" Robert looks out of the window. It is mid-July and he is in the middle of what he calls "a shit storm" of accusations and back talking. He sighs: "*It's a bloody mess of rumors and conspiracies, both about our change process and the swindling. And everything seems to be my fault. Shit, this is not fun anymore.*"

We are sitting in my office, eating takeaway salad. He feels abandoned and alone. Everyone seems to be against him. The fraud affair has kicked off a chain of troublesome events. The whole department is in turmoil and he is facing a totally different landscape. Reality has become rugged and the obstacles impossible to manage. He has gone astray and looped back to the landscape of inertia. We talk about leadership and the importance of staying the distance. I try to highlight the need for stamina, stubbornness and clarity: "*Don't abandon your direction but perhaps adjust the plan.*" He realizes as we reflect on the situation that his instrumental approach with milestones and deadlines needs to be substituted with "trial and error." We project his detailed master plan (a crammed Excel spreadsheet) on the wall and adjust tasks and timeframes. For the first time, he seems uncertain and vulnerable. This was not meant to be. When he notices my concern, however, he lightens up and grins: *"Hey man, don't worry, I won't give up. I am not lost. I am just pissed off and need a vacation."*

The CEO has bad memories of those weeks:

> We should have handled that fraud situation in a different way. I was really disappointed with our employers' organization. They advised us to play hard-ball, but then left us in the lurch. Well, one guy was convicted so that was nothing to talk about, but the other two ... It took too long and caused a lot of damage internally. Robert had to take plenty of beating.

The summer weather in the landscape of transformation is mediocre this year, but the change keeps pounding on. Robert builds an application for digitizing claims in Outlook together with a taskforce of progressive claims adjusters and sets up a scanning service with a subcontractor in Östersund—one of the deliverables from Project Toolbox. Overnight most of the documents "disappear" from cupboards and shelves and the conference room crammed with 200,000 acts can be ritually closed. *"People say it's no good but, hell, it's good enough! 70 percent right is better than 100 percent nothing ..."* Another important consequence is that the new digital workflow makes it more difficult to habitually refer cases to certain clerks. Robert is exhilarated:

> Yes! At last we have a common workflow. No more 'Aw ... this is Kalle's claim and he is not here. Please call again on Wednesday.' This is one small step for man, but one important step towards a mutual responsibility for our clients.

On the same day cake is served at afternoon coffee, and during an improvised ceremony around the cake Robert fetches the whiteboard and ritually ticks off 15 activities on the list. Inspired by this breakthrough, he establishes a "claims lab" where innovative people can meet on a regular basis, test new applications and continuously improve the new digitized workflow.

The autumn management seminar focuses on the "soft" aspects that Robert wanted us to neglect, by introducing coaching and feedback techniques. We also follow up the team properties set in January and discuss how well they have been complied with during the year. Reluctantly, Robert has to back down and accept that his instrumental worldview does not hold the ultimate truth—structural changes do not do the trick alone. As the management team builds trust by open and honest dialogue, his five team leaders dare to question motives and objectives. And he learns to listen.

In September our management seminar goes to Amsterdam. The purpose is to visit a modern Dutch insurance company and get some inspiration about smooth claims-handling processes besides the general follow-up of the change process back home. The last session, in December, we meet at a hotel in the center of Stockholm. The conference room is weird, sandwiched in behind the reception and a corridor.

We laugh and shake our heads. We perform a new calculation exercise like the one that failed in August 2006. This time, the awareness and urgency are tangible.

The KPI claims-adjusted/full-time employee has during the year improved by 33 percent but is still too slow. Stefan, the guy who took a swim in the Baltic Sea, shakes his head … *"This is much better but still not good enough. Too few are using our new paperless workflow."* After that, everyone is asked to draw an "energy line" of the year 2007 on the whiteboard and share highs and lows with each other. We both laugh and shudder. All the team leaders' curves converge and show an energy dip around July. *"Oh … what a shitty summer,"* says Stefan. It has been a really tough year, but it feels better now for everyone. Things are settling and people seek new solutions. "The new" is still a little chaotic, but the mindset is to look forward. Elisabeth, team leader of the front office, shares one of her best moments:

> A lot of new people started in September. Just the other day I saw a couple of them chit-chat at the coffee machine. I got curious and went there to listen in. And I became so glad! They talked about their work and how they could help each other, instead of running to me! Breakthrough!

When we interview Elisabeth four years later she looks back and emphasizes the importance of the claims-management team during this rough period of change:

> Honestly, I wouldn't have made it without this gang. We were tight. We had fun. We helped and supported each other. It was super and made this a good journey, despite all the mess along the way. For instance, I remember once when Anna and I just sat 40 minutes in a conference room without saying anything. We didn't have to because we both knew the situation we were in. It just felt good to be there in the same room together …

We end the December seminar by concluding that the change process is about to leave a period of turmoil and resistance and enter a stage of consolidation. All team leaders testify that the trust, alignment and good spirit in the new claims-management team established in January have been crucial. The new mindset is settling throughout the department and the comfort level is starting to return to sound levels, even if some individuals are displeased. Robert and I discuss activities to celebrate successes and goals achieved. A new baseline needs to be set, and behaviors need to be reinforced through training, tools and structures.

Arriving at the landscape of consolidation

In this the fourth and final landscape the topography is leveling out to new plains. The whole environment is opening up and easing off. The final year of this change process is characterized by enactment, maintenance of new patterns and a growing sense of contentment within the organization. People are terminating change processes and adjusting to a new common frame—"the new normal"—which will soon turn into new habitual patterns. This landscape can be seen as a terminus, and as the year goes by, Robert is eager to proceed to new challenges. His leadership focus is on securing resilience and new behavioral patterns. He also allows room for celebration and reward, as well as allowing people to remember the past.

January 2008. Two colleagues and I are assigned to facilitate the company's "dialogue days" which take place in the very beginning of January. This is the CEO's approach to gather the whole company and follow up the strategy deployment. The headline is: *"We are heading in the right direction—keep up the pace."* Some 500 people are attending, split into four occasions. This dialogue activity is well prepared. People follow a schedule and interact in small intensive group sessions. The whole idea of this process is to stimulate people's reflection of their current situation, to look forward and learn new things from colleagues. Many of the participants during these "dialogue days," including the staff in the consumer claims department, are aware that the old truths are being challenged but do not have a clear picture as to what the future plan is.

One station is called "Ask top management," where people can ask questions of the CEO and other senior executives. CEO Mats is both content and frustrated afterwards. *"I see a lot of positive energy and good spirit but the strategy deployment is too slow. People still don't understand. They haven't even bothered to read the business plan ..."*

Another station is about claims handling and productivity. We have rigged up an Excel application and some calculation exercises. The purpose is to get all employees (not just claims adjusters in the claims department) familiar with some key claims-handling measurements. To many, especially newly recruited claims adjusters and colleagues outside the claims department, this exercise is an eye opener since it explains workflows, concepts and costs in simple terms. Not all are impressed, however. *"Aw, this measurement hysteria!"* bursts out one of Robert's senior employees when her group comes to the station. *"It doesn't work like that! What about the quality! Everything is about figures these days ... I am so fed-up with all this ignorance."* Robert himself is a little taken aback by this outburst. Apparently everyone is not onboard yet, although the big restructuring process in his department has started to settle. Overall, this "dialogue day" signals that the shift in company mindset is still in process, although the CEO sketched out the new corporate strategy three years ago. *"Well, I suppose it takes a little longer to transform a culture that has matured for more than a century. Fluffy stuff is pretty hard after all,"* says Robert with a crooked smile.

29 February–2 March 2008. The flight into Ireland is bumpy. The claims department has reached set goals and is about to celebrate with a conference trip to Dublin. I am invited. We land safely and go by bus from the airport to a spectacular conference center at an old Guinness factory and museum. The mood is high. Both Robert and Eva are very appreciative and thank everyone for their efforts during the year of transformation. The vast majority of the group is glad and positive, but I also notice a few reserved individuals.

The purpose of the conference, besides celebrating wins, is to introduce, discuss and anchor team targets for 2008. However, I have a special assignment. My task is to work with the group that experienced the fraud affair last summer. That event is still an open wound and their team leader does not have enough management experience to resolve the situation. She has stayed home and will eventually leave for another job.

We sit in a dull, windowless room in the basement of the hotel. The night before was merry, and the group of seven claims adjusters that I am supposed to work with is a little worn. I arrange the chairs in a circle, so that we can talk face to face. The rest of the team leaders are conducting their own workshops based on a set agenda, but we will concentrate on discussing the after affects of the fraud affair. I start by asking everyone in the circle to say something. We talk all day about the feelings of losing a good comrade, about guilt and loyalty and rumors. My job is to listen, not to discuss or judge:

> They didn't have to go to the police. This could have been solved internally. Why?
> They were charged like criminals ... but I knew them. They were good guys ...
> Okay ... but one of them was convicted.
> No ... well ... aw ... hell, I don't know. I just feel bad about all this.

In the afternoon we talk about reconciliation and possible ways forward. The session ends with an air of relief. A burden has been lifted. After a pleasant dinner, the night ends in a crammed pub where cheerful group members offer me "Slippery Nipples" and other indecently named drinks. *"Jacob, you're one of us now,"* squalls one of the seniors. I share a Guinness with them and withdraw.

Two years later one of the participants from the basement in Dublin comes up to me when I am standing in their lunch restaurant waiting for Robert. I barely know the man and we have not talked much since that day. He says:

> I just want to say that you did a damn good job with us in Dublin. That day made a difference. I should have told you before but you know how it is ... Now that I saw you I figured what the hell, consultants also need praise.

He grins, shakes my hand and disappears. Apparently something good happened there.

Robert and I meet occasionally during the rest of 2008. The intensity in our collaboration is lower and the new organization seems to settle. Our journey eventually has ended up in a maintenance and termination stage. The activities on the 100 list from Project Toolbox are ticked off. Small assignments and projects are finalized and closed. The new structure is fine tuned. A new baseline is set and behaviors are reinforced through education, tools and structures. I observe that performance indicators are now displayed on large-screen TVs in the office and team meetings are held in a swifter way. Robert launches a huge investment in training called "the claims lift." The whole idea is to make the claims adjusters more versatile and adaptable. Newly recruited claims adjusters in the front office get a broad general education leading to a "claims driver's license," while experienced staff learn about different types of insurance so that they can adjust claims in several policy areas.

A new system for job rotation is also tested to facilitate skills development and learning. Claims adjusters may volunteer for "guest work" in neighboring teams. The ambition is to improve the interface between the front and back offices. Robert monitors and fine tunes, but is also a little restless. As things stabilize, he feels a need to develop new visions and plans based on new conditions. The organization's strategies, structures and people must be prepared for the next change, as the population slowly turns to a new mood of stability and comfort. He also feels that he is not getting enough internal praise for his achievements. The fraud affair still feeds rumors that stick to him. Everything is his fault. *"There are still people around who actually believe that I personally reported these three guys to the police because I didn't like them ..."* Some individuals call him "the devil." I notice as the year goes by that he starts to ponder about his future. *"What should I do when I grow up?"* is a recurrent question.

14 January 2009. This is the first time we meet after the Christmas holidays. Robert has been promoted and is very content. His new area of responsibility covers all delivery and support processes for both business units. He has also become a member of the executive management team and reports directly to the CEO. I notice his stylish new glasses with leather trim and tease him: *"Aha, you are a senior executive now—new suit, new glasses and a new car ..."* He grins: *"Yes, thanks to your fluffy talk about landscapes and maps, I managed to navigate all the way to the treasure."* We laugh. He has definitely taken a career step.

From an instrumental point of view this change journey is successful. The transformation has resulted in a significant productivity increase in two years with a retained level of customer and employee satisfaction. The number of employees has been reduced by 30 percent and the suit is no longer oversized. As mentioned in the introduction, the shortened lead times also made it possible to achieve SEK 40 million in settlement results and SEK 60 million in decreased costs for claims in merely 18 months. Robert's superiors are very pleased with that outcome. I ask him if he would be willing to talk about our mutual change journey at one of our external breakfast seminars. He agrees immediately.

On 24 April of that year Robert holds a presentation for some 40 of our clients and gets a lot of attention and appreciation. In his presentation he summarizes his own lessons learned, as described in Box 7.2.

BOX 7.2 A SAMPLE FROM ROBERT'S PRESENTATION, 24 APRIL 2009 (TRANSLATED FROM SWEDISH)

- Have a long-term plan—extend it every year and discuss it with a trusted advisor.
- Make sure you have a management team on board that fills the bill.
- Ensure resources to resolve issues not planned for (i.e. organic).

- Dare to take decisions without all the facts on the table.
- Keep an open and honest dialogue with the employees throughout the change process.

Afterwards, we leave the dim conference center and go out into the sunshine. The bright light makes us squint. We pause for a moment on a sunny street corner. Spring is in the air. Robert turns his face to the sun's warmth:

> You know, Jacob, this has been quite a personal leadership journey. When I took on this challenge I really rejected the soft side of things. Social interplay made me feel awkward, while plans, spreadsheets and figures made me feel safe. I know I scoffed about "fluffy stuff." Idiotic! Now I realize how important it is to keep people aware and in the loop. And how damn hard it is. But it is not either/or. Without a plan and clear objectives I would have lost track and failed. But without embracing all the "fluff" I would have failed nevertheless. So I guess that a combined approach is the most effective way to deal with these kinds of missions. Hey, did you just hear me say that feelings are important?! You had better watch out. One day I will dump my tie and show up in velvet pants.

He grins. I pat his back and say, "*See you.*" He nods and walks away to his car. So ends this story and another one begins.

3 March 2011. We meet Adam in the insurance company's new premises. He is one of the employees selected by Robert for our retrospective interviews. He has been around for 20 years, and it turns out that he has a lot to tell. In fact, he is very critical. For most of our conversation, he strongly criticizes the "*new era*" from 2005 onwards. Management has done "*weird and crazy stuff.*" Most leaders are "*narcissists*" and "*brainwashed.*" The solutions are "*crappy.*" Their invitations to collaboration have been "*false*" and "*dishonest.*" Very little has changed for the better. During the last minutes of our conversation, however, something happens.

> Well … reflecting about it retrospectively, I must admit that we have changed a bit after all. Before I met you, I attended a meeting with our colleagues at group headquarters. Recalling the conversations from that meeting I realize that the claims department is now much more proactive, enterprising and modern compared with some years ago. I might sound terribly negative, but here I must give some credit to the change process. There has actually been a change in our company culture.

Discussion

We have now narrated a story from a complex reality of organizational change and linked it to the concept of landscaping. We hope that this story clarifies aspects of how landscaping can contribute to effective organizational change in practice. Let us finally do a quick recap and exemplify how Robert (consciously and unconsciously) used the eight guidelines of sensemaking during the transformation of the claims department.

Robert started out in the landscape of comfort, where things were pretty stable, people seemed to be quite content and they went about their daily work without too much reflection and questioning about broader business issues. As CEO Mats told us, "*I came to a sleepy and introverted organization,*" "*folks said the right things, but nothing happened,*" "*We had to cut costs and felt intuitively that something was wrong at the consumer claims department, but we didn't know what. The productivity was low, but everyone seemed very busy.*" Or as Robert put it, "*Everyone is whining about all kinds of things, but no one wants to change anything.*"

In this landscape—and in the others for that matter—we can identify some of the eight guidelines of sensemaking: some are strongly deployed and some are less easy to recognize in the text. For example, we can see that Robert drove change through *logic of attraction*. He placed himself out in the open office, saluted everyone and tried to set a good example—wanting people to follow. Later in the story we also saw that he tried to deal with missing files himself and was talking to clients as well as handling claims. In the first workshop in spring 2006 he also performed *translation*, where he narrated a story (also an example of storytelling, see Chapter 4) full of symbols (see the section on symbolism in Chapter 4).

This activity is also an example of where he explicitly tried to translate the change so that it became more comprehensible and workable for employees (e.g. using different pictures and images). In a way, this activity also shows signs of *providing direction*, as it visualized the current crisis situation and the consequences of not changing. This guideline became more apparent on 21 June 2006, when he repeated the presentation from spring 2006 and combined it with a clearer presentation (and following interactive discussion) about the vision and plan (i.e. Project Toolbox). This occasion also had elements of translation since it provided some clarification of the plan of action.

There were several attempts to *converse candidly*. However, it seems that Robert is less skilled at having fruitful conversations and dialogue. This aspect of sensemaking is deeply problematic for Robert. He finds it difficult to calm down and listen—no balance between active talking and active listening—and to a certain extent he seems to think that conversation is a simple and immediate one-way transaction of information. There seem even to be problems with this kind of sensemaking during informal meetings and corridor talks, as people are afraid of interacting with him. Overall, candid conversation is an aspect of sensemaking that he struggles with throughout the rest of the change journey.

Moving on, at the beginning of the landscape of inertia Robert struggles with uninterested colleagues, inactivity and resistance: "*Why do we have to play around with figures? [...] What if we don't want to change?*" Eventually, in the latter parts of this landscape during fall 2006 there is even more hard feelings, resistance, growing uneasiness, and people are lost. Robert tries to counteract this development through making people *stay in motion*. For example, he proposes a "100 list" of improvements that is visibly displayed on a whiteboard and continuously updated using colors to signify development. Quick wins from the ticked-off 100 list are immediately celebrated to inspire people to more deeds and action. Robert accelerates people to stay in motion by introducing the "change breakfast" held every Friday. Here there is an update of the 100 list as well as general updates on what is going on and discussions about the biggest issues. The change breakfast and 100 list also serve as good examples of executing *look closely* and *update*, as it created situational awareness, a regular reassessment of plans and attention to important issues. In this landscape we also saw more attempts at candid conversation from Robert through a more structured approach on breakfast Fridays. However, this seems still to be an issue, and after actually having witnessed the breakfast Fridays we can say that the results were mediocre—far from being true dialogue—but a step in the right direction.

Further, in the landscape of transformation things really started to happen and, for example, a new organization was formally launched in January 2007, and a digitized workflow. There was also the unanticipated event of team leader Erik who left in a hurry and the swift action of using the resources at hand by putting Elisabeth in a new role. Later in the year the fraud affair forced Robert to handle both legal actions and internal turmoil. These incidents and other unexpected events make the spiral relapse and even on some occasions loop back to the landscape of inertia. However, Robert, hesitant and uncertain at first, has a growing awareness of the need to re-plan and adjust his leadership style, and he keeps pushing onward. Robert (and his management team) also becomes more accustomed to change conversation and dialogue and opens up for more of the "fluffy stuff." Here we see continued signs of *staying in motion*, and *looking closely* and *updating* in the management seminars, 100 list and Friday breakfasts. Besides the fraud affair and Erik leaving, the claims lab serves as a good example of the need to *improvise* and to test ideas out through trial and error.

Finally in consolidation, Robert and the employees seem to ride out the storm and enter a landscape that levels out into new flatter plains and things calm down. There is a celebration trip to Dublin, improved KPIs and reduced resistance. There are elements of the guideline *learning* in the structural initiative called "the claims lift" and the system for job rotation, the Dublin trip, as well as "dialogue days." These efforts aid the anchoring of the new behavior and allow people to reflect on the journey they have been through.

Conclusion

By now, when we have almost reached the end of this book, it is rather clear that the most challenging undertaking for change leaders today is to create broad-based awareness, understanding and meaning. This narrative shows that the heart of organizational change lies in human interaction, even if change initiatives often—as in this case—are initiated by structural overtones such as the launch of a new organizational design or new technology. The case testifies that change in real life is not rational and does not follow a series of predesigned steps—things happen along the way such as team leader Erik's departure and the unexpected fraud affair. Such things cannot be forecast and planned.

Robert, although raised in the ontology and perspective of planned change, was during this journey forced to realize that his idea of a "project" solely focusing on hard and structural aspects would not serve. In short, he was forced to reject the rationale of planned change. Instead, he was insightful enough to embrace the need for sensemaking as a means to handle the disruptive social systems within the claims department. However, he never abandoned his strong belief in a clear vision and concrete change objectives. Without this strategic clarity and his stamina and stubbornness Robert could have been dragged into a loop of resistance and denial, but his firmness gained respect and by means of sensemaking he was able to dismantle hindering forces and accelerate change in an environment where all his predecessors had failed. By adopting this integrated approach to change the structures, models and plans provided a foundation upon which to build the behavioral change, but the crucial success factor was Robert's newfound ability to lead through sensemaking. In this way, this case illustrates aspects of how leading change in practice is both about acknowledging local, emerging interpretations and constructions of meaning, and leading the change process in a systematic and structured way.

We can also claim that practice and theory converge, yet since the setting is complex we should perhaps be a little cautious in drawing too hasty conclusions. Access to a clean, objective, rational and value-free reality is probably impossible. In this case, not one of the interviewees from the retrospective interviews carried out in March 2011 could recall a coherent story from the studied period—not even Robert himself. Dates, events and even years were mixed up. These observations indicate that in *real time* this was more of an emergent change process since all stakeholders perceived a different reality from their respective viewpoints. Remember: "The world looks different from the bell tower than it does from the fields" (Reed 2011: 110).

The story holds many examples of this, for instance the different recollections of Robert's early attempts to provide direction and make people stay in motion. Employee Bertil recalled: "*Personally, I don't remember much from that time. Robert was anonymous back then. We didn't see him … No … I don't recall that I spoke to him at all …*"; while employee Carin tells a totally different story: "*My first impression of Robert was very good. I mean, he had an individual meeting with everyone!*" Although full access to reality is not given, it is fair to say that this in-depth case study shows how complex the reality of organizational change really is and that decisive management can change meanings through persistent sensegiving. The story also emphasizes the importance of "planning *and re-planning*" and a stubborn result orientation.

In this case, the capacity of the change leader in person seems to have been crucial. Leadership based on landscaping appears to overcome hindering forces if the leader is persistent enough to stay the distance and powerful enough to handle the landscape of inertia. It takes years to change a culture and resistance can be fierce. In the early stages Robert realized, perhaps a little unwillingly, that an "ordinary project" focusing on hard stuff would not do the job. Therefore, instead he embraced the need for sensemaking as a means to handle the hampering systems of meaning (e.g. the widespread illusion of productivity, the reluctance to change, the constant call for more resources, undemanding management, etc).[3] By doing so he could dismantle hindering forces and accelerate change. However, it can be discussed if he ever actually reached the point where the conversations turned into a true dialogue and where there was a meeting of minds on equal terms. As presented and discussed in Chapter 4, dialogue requires considerable skill and will not mature overnight. To undertake fruitful conversation and profound dialogue is perhaps one of the most demanding tasks when leading change through sensemaking.

Notes

1 This case study is based on participant observation by Jacob Hallencreutz following the research method of organizational ethnography. The research project took place between 2006 and 2009, and besides field notes during these three years (of approximately 50 pages) the empirical data consist of: ten in-depth interviews with Robert; 30 workshops with Robert's management team; 30 semi-structured field interviews; approximately 4,500 text files with a plethora of informal meeting notes and memoranda; approx. 500 internal documents consisting mainly of slideshows and reports; and 12 retrospective video-documented interviews conducted in 2011. The different data sources enabled extensive method triangulation both within and between the different datasets. In addition, to ensure reliability and validity, the research followed the ten sensibilities of organizational ethnography as postulated by Neyland (2007), as well as guidelines provided by other sources (Geertz 1973; Schwartzman 1993; Van Maanen 1979; Van Maanen 2011). Particularly for the accounts in this book, an effort has been made to strike a balance between rigor and relevance. The case study presented here is a hybrid-process story (Langley 1999; Riessman 2002) and this narration aimed to take different viewpoints from different stakeholders into consideration (Pentland 1999), to understand how the respondents "imposed order on the flow of experience" (Riessman 2002: 218), and to bring contextual richness to the story of enfolding events (Pettigrew 1990). The concept of landscaping as a whole is developed by an abductive research approach (Van de Ven 2007), based on this and three other case studies (implementation of a quality management system in a healthcare institution, deployment of Lean in an organization in the food industry, and the transformation of an IT department in a state agency—a sample of the empirical material from this last case is in the vignettes in the last section of Chapter 4).
2 All names in this case study have been changed to ensure the anonymity and confidentiality of participants.
3 When Robert tells the story today, he actually claims that he realized the need for sensemaking from the very beginning.

Bibliography

Geertz, C. (1973) *The Interpretation of Cultures: Selected Essays*. New York: Basic Books.
Langley, A. (1999) Strategies for theorizing from process data. *Academy of Management Review*, 24(4): 691–710.

Neyland, D. (2007) *Organizational Ethnography*. London: Sage.

Pentland, B. (1999) Building process theory with narrative: from description to explanation. *Academy of Management Review*, 24(4): 711–724.

Pettigrew, A. (1990) Longitudinal field research on change: theory and practice. special issue: longitudinal field research methods for studying processes of organizational change. *Organization Science*, 1(3): 267–292.

Reed, I. (2011) *Interpretation and Social Knowledge*. Chicago: The University of Chicago Press.

Riessman, C. (2002) "Narrative analysis." In A.M. Huberman & M.B. Miles (eds), *The Qualitative Researcher's Companion*. Thousand Oaks, CA: Sage, pp. 217–270.

Schwartzman, H.B. (1993) *Ethnography in Organizations*. Newbury Park, CA: Sage.

Van de Ven, A. (2007) *Engaged Scholarship: A Guide for Organizational and Social Research*. Oxford: Oxford University Press.

Van Maanen, J. (1979) The fact of fiction in organizational ethnography. *Administrative Science Quarterly*, 24(4): 539–550.

Van Maanen, J. (2011) *Tales of the Field: On Writing Ethnography*. Chicago, IL: University of Chicago Press.

8

SUMMARY, LESSONS LEARNED AND CONCLUDING THOUGHTS

We have arrived at our last chapter and it is time to wrap up and discuss some conclusions. Let us do so with a reflective recap of our journey, the lessons we have learned and some final thoughts.

Summary

We embarked on this journey by discussing the discouraging fact that we—scholars as well as practitioners—seem to accept a poor outcome from change initiatives. In recent decades there has been a general consensus between practitioners and scholars that few are successful when leading organizational change. We proclaimed that leaders need to explore seriously their practices and attitudes toward the people side, especially on how to gain broad-based empowerment during change processes. The tendency to dismiss this "soft side" of organizational change in favor of using a set of quick prescriptive steps or no structure at all is simply not good enough. In an effort just to get it done, managers underestimate the need for sensemaking and the effort it takes to create awareness, understanding and meaning. One reason why managers overlook this aspect of change leadership is because up until now there have been few, if any, books that explain how change can be led through a sensemaking approach.

In the subsequent chapter we engaged in defining and discussing the nature of change and its different perspectives. Here we tried to conceptualize change by using a story about five monkeys that encapsulated some of the cornerstones of the theoretical foundation. Then we discussed at length different perspectives of change. The reason why we did so is because "[t]he language of change can be a liberating force or an analytical prison" (Pettigrew et al. 2001: 700). In other words, the words and language we use about change can help us comprehend and discuss change but they also carry with them certain underlying assumption that guide our action. We are imprisoned by the way we think and talk about change, and if we do not acknowledge that change has different facets, approaches and assumptions then in the long run this can impede the change process as such.

Therefore, large parts of Chapter 2 were devoted to opening the monolithic concept of change and uncovering some of its underlying assumptions. We started doing so by showing that earlier work tended to make sense of different types of change by classifying it according to scope and scale, or according to rate of occurrence, and we elevated this into a matrix. We also illustrated that change can be categorized depending on if it is a planned activity that progressively moves from one stable state to another, or an emergent process consisting of many loosely coupled activities that evolve over time. Some of the different arguments for and against these perspectives were considered and we complicated things further by claiming that on the whole, both perspectives are to some extent present in a change process depending on, for example, the standpoint of the observer.

We increased the philosophical focus by exploring what change actually is, what it is composed of, how it comes into being and how we can study it. This subject was counteracted by moving away from the questions that occupy scholars towards issues that practitioners often discuss: why as many as 70 percent of change initiatives fail. We came closer to an answer by looking at the evidence and reasons for failure, concluding, for example, that there are no reliable data for such a claim, that there are multiple aspects and accounts of change, and that the importance of context is completely overlooked—the belief that success can be replicated anywhere. We also contributed to the riddle of defining success and failure of organizational change by illustrating that measuring success and failure is an extremely complex, if not impossible, endeavor. We finished by conveying the messages that it is pointless to try to establish validity in any external or objective sense because each of us has experiences from our own point of view and each of us experiences a slightly different reality from anyone else. My landscape of meaning varies from yours. Therefore, there might not be such a thing as a single, generalized organizational recipe for success.

Chapter 3 began by defining sensemaking, organizational sensemaking and sensegiving. Here we stressed the social nature of sensemaking and its reciprocal and cyclical relationship with sensegiving: you are performing sensegiving to others and they make sense of this together with other stimuli, and in turn perform sensegiving that influences your sensemaking, and so on. After this we dug deeper by explaining Weick's seven properties of sensemaking (as well as the more recent property of prospective sensemaking), which can be summarized as: "Once people begin to act (enactment), they generate tangible outcomes (cues) in some context (social), and this helps them to discover (retrospect) what is occurring (ongoing), what needs to be explained (plausibility), and what should be done next (identity enhancement)" (Weick 1995: 55). Finally, we tried to decode, summarize and to some extent simplify matters of sensemaking by comparing it with the making of maps.

In Chapter 4 we transferred from a theoretical scene into a more real-world context as we discovered some of the sources of cues that people extract to make their world workable and sensible. The intention was to provide insight into some, but by no means all, classical and more recent studies, and this was done through an implicit structure of looking closely at how we make sense of what we hear, what we see, what we feel and what we use. We learned that we make the world more comprehensible by hearing and conveying different meanings that are carried in everyday narratives. We stressed the importance of leaders' willingness to listen to the different narratives that flow throughout an organization. Subsequent sections explained how leaders can take an active part in the language game and discourse connected to change by describing different change conversations and their risk for breakdowns, uncovering the different roles people play when they perform speech acts, affording principle for fruitful dialogue, and finally showing different ways in which storytelling can snare the message of change.

We then travelled from the area of language into the more subtle area of symbolic communication. Here we showed how symbols can take almost any form and be carried in any communication vehicle. This was illustrated partly by showing how leaders often send symbolic messages that influence the sensemaking of others in, for example, the organizational rituals that they often orchestrate and in organizational systems and processes such as control systems. However, we also issued a warning, as symbolic communication often backfires when people misinterpret the message. Some researchers' informed advice was given, such as the importance of a strategic and systematic approach, the identification and elimination of symbols that uphold the status quo, context sensitivity, and varying the different forms and ways in which the symbolic message is conveyed.

The chapter went on to explain that the cues that people extract for their sensemaking not only stem from imperceptible practice and ambiguous areas such as language, discourse and symbols, but also from our bodily movement and use of material artifacts and technology. This was illustrated mainly by showing how IT is both a social and material artifact (sociomaterial) and how such technology plays a pivotal role in shaping people's sensemaking processes: they give something to talk about, to reflect upon and to discuss with others which together (it is hoped) reduce their feelings of equivalence as well as providing energy to move forward. Finally, we finished Chapter 4 by providing three workshop exercises and vignettes from a real-world change project. The exercises were connected to symbolism, change conversations and embodiment, presented earlier in the chapter, and they illustrated how sensemaking can be enhanced in practice.

Earlier chapters served to enrich understanding of the various aspects of change and sensemaking in particular. They functioned as a backdrop and background to the main picture that we would explore in Chapters 6 and 7: the connection between sensemaking and leadership. At this juncture, our journey had come to the part where we really started to address more directly our guiding question of this book, about what it is that managers actually do when they perform sensemaking.

We did so in Chapter 5 by beginning to translate some of the leadership research that told us about the pivotal role of mastering conversations and setting the scene of such verbal exchanges. We also learned that leaders often act as facilitators by provoking unconventional thoughts, by disrupting ingrained ways of thinking and by making others see and understand what lies beyond the current mythcycles of the organization. Next we moved on to a colorful poem about lost soldiers in the Alps using a map they falsely believed was a map of the Alps, but which was actually of the Pyrenees. This poem yielded some thoughtful notions about leadership and the role of change programs, and by doing so the poem also aided our transition to the review of the eight guidelines of leading sensemaking: stay in motion; provide a direction; look closely and update; converse candidly; unblock improvisation; facilitate learning; translate; and change through logic of attraction.

These guidelines provided us with the answer to the activities that managers perform when they perform sensemaking. We then elevated our discussion into the process of leading sensemaking. In the theoretical Chapter 2 we had learned that the trajectory of planned change often resembles an arrow from the present to a clearly defined future, often chopped up into different phases or steps. At the other extreme we had learned that the advocates of emergent change favor a view of change that follows a continuous, processual and cyclical trajectory which seeks equilibrium and goes through different phases that are revisited in altered form. We proposed that in a leadership viewpoint the sensemaking process is neither a straight arrow from past to future nor a continuous circle. Instead, it evolves like an upward spiral that is fueled by the eight guidelines.

Chapter 5 was insufficient in explaining the details of how sensemaking in a leadership perspective emerges, develops, grows or terminates over time. This was the purpose of Chapter 6, which developed the concept of landscaping, taking us inside the spiral of sensemaking and explaining that it moves through the landscapes of comfort, inertia, transformation and consolidation.

We learned that the landscape of comfort is constituted by compliance and habitual behavioral patterns and the role of the leader is to get people's attention, create an understanding of the need for change and sell the problem rather than the solution. The rougher landscape of inertia includes feelings of uncertainty and resistance, counteracted by information transparency, providing direction and maintaining people's motion. Ideally, the spiral continues upward to the landscape of transformation, where people alternate between action and relapse, and where leaders try to keep the change moving forward by confronting losses and gains as well as nurturing a climate for testing and "learning from mistakes." Finally, in the landscape of consolidation people begin to adjust to "the new normal" and leaders focus on securing new behavioral patterns through reward and celebration at the same time as they are honoring the past and the journey they have been through. When the dust has settled and time has passed, the landscape of consolidation slowly transforms into a landscape of comfort and a new intensive change spiral is about to start once more.

Finally, Chapter 7 illustrated the landscaping perspective through a thick descriptive case study. The objective was to tell a story from the complex reality of organizational change and link it to the concept of landscaping outlined in the previous chapter. The story evolved around aspects of how landscaping contributed to effective organizational change in practice. We examined a three-year change journey in a Scandinavian insurance company which covered transformation of organizational structures, business processes, and leadership style and culture.

Lessons learned

The discouraging fact that everyone seems to accept a poor outcome from change initiatives was our starting point. In the book we come to the conclusion that the widespread notion that 70 percent of all change initiatives fail should be scrutinized. As discussed in Chapter 2, there is no empirical evidence for this figure. In fact, there seem to be no clear standards or performance indicators to define the outcome of change initiatives at all. Measuring success and failure is extremely complex, if not impossible. Thus, the discussion about success and failure in organizational change needs to be reframed. We should embrace the multiple landscapes of change experience and notice that the experience of success and failure is context dependent and relies on who, when and how you ask such a question. So, our first lesson learned is:

> The question of success and failure is obsolete. Instead we should focus on moving towards an understanding of how we can manage, lead and align the journey through multiple landscapes of meaning which together make up a change process.

However, even if the figures are questionable, it is unwise to overlook the substantial number of studies indicating that change processes actually often fail to reach intended objectives. The ordeal to lead an organization from a current state to a desired future state often seems to end somewhere else (which does not necessarily mean that the whole venture is a failure). So, what is the ghost in the machine? Our own research, two decades of management experience and numerous discussions with senior executives, prominent researchers and illuminated colleagues in seminars, around lunch tables and coffee machines in the process of writing this book have strengthened our belief that one of the most vital causes of change failure is a widespread tendency to dismiss behavioral aspects of organizational change and a consequent underestimation of the need for sensemaking. To create awareness, understanding and meaning is quite an effort and managers often fail to win over the hearts and minds of the people in the organization. Thus, our second lesson learned is:

> Change leaders underestimate the effort it takes to create awareness, understanding and meaning, and effective organizational change hinges first and foremost on our ability to lead such behavioral change.

A key point to take away from this book is the landscaping metaphor. Social systems should be described as "landscapes of meaning." However, a word of caution could be placed here: we do not claim that organizations should be seen as unitary systems. We all cope with change in different manners and at different speeds. Some of us are early adopters equipped with swift sensemaking processes, always willing to take on change challenges. Most of us will await the change process to grow, calculate pros and cons and eventually decide to embrace the new. Some individuals might not want to change at all. In this book we stress that the diffusion of behavioral change is not a linear process (this cannot be repeated enough). It is impossible to calculate exactly how and when individuals will act and react. Individuals' respective sensemaking processes will take different times, and habitual patterns within organizations are strong hindering forces. This is what people often refer to as "cultural resistance." Surprisingly, we have often found that change leaders tend to be deeply occupied with the percentage of late adopters, coaxing and convincing them to change, which is understandable because many books emphasize the importance of handling resistance. However, what we have learned is that change leaders should do the opposite. Management attention should be on the 80 percent who actually embrace the change. We should allow early adopters to experiment, conduct pilot testing and be forerunners. Good examples should be highlighted and quick wins celebrated. Thus:

> Proactive change leaders should be catalysts and embrace the early adopters and open up for experimenting and pilot testing.

Because there is a gap between rhetoric and reality, we also attempted to define and discuss the nature of change and its different perspectives. Since we believe that the world is constructed, interpreted and experienced by people in their interactions with each other, our conclusion is that the classic instrumental change discourse should be abandoned (i.e. the planned perspective). The heart of organizational change lies—as good as always—in human behavior, even if the change as such is often triggered by "hard stuff" such as new technology and structure. Thus, change in reality is *not* rational and does *not* follow a series of predesigned and clear steps. Change consists of people, and people are different and live in the messiness of everyday life. They adapt to change in different ways, they make sense of change in different ways and they act in different ways. Therefore, change should be managed accordingly.

On the other hand, we are also skeptical of the most extreme position of the emergent change discourse suggesting that change proceeds in a circular trajectory that is caged because of its pre-figured program of different phases—many loosely coupled events and activities that abide to an underlying code. In this sense, processes are all there is and change becomes to some extent a process of "going around in circles," never breaking free and never to a greater extent freeing oneself from the "vicious circle." We believe that this school of theory leaves the pragmatic change leader empty handed: if change just consists of circular processes, can it be managed at all? Is everything organic and emergent? Is there no structure to the messiness of all this? A manager trying to follow a truly emergent approach to change will sooner or later discover that this movement lacks a clear and united focus on how to manage, deal and drive change forward as well as a great dearth of any agreement on model or approach.

The standpoints of planned versus emergent change can be considered as two extremes, both of which depict some of the realities of change. In this sense, both types of trajectory tell us something about the nature of organizational change, but with their own respective significant drawbacks that are not properly addressed. Instead we believe that in reality, and through the lens of sensemaking theory, change should be portrayed as a spiral of events that moves upward. We embrace the idea that organizational change emerges in a spiral motion that is energized by sensemaking. Or, as Weick and Quinn (1999: 373) note, "change is not a linear movement through the four stages but a spiral pattern of contemplation, action, and relapse and then successive returns to contemplation, action, and relapse before entering the maintenance and then termination stages." This spiral metaphor proffers that understanding is constantly changing and never returns to an earlier point. Interpretations emerge in a spiral motion between our current understanding and our encounters with new experiences and ideas, which lead to new understandings, which in turn will guide future interpretations and movements. The growing sense of and answer to the question "what's the story?" build into an understanding that informs and guides future action. This action fuels more sensemaking which enables you to act yet again. This leads us to our fourth lesson:

> Organizational change moves upward (or downward) following a spiral trajectory that is slippery because of the messiness of everyday life and because of multiple landscapes of meaning, but this spiral pattern can still to some extent be foreseen, planned and managed.

In our theoretical review in Chapter 2, we discussed how different ontological assumptions about organizational change influence the view of how change leadership should be executed. Basically, this was a discussion about different philosophies of science. If our theories are grounded in a reductionist and "hard systems" approach, we probably believe that the world is objective and rational and that change follows natural steps. The world is a single unitary reality apart from our perceptions which follows some sort of natural law. We would probably claim that change processes can be observed and measured, and successes can be brought out of context and be replicated and generalized. From this perspective the mission of a change leader is simply to learn from success and failure of change and then replicate it and "make it happen" (Greenhalgh et al. 2004).

The antithesis, advocated by the school of emergent change, is that change leadership is about acknowledging local, emerging interpretations and constructions of meaning. The change leader can do nothing but facilitate the process and "let it happen" (Greenhalgh et al. 2004). Our synthesis is that an effective change leader is neither just a specialist nor just a facilitator, but more of a catalyst with the ability to combine competencies and alter leadership styles. The conclusion is that leading change is both about acknowledging local, emerging interpretations and constructions of meaning *and* leading the change process in a planned, project-like manner. Thus, an effective change leader should "help it happen" (Greenhalgh et al. 2004). This is what leading through sensemaking is all about, and the fifth lesson is:

> Change leadership is about acknowledging local, emerging interpretations and constructions of meaning as well as leading the change process in a planned, project-like manner: "help it happen."

In Chapters 6 and 7, we elevated the discussion about sensemaking and behavioral change to an organizational level and showed what the consequences were for the change leader. The concept of landscaping is our response to the call for means to embrace the people side of change. During a change process, a social system goes through four imaginary landscapes of meaning: comfort, inertia, transformation and consolidation. We explored how interpretations during a change spiral through these landscapes of meaning, and unraveled how this spiral motion of activities could be fuelled by systematic and proactive sensemaking. The concept of landscaping emphasizes the importance of decisive leadership, a stubborn result orientation and an agile ability to "plan and re-plan" as the change process unfolds. This is the sixth lesson learned:

> During a change process a social system goes through four imaginary landscapes of meaning, consisting of comfort, inertia, transformation and consolidation.

We further illustrated that inside the spiral of sensemaking it is pivotal to stay in motion and push the change upward. The pace of the movement up the spiral is very much set by the leader's skill in deploying the eight guidelines of sensemaking presented in Chapter 5, as well as using the different types of cues presented in Chapter 4. If a change leader can provide a direction for the people, instill confidence and show where to go, the spiral will most likely move upward. Likewise, if one can encourage improvisation and allow people to test things and learn by doing, the motion swings upward. Of course, this production of ideas can also backfire. Generation of "hot air," endless analysis and talk, talk, talk can be the only outcome. Then people might get stuck in a negative loop of action and relapse. This is our final insight:

> The spiral is fueled by the leader's skill in deploying the eight guidelines of sensemaking and managing cues, and these together influence the effectiveness of the change.

Concluding thoughts

By writing yet another management book about organizational change, we are fully aware of the risk that we have slipped into the same hole as many other authors in the field. However, we believe that our concept of landscaping offers a way forward that sets it apart from many other works in the field. Landscaping provides us with a new starting point for describing social systems and change more comprehensibly than earlier research and practice has offered.

In real life, leadership based on landscaping appears to overcome many of the hindering forces of change if the leaders are persistent enough to go the distance and powerful enough to navigate the landscape of inertia. It takes years to change behavioral patterns and change resistance can be demanding, and it is our belief that in such situations the personal capacities of the change leaders are paramount. The people in Chapter 7, in particular our friend Robert, realized, perhaps a little unwillingly, that an "ordinary project" focusing on hard, structural stuff would not do the job. Instead, he embraced the need for different forms of sensemaking as a means to handle the hampering systems of meaning. By doing so, he could dismantle hindering forces and accelerate change in an environment where all his predecessors had failed. In this way, enabling structures, models, plans—the hard stuff of change—are important, as they provide a foundation to build upon. These elements are "the order qualifiers" of change. However, it is the leaders and their ability to be sensemakers and the people who surround such leaders that are the tipping-point factors that ultimately influence the success of the change. These elements are "the order winners" of change which serve as competitive advantage that determine effectiveness.

As mentioned earlier in this book, we believe that the world is complex and dynamic, and is constructed, interpreted and experienced by people in their interactions with each other and with wider social systems. However, we also strongly believe that this world can, at least to some extent, be planned and managed by means of management models. In this book we have tried to decode the theories on sensemaking and bring them closer to reality. We have visualized how a proactive change leader can guide people through four different imaginary landscapes of meaning: comfort, inertia, transformation and consolidation. We have also highlighted that key leadership tools are the eight guidelines of sensemaking. We do not claim to have unraveled the ultimate truth, but we strongly believe that we have shed some new light on how sensemaking effectively can guide organizations through the challenges of the change process.

So what is our keystone conclusion? Managers should zoom out and understand the complex reality of organizational change before they rush into new change assignments. What do surgeons and pilots do when they want to progress? They learn new things. It is now time for managers, especially senior managers, to start to see organizational change as an area of expertise—but with a competence gap that needs to be addressed. Take this gap seriously and do the following: build your knowledge of the underlying human dynamics of change, inherent in whatever change model you choose. Read this book again. And learn to lead through sensemaking.

Bibliography

Greenhalgh, T., Robert, G., Macfarlane, F., Bate, P. & Kyriakidou, O. (2004) Diffusion of innovations in service organizations: systematic review and recommendations. *Milbank Quarterly*, 82(4): 581–629.

Pettigrew, A., Woodman, R. & Cameron, K. (2001) Studying organizational change and development: challenges for future research. *Academy of Management Journal*, 44(4): 697–713.

Weick, K.E. (1995) *Sensemaking in Organizations*. Thousand Oaks, CA: Sage.

Weick, K.E. & Quinn, R.E. (1999) Organizational change and development. *Annual Review of Psychology*, 50(1): 361–386.

INDEX

Entries in **bold** denote tables and boxes; entries in *italics* denote figures.

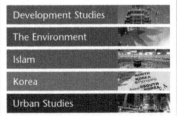